❧ HOMEWORK ❧
FOR
GROWN-UPS

∽ HOMEWORK ∽
FOR
GROWN-UPS

Everything You Learned at School . . .
and Promptly Forgot

E. FOLEY & B. COATES

■ SQUARE PEG

Published by Square Peg 2008

8 10 9

First published in Great Britain in 2008 by
SQUARE PEG
Random House, 20 Vauxhall Bridge Road,
London SW1V 2SA

www.randomhouse.co.uk

Addresses for companies within The Random House Group Limited
can be found at: www.randomhouse.co.uk/offices.htm

The Random House Group Limited Reg. No. 954009

A CIP catalogue record for this book is available from the British Library

ISBN 9780224082662

The Random House Group Limited makes every effort to ensure that
the papers used in its books are made from trees that have been legally sourced from
well-managed and credibly certified forests. Our paper procurement policy
can be found at www.rbooks.co.uk/environment

Mixed Sources
Product group from well-managed
forests and other controlled sources
www.fsc.org Cert no. TT-COC-2139
© 1996 Forest Stewardship Council
FSC

Designed and typeset in Bembo by Peter Ward
Printed and bound in the UK by
CPI Mackays, Chatham ME5 8TD

Ꮳ CONTENTS Ꮳ

ᗏ INTRODUCTION ᗏ

Where did it all go? Everything we learned at school now seems a distant memory. We sit slack-jawed when our children ask us which planet comes after Jupiter, or what the capital of Bulgaria is, or what quid pro quo actually means. Have you ever found yourself making up your own version of Pythagoras' theorem in order to avoid the humiliating scorn of your offspring? Have you ever started blithely on a list of Henry VIII's wives, while your little one looks up at you full of admiration, only to find yourself with too many Catherines? Have you ever succumbed to the temptation to use the embarrassing get-out clause 'Ask your father/mother'?

Even simple queries like 'Why is the sky blue?' have many parents scratching their heads. All we can remember is that we used to know the answer. A recent study revealed that even though most pupils learn French for five years, by the time they are adults the sum total of their knowledge stretches to – at best – four words. In these days of high-speed Internet connections and calculators on mobile phones, we rarely have to use the information that was drummed into us in our schooldays. The good news is that it's still all there. And even better, it's surprisingly easy to revive those dormant grey cells and hold your head up with pride when you're next asked to help with homework.

Homework for Grown-ups is a revision guide for adults that will put you back on track. We aim to entertain you as well as exercise your brain and equip you with the basics, so you can impress your friends or handle homework without humiliation.

Homework for Grown-ups is organised in ten chapters, each covering a school subject: English, Maths, Home Economics, History, Science, Religious Education, Geography, Classics, Physical Education and Art. After reading it we hope you'll be as sharp as a tack, as bright as a

I

button and as clever as when you were a fresh-faced youngster in grey socks and a blazer.

Wouldn't it be great to slip a couple of Latin phrases into a conversation with your boss, or pontificate on the qualities of a tetrahedron at a cocktail party, or list the kings of England in your head while the dentist is giving you a filling? *Homework for Grown-ups* is the way to get back your self-respect and also show the kids a thing or two.

ENGLISH LANGUAGE
AND
LITERATURE

'**English** *n.* the language of England, now used in
many varieties throughout the world'
Oxford Concise English Dictionary

'For words, like Nature, half reveal
And half conceal the Soul within'
ALFRED, LORD TENNYSON (1809–92), *In Memoriam A. H. H.*

Our mother tongue is a rich and flexible beast. It contains such beauteous and varied words as 'tatterdemalion',* 'punch', 'vulpine',† 'mendacious',‡ 'croak', 'badger', 'Saturday' and 'snow'. It has the power to communicate a huge spectrum of emotions in a compact, vague phrase ('I love you', 'I'm not sure about that') and also to express accurately very specific notions ('He's a little ochlophobic',§ 'Pass me the potassium permanganate'). The shapes and sounds of our words are hugely varied, often depending on whence our magpie language has picked up specific terms: the vowel-heavy, melodic 'anaesthesia', 'echo' and 'chaos' from the ancient Greek; the concise, muscular 'belch', 'night' and 'cow' from our Anglo-Saxon forefathers; and the sleek 'cuisine', 'blonde' and 'rendezvous' from the French, for example.

In fact, the history of the British Isles is written in our words, from Viking borrowings ('bark', 'cake', 'akimbo') to the souvenirs of empire ('pukka', 'bungalow', 'trek'). Today English is an official language of more than fifty countries including Madagascar, Belize, Fiji and Singapore and is spoken by more people on Earth than any other. The

---

*A ragamuffin   †Like a fox   ‡Untruthful   §Afraid of crowds

Oxford English Dictionary contains definitions for over 500,000 words in current use (some studies record over 900,000 English words), and the average person probably uses about $1/60$ of these in their lifetime. More impressively, Shakespeare's vocabulary is reckoned to have run to over 24,000 words. In order to appreciate properly the wonderful works of literary giants like Shakespeare, or indeed to create your own, it is vital to have a basic grasp of how the language works. Grammar provides the building blocks from which the castles of great literature are built.

We are extremely lucky to have such a rich heritage of literature in our language to turn to – whether John Milton, Jane Austen or James Joyce is your thing. Literature can educate, console, amuse, enrage, challenge, move and even morally guide (as long as one reads 'improving books'). Your reading could be made up of the instructions for the windscreen wipers on your car or it could be the poetry of T. S. Eliot, but either way you need to understand your language and its literary heritage to get the best out of the world.

ENGLISH LANGUAGE

WAYS WITH WORDS:
THE BASIC RULES OF GRAMMAR

As we have seen, there are thousands of words to choose from in our generous language, but it may surprise you to learn that there are only nine *kinds* of word (although in some circumstances a word can belong to more than one class).

1. **Nouns** are 'naming' words. They name people, places or things. There are three kinds of noun. **Proper nouns** are specific names of people and places and are written with capital letters at the start of them: 'America', 'Danny'. **Abstract nouns** are things or concepts that you can't touch: 'shyness', 'romance', 'happiness'. **Common nouns** are the words for everything else: 'car', 'jacket', 'cinema'.

2. **Verbs** are words indicating action or change: 'to sing', 'to kiss', 'to be', 'to eat'. Many verbs have a basic root form and usually different endings are added to this root depending on the subject of the verb and the tense: 'I dance', 'he dances', 'they dance', 'I danced', 'he danced', 'they danced'.

The **subject** of a verb is the person or thing who is carrying out the action of the verb and the **object** of a verb is the person or thing that the verb is being carried out upon. In the sentence 'Danny kissed Sandy.' 'Danny' is the subject, 'kissed' is the verb and 'Sandy' is the lucky object.

In order to express some of the different tenses (present, future, past, etc.), a verb can become a **verb phrase**, incorporating auxiliary verbs to indicate timing. For example, in the sentence 'Danny had been kissing Sandy', 'had been kissing' is a verb phrase.

There is a particular subgroup of auxiliary verbs called **modal verbs**, such as 'may', 'must' and 'can'. These express how likely or possible an event is. In the sentence 'Danny can kiss Sandy', 'can' is the modal verb.

3. **Adjectives** are words that modify and describe nouns. In 'the shiny car', 'shiny' is the adjective. Adjectives can themselves be modified, in which case they become **adjectival phrases**: 'the impressively shiny car'.

4. **Adverbs** tell us how, where or when something is done. In other words, they describe the manner, place or time of a verb. Many adverbs are created by adding 'ly' to the end of an adjective: so 'slow' becomes 'slowly'.

5. **Pronouns** are the words that replace nouns in a sentence. Pronouns like 'he', 'which', 'none' and 'you' are used to make sentences less cumbersome and less repetitive. Without pronouns we would end up with childish sentences like: 'Danny took liberties with Sandy at the drive-in so Sandy slapped Danny and left Danny.'

6. **Conjunctions** are used to link words, phrases and clauses, as in: 'I want the burger **and** the milkshake', or 'Tell me **when** you are ready'.

7. **Articles** are very easy to remember as they only consist of 'a', 'an' and 'the'. 'A/an' is the **indefinite article** – it can refer to any member of a group: '**A** boy kissed her'. The **definite article** is used when the specific subject is known: '**The** boy kissed her'.

8. **Prepositions** link nouns, pronouns and phrases to other words in a sentence. Prepositions usually indicate relationships in space or time. Examples are: 'under', 'above', 'behind', 'from', 'with', 'at' and 'for'.

9. An **interjection** is a word added to a sentence to convey emotion. It is not grammatically related to any other part of the sentence. Interjections are often followed with an exclamation mark. Examples are: '**Ouch**, that hurt!', '**Hey**! Leave me alone!'

SATISFYING SENTENCES

When speaking we are often regrettably casual in our manner and fail to communicate in complete units of sense – also known as sentences. It is natural for oral communication to sometimes consist of fragments, or even of hand gestures and grunts, but for clarity on the page we should attempt to write in full sentences. (Unless of course one is composing an experimental surrealist haiku or some other advanced form.)

Sentences are made up of one or more **clauses**. A clause is a group of words that includes a verb and usually also a subject. There are two types of clause: **main clauses** and **subordinate clauses**. Main clauses are complete units of sense and must contain a verb and a subject – every sentence must include a main clause. Subordinate clauses are dependent on the main clause and do not have to be complete units of sense. For example, in the sentence 'The acrid stench of exhaust fumes filled the air, reminding Sandy of Danny and encouraging her to change her dress sense', the main clause is 'The acrid stench of exhaust fumes filled the air.' The clauses 'reminding Sandy of Danny' and 'encouraging her to change her dress sense' are both subordinate.

THE HUMBLE GERUND

A gerund might sound like a shy woodland creature, who whiles away his days in a burrow and munches on water lilies, but the true meaning of the word is far more grammatically intriguing. The gerund in English is identical in form to the present participle ('running', 'spitting', 'drinking', 'fighting') but it is a verb that functions in sentences as a noun either by itself or as part of a clause.

For example, in the sentence 'Fighting is fun', 'fighting' is a gerund and acts as a noun, and in the sentence 'Fighting the system is fun', 'fighting the system' is a whole clause that acts as a noun.

COMMON GRAMMATICAL MISTAKES

'THAT' OR 'WHICH'?: RELATIVE PRONOUNS AND CLAUSES

In grammar, as in life, people are often confused and frustrated by relatives. Happily, the world of grammar is more logical and serene than the world of grandmas.

Relative pronouns join clauses together in a sentence and begin subordinate clauses that give more information about the main clause – this kind of clause is called a **relative clause**. Who, whom, which, that, whose, when, where and why are all relative pronouns.

There are two types of relative clause: **restrictive** (also called **defining**) and **non-restrictive** (also called, you guessed it, **non-defining**).

A restrictive relative clause identifies what is being referred to by the previous noun or pronoun. For example, in the sentence 'The jumper that I wore yesterday was pink,' the relative clause is 'that I wore yesterday' and it is a restrictive relative clause because it identifies 'the jumper'. Restrictive relative clauses cannot be removed from the sentence without affecting its meaning and they are never preceded by a comma.

A non-restrictive relative clause gives us more information about the preceding noun or pronoun but is not essential to the meaning of the sentence. Non-restrictive clauses are displayed inside commas to separate them from the rest of the sentence. For example, in the sentence 'The jumper, which was bright pink, was knitted by my aunt' the non-restrictive relative clause is 'which was bright pink,'. You could remove this from the sentence without losing the sentence's central meaning.

- **'That' or 'which' can be used in restrictive relative clauses**, although 'that' should be the preferred choice unless the clause begins with a preposition, or you need to add emphasis or avoid the repetition of the word 'that'.
- **Only 'which' can be used in non-restrictive relative clauses**. 'The jumper, that was bright pink, was knitted by my aunt' is incorrect.

DARLING, YOUR PARTICIPLE IS DANGLING: THE DANGERS OF DANGLING PARTICIPLES

Dangling participles may sound like a bizarre threat but you should keep a sharp eye out for them and always give them a wide berth. A dangling participle is a clause containing a present participle with no subject, followed by a main clause with a different subject to the subject of the participle. This inelegant and nonsensical construction should be avoided at all costs.

For example: 'Having read the book, a bottle of wine was opened' is incorrect. The bottle of wine did not read the book. This should be reworded along the lines of 'Having read the book, she opened a bottle of wine'.

DIVIDE AND OVERRULE: SPLIT INFINITIVES

Split infinitives should be avoided if possible although sometimes they are necessary and you should boldly face down any irate grammarians who object. A split infinitive is where the infinitive form of a verb – for example 'to cook', 'to go', 'to kill' – is interrupted by an adverb. The opening lines of *Star Trek* contain the most famous split infinitive of all time: 'to boldly go'. This should strictly be 'to go boldly'.

KNOWING ME, KNOWING YOU: 'ME', 'MYSELF' AND 'I'

Surprisingly, considering how central we all are to our own universes, many people make mistakes when referring to themselves in sentences. 'I' is used when you are the subject of the sentence and 'me' should be used only when you are the object. 'Tristan and me smoked a hundred fags today' is incorrect – the sentence should be 'Tristan and I smoked a hundred fags today'. The way to work this out is to remove Tristan from the sentence: you wouldn't say 'Me smoked a hundred cigarettes today', you would naturally say 'I smoked a hundred cigarettes today'. The same rule applies if you are confused about when to use 'she' or 'her' and 'he' or 'him'. 'Tristan and she smoked a hundred cigarettes today' is correct, rather than 'Tristan and her smoked a hundred cigarettes today'.

'Myself' is a **reflexive pronoun**. Reflexive pronouns are pronouns that refer back to the subject of a sentence: e.g. 'oneself', 'himself', 'yourself', 'themselves'. They are used when the subject and object of a sentence are the same, such as in the sentence 'I love myself a bit too much'. 'Myself' should never be used as a substitute for 'me' or 'I'. 'He gave myself the tax return' is incorrect. It should be 'He gave me the tax return'.

!??..:,,?!!: PUNCTUATION

Except for in the work of very clever novelists, sentences in prose are broken up into logical parts using punctuation marks. In speech, these represent pauses but in written language there are certain rules that should be followed.

Full stops divide sentences from other sentences. They are the strongest form of punctuation. 'Gwendoline is rather nasty. She is holding Mary-Lou under the water.'

Question marks are used in the place of full stops when the sentence is a question. 'Is Mary-Lou all right?'

Exclamation marks are used after words, phrases or sentences that are exclamatory, hortatory (i.e. giving encouragement or advice), particularly enthusiastic or full of wonder or contempt. 'What a horrible cow!'

Colons are used to introduce lists or to separate main clauses in a sentence where the following clause explains, paraphrases or gives an example of the preceding clause. 'Darrell had a short temper: she lost control and smacked Gwendoline in the face.'

Semicolons are used between two main clauses when they are connected together more strongly than warrants a full stop. They are also used to divide sentences that complement or parallel each other in some way or to divide up lists if commas aren't clear enough to mark the divisions. 'Miss Grayling, the headmistress; Miss Potts, the first-form teacher; Mr Young, the music teacher; Mam'zelle Dupont, the French teacher'.

Dashes are used to indicate a pause or to introduce a list or explanation. Pairs of dashes are often used in the place of parentheses or commas. 'Mary-Lou is timid – some would say positively wet – and rather small of stature.'

Parentheses (also called brackets) are used to separate off extra information or explanations from the rest of the sentence. Square brackets are used to indicate material that has been inserted by an editor, or someone other than the author of the rest of the text. 'Gwendoline broke Mary-Lou's most treasured possession [an expensive fountain pen] and tried to frame Darrell for the crime.'

Commas are used as light divisions to make the structure and meaning of sentences clear, for example in lists. They are also used to mark non-restrictive relative clauses. They are useful tools to avoid ambiguity. The famous sentence 'He eats shoots and leaves', means something entirely different when a comma is added: 'He eats, shoots and leaves.' Some people use commas more than others so the rules are slightly more flexible than for other forms of punctuation. However, you should *never* separate a subject from its verb with a comma or a verb from its object. In the sentence above separating the verb 'eats' from its object 'shoots and leaves' utterly changes the meaning of the sentence. You also cannot link two main clauses using a comma, you must use a conjunction instead. For example, 'Gwendoline is a spoilt brat, she also has blonde hair' is wrong. This should read 'Gwendoline is a spoilt brat and she also has blonde hair'.

Apostrophes are used to indicate possession ('Mary-Lou's pen', 'Darrell's temper'). The apostrophe comes before the 's' for singular nouns and after the 's' for plural nouns: 'Mary-Lou's pen'; 'the girls' swimming lesson'. However, for nouns that don't add an 's' in the plural, you need to add ''s', e.g. 'the women's conversation'. Apostrophes are also used to indicate missing letters ('she'll' is a contraction of 'she will'). Please be sure to remember that 'its' means 'belonging to it' and 'it's' means 'it is'.

Quotation marks are used to indicate quotations and direct speech. '"It wasn't me," she answered.'

Hyphens are used in some compound words such as 'musk-rose' and 'non-infectious'. They are also used to connect words that would look awkward or unclear if they were put together to make one word, e.g. re-enact, drip-proof, part-time. Hyphens are also used to link words used to describe an attribute of the noun, such as 'well-known villain', 'in-depth investigation', and to avoid ambiguity – the 'deep-blue sea' is different to the 'deep blue sea'.

BELLS AND WHISTLES: FIGURES OF SPEECH I

The very best authors use linguistic effects to add variety and imaginative emphasis to their writing. Figures of speech involve uses of words that go beyond the words' literal meaning and have been popular since the glory days of rhetoric in the Roman Empire, when they were used to bolster the persuasiveness of political arguments in debates as well as in literary works. You will find that you naturally use different stylistic effects in everyday speech without realising it: 'I'm boiling hot,' 'He's a bastard,' 'It scared the hell out of me.' It can become tiresome to listen to someone pontificating in continual metaphor, but it is a useful exercise to try to pepper your literary endeavours with a few of the following:

Metaphor: The use of a term for an object or action that feels imaginatively true but is not literally relevant. For example, referring to an intimate friend as an 'old flame', does not literally mean that he or she is aged and on fire but that metaphorical language is being used to describe desire in terms of fire conjuring up a sense of its uncontrollable and overwhelming quality.

Simile: Similar to metaphor but involving comparisons, for example 'He is as mad as a badger'. You can spot the difference between similes and metaphors because similes use the words 'like' or 'as'.

Pathetic fallacy: The term used when inanimate things are invested with human feelings or actions. Here is an example from Shelley's poem 'To Jane': 'The stars will awaken / Though the moon sleep a full hour later'. If you pay proper attention to the Geography chapter you will know that the moon and stars never go to bed or get up.

Euphemism: The substitution of a milder or more genteel phrase to describe something that might be seen as offensive or unpleasant. Some examples are 'We're going to have to let you go' = 'You're sacked', 'She passed away' = 'She died', 'I'd like us to be friends' = 'You're dumped', 'Follically challenged' = 'Bald'.

Hyperbole: Extreme exaggeration. For example: 'I'm so hungry I could eat a horse'; 'You are the worst driver in the world'; 'He weighs about fifty stone'.

Synecdoche: This is where the part is used to represent the whole or vice versa. The phrases 'hired hands' and 'mouths to feed' are synecdoches.

Litotes: Ironic understatement, particularly where a negative construction is used: 'No small problem'; 'I was not entirely happy'.

Prosopopoeia: The personification of an inanimate thing or the representation of the speech of an absent or imaginary person. 'The cake was calling to me' is an example of prosopopoeia.

Oxymoron: A figure of speech where opposite or contradicting words are combined. 'Thunderous silence' is an example of an oxymoron.

A GOOD MOOD: THE SUBJUNCTIVE

It is quite possible to wander carelessly through life in blissful ignorance of what actually constitutes the subjunctive, but most native English speakers use it intuitively all the time so it is worth closer inspection.

The subjunctive is what is known as a **grammatical mood**. Grammatical moods describe the relationship a verb has to reality and intent. There are both **realis moods** and **irrealis moods**.

Realis moods indicate that something is, or is not, actually the case. The easy way to remember this is that realis moods are based on reality. The everyday indicative mood that all of us use all the time for making factual statements is a realis mood. For example, 'Zammo is a heroin addict'.

Irrealis moods indicate that the situation described is not known to have definitely happened. The subjunctive is an irrealis mood. The subjunctive is used for statements that discuss hypothetical or unlikely events, express opinions or emotions, or make polite requests: 'If I were you, I'd sell your mother's silver'; 'I suggested that he seek professional help'.

The subjunctive looks exactly like the indicative except for: – in the verb 'to be' where 'be' is used for all persons* of the present subjunctive and 'were' for all persons in the past subjunctive (as in 'If I were you . . .') – in all other verbs in the third-person present singular where the verb drops its normal 's' ending (as in 'I suggested that he seek . . .' rather than 'he seeks').

---

*A REMINDER OF THE PERSONS OF A VERB

first person = I	first-person plural = we
second person = you	second-person plural = you
third person = he, she or it	third-person plural = they

NIMBLE -NYMS:
SOME DISTINCTIVE WORD TYPES

Homonym: A word with the same sound and spelling as another word but a different meaning: 'mouse' meaning small, furry rodent and 'mouse' meaning a device to move the cursor on a computer are homonyms.

Synonym: A word that means the same, or nearly the same, as another word: 'scared' and 'frightened' are synonyms.

Metonym: A word that means one thing but is used to refer to a related thing: 'the Crown' can mean 'the monarchy', 'plastic' can be used to mean 'credit card'.

Hapax legomenon: A word that occurs only once in a language's recorded texts or in an author's body of work. 'Honorificabili-tudinitatibus' appears only once in all Shakespeare's plays (in *Love's Labour's Lost*) and is therefore a hapax legomenon of these works. (By the way, 'honorificabilitudinitatibus' means deserving of respect).

Neologism: A word that has just been invented.

Nonce word: A word that is made up for a particular occasion and not expected to be used again.

Portmanteau word: '*Portmanteau*' is a French word for suitcase and a portmanteau word is a word that blends two separate words together to make a new word. The term comes from Lewis Carroll's book *Through the Looking-Glass* where it is used to describe the nonce word 'slithy' which is a mixture of 'lithe' and 'slimy'.

Palindrome: A word, phrase or sentence which reads the same forwards or backwards. 'Deed', 'madam', and 'I prefer pi' are all palindromes.

SP: SOME COMMONLY
MISSPELLED WORDS

Very few people have a 100 per cent hit rate with their spelling. Even the most learned lexical geniuses can occasionally be stumped by particularly difficult terms, or make the odd careless error with familiar words. It's true that it's more of a wrestling match for some people than others but with a little practice we can all master our own blind spots, be they 'they're' for 'their', 'you're' for 'your' or more complicated constructions like 'psittacine' (meaning 'of the parrot family', in case you're wondering), 'sciatica', or 'Mississippi'.

Here are a couple of rules to help you with some common spelling difficulties, although naturally there are exceptions to every rule:

- In words that feature the combination of letters 'i' and 'e', the 'i' usually comes before the 'e' except when the letters follow the letter 'c'. The rhyme to help you remember this is '"i" before "e" except after "c"'.
- It is also useful to remember that in British English '-ce' endings usually indicate nouns and '-se' endings indicate verbs; e.g. 'practice' and 'practise', and 'licence' and 'license'. American English uses '-se' for both nouns and verbs.

We've compiled a list of frequently misspelled words here for you to learn by heart to avoid future humiliating errors:

accommodate	drunkenness	manoeuvre	rhythm
cemetery	harass	millennium	sacrilegious
daiquiri	inoculate	minuscule	satellite
diarrhoea	leisure	occurrence	supersede
discreet*	liaison	parallel	weird

(*this means 'circumspect', the other spelling – 'discrete' – means 'separate')

TINSEL AND BAUBLES: RHETORICAL EFFECTS

There are so many wonderful words to describe the inventive use of words that we couldn't resist adding a few more here for your delectation. Be sure to look out for these clever constructions in the next book you read, and then talk about them loudly on the bus in order to draw impressed looks of admiration from your fellow passengers.

Onomatopoeia: The use of words that sound like what they are referring to: 'cuckoo', 'snap' and 'mellifluous' are examples of onomatopoeic words.

Anacoluthon: A sentence that lacks correct grammatical structure sometimes used in literature for rhetorical purposes or to indicate realistic thought processes: 'If only I had been there – nothing could've saved him.'

Anaphora: The repetition of a word or words at the start of successive phrases or sentences. 'Never take unnecessary risks. Never agree to carry out dangerous dares. Never climb on to the roofs of multi-storey car parks.'

Chiasmus: Two parallel phrases where the order of words in the first is reversed in the second. This term comes from the ancient Greek word '*chiasma*' meaning 'cross'. 'He plunged from on high and from below we looked on' is a chiastic sentence.

Alliteration: The repetition of sounds or letters at the start of successive or closely positioned words: 'He was a sad, silly show-off.'

Assonance: Repetition of the same sounds, particularly the repetition of the same vowel sounds in successive or closely positioned words or phrases: 'Why lie? He died.'

Consonance: The repetition of similar-sounding consonants in successive or closely positioned words or phrases: 'It seems like such a shocking shame.'

Zeugma: A verbal construction where one word is applied to two others with differences in meaning for each. This comes from the ancient Greek word '*zuegnunai*', meaning 'to yoke together'. For example: 'He lost his footing and his life.'

Allegory: A work of literature where the meaning or message is represented symbolically rather than realistically. *Pilgrim's Progress* by John Bunyan is a famous allegorical story. At first look it appears to be a story about a difficult trip undertaken by a man called Christian. In fact, his journey is a symbolic representation of the Christian soul's journey to heaven.

ENGLISH LITERATURE

SPEED-READING: A VERY SHORT GUIDE TO SOME KEY WORKS OF LITERATURE

Pride and Prejudice (1813) by Jane Austen – Sassy woman with nightmare family meets snobby rich boy. After various intrigues everyone ends up married.

Oliver Twist (1837–8) by Charles Dickens – Orphan asks for more gruel and ends up on the streets, is cruelly treated by adults, makes friends with criminal gang, gets implicated in robbery, and is rescued by kind-hearted honest folk who turn out to be relatives. Prostitute pal doesn't fare so well.

Wuthering Heights (1847) by Emily Brontë – Love triangle on the Yorkshire moors between dark, moody ruffian, spoilt, vivacious blonde and weedy nice-guy ends with all of them dead but their children getting on like a house on fire.

War and Peace (1865–9) by Leo Tolstoy – Napoleon is winning the war against Russia. No he isn't! Yes he is! No he isn't! Sparky Natasha loves ambitious Andrei but nearly runs off with sleazy Anatole before eventually ending up with thoughtful but bumbling, ex-Freemason, ex-aspiring political assassin and ex-prisoner-of-war, Pierre.

Ulysses (1918–20) by James Joyce – One day Leopold Bloom, having trouble with his missus, wanders around Dublin and bumps into Stephen Dedalus. After 933 pages Bloom ends up in bed with Mrs Bloom.

To the Lighthouse (1927) by Virginia Woolf – Holidaying family attempt to visit the local lighthouse and finally get round to it ten years later.

Of Mice and Men (1937) by John Steinbeck – Little clever guy and big stupid guy get jobs on California farm, but clumsy big guy accidentally kills the boss's wife. Little guy shoots big guy to save him from lynching, while promising him a rabbit farm.

An Inspector Calls (1947) by J. B. Priestley – Inspector questions nouveau riche family about a girl's suicide. Turns out they all did it. Then it turns out the inspector wasn't an inspector.

Lord of the Flies (1954) by William Golding – Schoolboys survive plane crash but quickly start killing each other and end up crying on the beach.

DYNAMIC DICKENS'S DAZZLING DRAMATIS PERSONAE

One of our best-loved novelists, and probably the first ever international literary celebrity, Charles John Huffam Dickens was born on 7 February 1812 in Landport, Portsmouth. His father was a clerk in the Navy Pay Office who wasn't very good at taking care of his pennies and, when Charles was twelve years old, Dickens pater was imprisoned in the Marshalsea jail in Southwark for debt (please read our Household Management section in the Home Economics chapter to avoid a similar fate).

As a result of this Charles was forced to go to work in a shoe-polish factory, which he apparently described to his biographer John Foster as 'a crazy, tumbledown old house . . . literally overrun with rats'. Thankfully an inheritance saved the day and young Charles was able to leave his dreary work pasting labels onto jars and go to school.

The only way was up from this point on: having worked as a law clerk and a journalist, at the age of twenty-one Dickens began to publish short stories and essays in newspapers and magazines. *The Pickwick Papers*, his first commercial success, was published in 1836, the same year that he married Catherine Hogarth, with whom he went on to have ten children.

Many other novels followed and Dickens became incredibly popular in America as well as Britain. He was celebrated for the animated readings of his work and his author tours were spectacular successes. However, on his final tour in 1870, the strain of reading his brutal description of Bill Sikes's murder of Nancy from *Oliver Twist* has been attributed by some biographers to worsening his already frail health. Charles Dickens died on 9 June of that year leaving his last novel, *The Mystery of Edwin Drood*, unfinished. He is buried in Westminster Abbey.

Dickens is widely admired for the exceptionally colourful characters that gambol, skip and creep through his work, some of whom were based on figures from his own life. The famous ones like Ebeneezer Scrooge, Mr Micawber, Miss Havisham, Uriah Heep, Mr Pickwick, Fagin, Mr Gradgrind and Little Nell are familiar to us all and many of them have the dubious honour of having public houses named after them all over the world. However, Dickens invested even his bit players with engaging and surprising traits. Below you will find a list of five of the most memorable of the great Charles's minor creations:

The Fat Boy (*The Pickwick Papers*, 1836-7) – Actually called Joe, the Fat Boy is an obese child who falls asleep all the time, often standing up, and after whom the medical condition Pickwickian syndrome, where obesity negatively affects a patient's sleep, is named.

Bull's-eye (*Oliver Twist*, 1837-8) – A 'white shaggy dog, with his face scratched and torn in twenty different places', belonging to the villain Bill Sikes with 'faults of temper in common with his owner'. Bull's-eye terrorises poor Oliver and later witnesses Bill's murder of Nancy (and gets his paws covered in her blood), thereafter becoming a liability to Bill who attempts to drown him. Evidently forgiving this insult, at Bill's death, Bull's-eye throws himself off a building with 'a dismal howl'.

The Marchioness (*The Old Curiosity Shop*, 1841) – A mysterious tiny-framed child, the Marchioness works for the 'amazon at common law' Sally Brass, and is locked in her downstairs kitchen every night. She never has 'a clean face ... or ... any rest or enjoyment whatever'. She is known simply as the 'small servant' until Richard Swiveller christens her 'the Marchioness' during an illicit card game. She proves crucial to the plot, thanks to her eavesdropping skills, and, after being rescued and sent off to school by Swiveller, balances out Little Nell's sad ending by eventually becoming his happily married wife, 'And they played many hundred thousand games of cribbage together.'

Mr Krook (*Bleak House*, 1852–3) – The 'short, cadaverous, and withered' owner of a Rag and Bottle and Marine Stores Shop (he even seems to sell cat skins and sacks of ladies' hair) and a vicious grey cat called Lady Jane. Krook is partial to a drop of the hard stuff but mainly noteworthy for his unusual demise – in Chapter 32 he spontaneously combusts.

Aged Parent (*Great Expectations*, 1860-1) – Aged P. is more an example of warm-hearted comic colour than central to the plot of *Great Expectations*. He is Pip's friend Wemmick's ancient father: 'a very old man in a flannel coat: clean, cheerful, comfortable, and well cared for, but intensely deaf'. He lives with his son in Walworth in 'a crazy little box of a cottage' decked out to look like a castle, where every night they set off a gun and every Sunday the deaf old man reads out the newspapers. He is very fond of buttered toast and sausages.

THAT FORBIDDEN TREE: MILTON'S *PARADISE LOST*

John Milton (1608–74) is arguably our nation's greatest epic poet. A Renaissance man, he excelled at school and was passionate about languages – in later life he could speak French, Spanish, Italian, Greek, Latin, Aramaic, Hebrew and Anglo-Saxon. He was fervently political and religious and wrote campaigning pamphlets on various subjects – including a surprisingly modern tract on divorce after his wife deserted him.

His eyesight deteriorated when he was in his thirties and by the age of forty-six he was blind. He conceived of the idea of an epic poem, the first to be written in English, as a teenager, but it wasn't until he was forced by the Restoration to go into hiding that he was afforded the time to write it. He chose the Book of Genesis as his subject and dictated the poem in blank verse over several years to his two long-suffering daughters. *Paradise Lost* was finally published in 1667, with a revised version appearing in 1671.

Drawing inspiration from classic epics such as Homer's *Odyssey* and Virgil's *Aeneid*, Milton set out to write a poem that would 'justify the ways of God to man'. Arranged in twelve books, *Paradise Lost* tells the story of Satan's exile from heaven and his efforts to compete with God by meddling with His best creation: humankind.

In order to attack God, Satan travels to Paradise and the Garden of Eden, where the first people, Adam and Eve, live in bliss. He disguises himself as a toad to try to persuade Eve to disobey God's prohibition against eating fruit from the Tree of Knowledge. However, the Archangel Gabriel, who guards Eden, finds Satan and kicks him out, and the Archangel Raphael is dispatched to talk to Adam and Eve about the threat from their sly enemy.

After sharing a meal together, Eve leaves the table and Raphael tells Adam of the war fought between the angels and Satan, of Satan's jealousy of the Son of God, and of the tricksy ways that Satan might try to corrupt Adam and Eve. He also tells the story of how the world was made and how Adam was created. Adam confesses how attracted to Eve he is but Raphael urges him to calm down and try to love her in a spiritual rather than physical way.

Eight days after leaving the garden, the incorrigible Satan returns disguised as a serpent and this time he successfully seduces Eve into eating from the forbidden tree. When he discovers what has happened, Adam decides he would rather be punished with his beloved than lose her and so eats the fruit as well. For this crime, the pair, and all their future progeny, are sentenced by the Son to endure the afflictions of death and sin. Eve is also cursed with the pain of childbirth and the serpent is condemned never to walk upright. The glorious weather the Earth has enjoyed up until this point is also made more inhospitable to the fallen couple.

Adam and Eve repent of their sins and decide to try to redeem them-selves, and ultimately beat Satan, by staying obedient to God in the future. The Archangel Michael escorts them out of the garden and shows Adam a vision of their future, of generations devastated by death and sin. He then shows him a more positive vision of Noah, along with other scenes that appear in the Bible. Finally, Adam and Eve leave Paradise hand in hand.

This majestic poem is enormously rich and reflects on themes such as man's place in the world, the role of women and sex, concepts of free will, hierarchy and redemption; yet it is perhaps most powerful in its remarkable depiction of Satan. Rather than being a simple embodiment of evil, Satan is rendered as an incredibly complex character by Milton:

he struggles with his own failings, he suffers jealousy, emotion, pride, and in the opening books he is endowed with an extraordinary heroism – refusing to be frightened of God, and courageously accepting his fate of eternal damnation. Some have suggested that this heroism is a deliberate narrative device, demonstrating to us as readers how easy it is to be tempted by evil. Others have suggested that, even if he wasn't completely aware of it himself, Milton had a revolutionary sensibility, and was drawn to his anti-hero's pluck and boldness.

METRE MATTERS:
PERFECT YOUR PROSODY

Prosody is another term for the laws of **metre** in verse and metre is simply the official term used to describe poetic rhythm – the magic ingredient that sets verse apart from common-or-garden prose. Poets often use particular structures and rhythms for their works, above and beyond the innate beats and musicality of the way we naturally speak.

Although we don't use written accents much, like French or Italian, English is an accentual language. This means that words all have different patterns of stress – you'll find that you naturally say one syllable (unit of sound) of the word 'postman' with more emphasis than the other syllable. 'Postman' is generally pronounced with a stress on the first syllable '**post**man' rather than on the second syllable 'post**man**'. The stressed syllables in words can differ depending on regional accent.

Most English poetry is made up of different patterns of word stress and numbers of syllables: this is called **accentual-syllabic metre**. In other languages, such as Latin, poetic metre is defined by the length of sounds of the syllables rather than the stress on them, which is known as **quantitative metre**. It is also possible to have purely **syllabic metre** (based on the number of syllables in a line), as in Japanese **haiku**, although this isn't common in English poetry. Purely **accentual metre**, where the number of stresses in a line is fixed but the total number of syllables can alter from line to line, used to be common in Anglo-Saxon poetry, such as the marvellous eighth-century Old English epic poem *Beowulf*.

However, much as all these different flavours of metre are enthralling in their own rights, you'll be glad to know that we are only going to pay close attention to accentual-syllabic metre here. The key thing to remember about this is that *the number and pattern of stresses in a line of poetry define its metre.*

Now that you've got metre, syllables and stress clear, it's time to recall that lines of poetry are divided into **feet**. Each foot has a particular pattern of stressed and unstressed syllables that is then repeated a set number of times in the line. This fancy footwork constitutes the metre. For example, an **iambic pentameter** is a line of five feet (the word pentameter comes from the ancient Greek meaning 'five measures') where each foot is a specific pattern of one unstressed syllable followed by one stressed syllable called an **iamb**.

The best examples of the great iamb at work in this way are to be found in the works of Shakespeare: 'Shall **I** | com**pare** | thee **to** | a **summ** | er's **day**?' is a perfect iambic pentameter. Shakespeare is famous for his masterful use of **blank verse**, which simply means unrhymed iambic pentameters. Words that are naturally iambic when standing alone include 'achieve', 'delight' and 'reproach'.

DIFFERENT TYPES OF METRE

dimeter . . . . two feet
trimeter . . . . three feet
tetrameter . . . . four feet
pentameter . . . . five feet
hexameter . . . . six feet

There are other types of metre, with greater numbers of feet, but these are the ones you really need to get a fix on as they are the most common in English poetry. All their names are taken from the ancient Greek numbers for the quantity of feet they contain.

DIFFERENT TYPES OF FEET

This table shows some different varieties of metric feet. The most common ones used in English poetry are **iambs**, **trochees**, **dactyls** and **anapaests**. There are many more but we have only listed the feet that consist of two and three syllables below.

− = unstressed	/ = stressed
iamb	− /
trochee	/ −
spondee	/ /
pyrrhus	− −
anapaest	− − /
dactyl	/ − −
amphibrach	− / −
amphimacer	/ − /
bacchius	− / /
antibacchius	/ / −
molossus	/ / /
tribrach	− − −

Usually, the carefully chosen pattern of words in a line creates the metre but individual words each have their own natural metre as well. The word 'suspect', when it is being used as a verb is naturally iambic: 'I sus**pect** him of tax evasion'. However, when this word is used as a noun ('They arrested the **sus**pect') or adjective (I found his alibi a little **sus**pect'), it takes the stress on the first syllable and is therefore a trochee. The words 'arrested' and 'evasion' are amphibrachs and 'alibi' is a dactyl.

Obviously, normal prose sentences have no ordered metre. Poets use meticulously selected combinations of words to create their rhythms rather than simply relying on the individual words' inherent stress patterns.

Here are some lines of different regular metres, to help you get a feel for them.

First, a hurtling anapaestic tetrameter by the dashing Lord Byron:

> The Assyrian came down like the wolf on the fold,
> And his cohorts were gleaming in purple and gold;

Next, a vivid trochaic tetrameter from William Blake, with the added twist of a dropped final syllable creating a **strong** or **masculine rhyme**:

> Tyger! Tyger! burning bright
> In the forests of the night.

A strong rhyme, often also called a masculine rhyme (because, of course, all men are strong and brave like stressed syllables), is where the final syllable of the line is stressed. In contrast a **weak** or **feminine rhyme** is where the final syllable of the line is unstressed.

Here we have a beautifully melancholy iambic pentameter from Christina Rossetti:

> Remember me when I am gone away,
> Gone far away into the silent land.

If you're having trouble remembering which metre is which, there is an ingenious poem by Samuel Taylor Coleridge (1772–1834), written to help his son remember the different metrical feet. Here is the first stanza:

> Trochee trips from long to short;
> From long to long in solemn sort
> Slow Spondee stalks, strong foot!, yet ill able
> Ever to come up with Dactyl's trisyllable.
> Iambics march from short to long.
> With a leap and a bound the swift Anapaests throng.
> One syllable long, with one short at each side,
> Amphibrachys hastes with a stately stride.
> First and last being long, middle short, Amphimacer
> Strikes his thundering hoofs like a proud high-bred Racer.

Now that you've got a firm grasp on the laws of metre it's important to learn that these particular rules are made to be broken. Poets are wild and zany creatures who like to mess around with the regular rhythmic structures imparted by set metres. There are many effects that they use to give life, emotion and style to their poems. Sometimes they will add odd feet of different types into an otherwise ordered pattern for emphasis or surprise, sometimes they leave pauses called **caesuras** in the middle of their lines, sometimes they arrange patterns of rhyming words at the ends of certain lines in their work and sometimes they disrupt the rhythm by adding extra syllables or dropping them altogether.

Modern poets often work without regular metre at all, using patterns of stress and stylistic effects that vary from line to line: this is known as **free verse** or *vers libre*. This form wasn't used extensively before the nineteenth century but is very popular nowadays. Free verse is not without rhythm (if it was, it would be prose of course) but the patterns of rhythm and cadence are irregular.

STANZA FORMS

If we push back our spectacles, blink at the light and move up a level from the individual combinations of words that make a poetic line, we come to the overall structure of a poem. A whole poem is often divided into different sections called **stanzas**, a bit like paragraphs in prose. There are certain verse forms that always have the same number and arrangement of lines in their stanzas, or patterns of rhyme at the end of lines. Some of the most famous are listed below.

Petrarchan sonnet	One stanza of eight lines (called an **octave**) ending in rhymes in the pattern ABBAABBA (i.e. line one rhymes with lines four, five and eight and line two rhymes with three, six and seven). This is followed by one stanza of six lines (called a **sestet**) traditionally rhyming in the pattern CDECDE but nowadays also encompassing different schemes. Petrarchan sonnets are usually composed of iambic pentameters.

Shakespearean sonnet	Three stanzas of four lines (called **quatrains**) rhyming ABAB CDCD EFEF followed by two lines (called a **couplet**) rhyming GG. Usually in iambic pentameters.
Spenserian sonnet	Three quatrains rhyming ABAB BCBC CDCD followed by a couplet rhyming EE. Usually in iambic pentameters.
Ballad	Poems usually involving quatrains with alternating tetrameters and trimeters.
Ballade	Three stanzas each with the same pattern of three rhymes followed by one short concluding stanza.
Terza rima	Poems involving **tercets** (sets of three lines) where the middle line of each tercet rhymes with the first and last lines of the following tercet.
Ottava rima	Poems involving octaves of iambic pentameters with the rhyme scheme ABABABCC.
Villanelle	Five stanzas of tercets followed by one quatrain, all using only two rhymes.
Sestina	Six sestets followed by one tercet with lines ending in set patterns of repeated words.
Heroic couplet	Two rhyming lines of iambic pentameter.

A PORTRAIT OF A POEM:
HOW TO ANALYSE POETRY

'To His Coy Mistress' by Andrew Marvell

Had we but world enough, and time,
This coyness, lady, were no crime.
We would sit down and think which way
To walk, and pass our long love's day.
Thou by the Indian Ganges' side
Shouldst rubies find: I by the tide
Of Humber would complain. I would
Love you ten years before the Flood:
And you should, if you please, refuse
Till the conversion of the Jews.
My vegetable love should grow
Vaster than empires, and more slow.
An hundred years should go to praise
Thine eyes, and on thy forehead gaze.
Two hundred to adore each breast:
But thirty thousand to the rest.
An age at least to every part,
And the last age should show your heart.
For, lady, you deserve this state,
Nor would I love at lower rate.

But at my back I always hear
Time's wingèd chariot hurrying near:
And yonder all before us lie
Deserts of vast eternity.
Thy beauty shall no more be found,
Nor, in thy marble vault, shall sound
My echoing song: then worms shall try
That long preserv'd virginity:
And your quaint honour turn to dust;
And into ashes all my lust.
The grave's a fine and private place,
But none I think do there embrace.

★

Now therefore, while the youthful hue
Sits on thy skin like morning dew,
And while thy willing soul transpires
At every pore with instant fires,
Now let us sport us while we may;
And now, like am'rous birds of prey,
Rather at once our time devour,
Than languish in his slow-chapp'd power.
Let us roll all our strength, and all
Our sweetness, up into one ball:
And tear our pleasures with rough strife
Thorough the iron gates of life.
Thus, though we cannot make our sun
Stand still, yet we will make him run.

If you want to really get under the skin of a poem, there are certain steps you can take and points you can consider that may enhance your enjoyment and understanding. First of all, it's worth looking at the shape and pattern of the poem on the page. You may be able to identify the verse form by doing this and you'll also get an initial idea of the poet's intentions. Is the poem one long monologue? Is it broken down into bouncy rhyming couplets? Does it stretch on for pages and pages suggesting an epic bent in its ambitious creator?

The next step is to read the poem through in one go and then pause before reading it again slowly. It really is worth taking the time to read any poem you come across twice even if you go no further than this. Poems are not made to be raced through in order to grab information quickly, like recipes or instruction manuals. You should revel in the choice of words and the rhythm of the lines as well as thinking about the subject matter – you could even read the poem out loud if you feel so inclined and you won't be alarming anyone.

After this, hopefully you will have some idea of the purpose and style of the work you're considering. There are then various other factors that you can consider or research to help you delve further into the poem's secrets. Some helpful details about 'To His Coy Mistress' are given below.

Context

Depending on how inquisitive you're feeling, you can find out as little or as much as you like about the background and history of a poem. Poets can write very personally about themselves or adopt personas or write on subjects that have absolutely no connection with their actual lives. Some critics believe that a sense of context is imperative to understand poetic works properly, but others are equally adamant that poems should be looked at in isolation without the influence of knowledge about the poet's life. If you are of the latter persuasion then skip to the end of this section.

Andrew Marvell was born in 1621 in Yorkshire, the son of a clergyman. He entered Cambridge at the age of twelve and received his BA in 1639. After university he travelled the world before working as a tutor. He was John Milton's assistant in his post as Latin Secretary from 1657 to 1659 and from then until his death in 1678 he was MP for Hull.

Marvell, along with poets like John Donne and George Herbert, is referred to today as being one of the metaphysical poets. These poets considered metaphysical concerns such as the nature of being and the universe in compositions that typically showed great wit, lyricism and ingenuity of style.

'To His Coy Mistress' is a poem on the *carpe diem* theme. This means that it puts forward a similar attitude to one of the Latin poet Horace's celebrated odes which contains the phrase '*carpe diem*' or 'seize the day'. It's a theme celebrated in several works of literature including poems by Christopher Marlowe and Robert Herrick.

Structure

If you look closely, you will see that the structure of 'To His Coy Mistress' represents a perfect marriage of passion and logic. The poem takes the form of an appeal from a young man to his girlfriend to remember that life is short and therefore she should sleep with him while there is still time for them to enjoy it. It is a seduction poem that is carefully structured in three paragraphs which work syllogistically – there is an opening statement, a qualifying argument and finally a resolution.

In the first stanza the poet sets out his argument, stating 'Had we but world enough, and time, / This coyness, lady, were no crime', and goes on to give examples of the slow romancing they could enjoy if this were the case. In the second stanza he reminds his mistress that, in fact, death is only just round the corner and time is fleeting: 'But at my back I always hear / Time's winged chariot hurrying near'. The third stanza closes the poem with the exhortation to seize the day: 'Now let us sport us while we may'.

The poem is written in iambic tetrameter with rhyming couplets: the rhyme scheme is AA BB CC DD EE, perhaps to emphasise the poem's praise of union.

Language
Moving on from looking at the structure to the individual words, you will spot that 'To His Coy Mistress' employs lyrical language stuffed with religious and historical metaphors to emphasise the poet's logical argument, and at the same time to flatter his mistress. There is also a great deal of natural imagery: his love for her, if they had time, would be 'vegetable'; they should make love with the passion of hunting birds, while her skin is as new and young as the 'morning dew'. Pronouns are used extensively in the first stanza, but, as 'Time's winged chariot' appears, the pronouns disappear as the language compresses and literally speeds up, cleverly reflecting the increasing urgency of the speaker's feelings and the sense of time passing swiftly.

RHYMES TO REMEMBER: POEMS TO COMMIT TO MEMORY

It is not just a useful exercise in self-discipline and mental agility to memorise poetry – although these are certainly valid enough skills to sharpen up. Becoming intimately and permanently acquainted with a poet's creation brings a special joy of its own. On a more frivolous level, every cultured person should have a couple of decent poems up their sleeves in case they are called upon to do a turn at a party (recitation is much more elegant than belting out a karaoke hit). It is also useful in situations of stress – such as getting stuck on top of a ferris wheel or at a child's fourth birthday party – to have a poem lodged away in the archives of your mind to recite to yourself in a calming way. It helps with insomnia too. The following works particularly lend themselves to memorisation and recitation.

'The Tyger' by William Blake (1757–1827)

Tyger! Tyger! burning bright
In the forests of the night,
What immortal hand or eye
Could frame thy fearful symmetry?

In what distant deeps or skies
Burnt the fire of thine eyes?
On what wings dare he aspire?
What the hand dare seize the fire?

And what shoulder, & what art,
Could twist the sinews of thy heart?
And when thy heart began to beat,
What dread hand? & what dread feet?

What the hammer? what the chain,
In what furnace was thy brain?
What the anvil? what dread grasp
Dare its deadly terrors clasp?

When the stars threw down their spears,
And watered heaven with their tears,
Did he smile his work to see?
Did he who made the Lamb make thee?

Tyger! Tyger! burning bright
In the forests of the night,
What immortal hand or eye
Dare frame thy fearful symmetry?

'Auld Lang Syne' by Robert Burns (1759–96)

Should auld acquaintance be forgot,
And never brought to min'?
Should auld acquaintance be forgot,
And auld lang syne?

For auld lang syne, my dear,
For auld lang syne,
We'll tak a cup o' kindness yet,
For auld lang syne.

We twa hae run about the braes,
An pu'd the gowans fine;
But we've wandered mony a weary foot
Sin' auld lang syne.

We twa hae paidled i' the burn,
Frae morning sun till dine;
But seas between us braid hae roared
Sin' auld lang syne

And there's a hand, my trusty fiere,
And gie's a hand o' thine;
And we'll tak a right guid-willie waught,
For auld lang syne.

And surely ye'll be your pint-stowp,
And surely I'll be mine;
And we'll tak a cup o' kindness yet
For auld lang syne.

'Daffodils' by William Wordsworth (1770–1850)

I wander'd lonely as a cloud
That floats on high o'er vales and hills,
When all at once I saw a crowd,
A host, of golden daffodils;
Beside the lake, beneath the trees,
Fluttering and dancing in the breeze.

Continuous as the stars that shine
And twinkle on the Milky Way,
They stretch'd in never-ending line
Along the margin of a bay:
Ten thousand saw I at a glance,
Tossing their heads in sprightly dance.

The waves beside them danced; but they
Out-did the sparkling waves in glee:
A poet could not but be gay,
In such a jocund company:
I gazed – and gazed – but little thought
What wealth the show to me had brought:

For oft, when on my couch I lie
In vacant or in pensive mood,
They flash upon that inward eye
Which is the bliss of solitude;
And then my heart with pleasure fills,
And dances with the daffodils.

'How Do I Love Thee?'
by Elizabeth Barrett Browning (1806–61)

How do I love thee? Let me count the ways.
I love thee to the depth and breadth and height
My soul can reach, when feeling out of sight
For the ends of Being and ideal Grace.
I love thee to the level of everyday's
Most quiet need, by sun and candle-light.
I love thee freely, as men strive for Right;
I love thee purely, as they turn from Praise.
I love thee with the passion put to use
In my old griefs, and with my childhood's faith.
I love thee with a love I seemed to lose
With my lost saints, – I love thee with the breath,
Smiles, tears, of all my life! – and, if God choose,
I shall but love thee better after death.

THE BRILLIANT BARD:
WILLIAM SHAKESPEARE (1564–1616)

You should be proud to number yourself among the 'happy few' who can claim William Shakespeare as their compatriot. Even though he may have had, as Ben Jonson said, 'small Latin and less Greek', this 'man of men' was an unequivocal genius who has exercised an unrivalled influence over the popular imaginations and language of our 'precious stone set in a silver sea'.

We know only the bare bones about William Shakespeare's life: he was 'of woman born' in Stratford-upon-Avon on or about 23 April 1564; he married Anne Hathaway in 1582 and they had three 'pretty chickens' – a daughter called Susanna and twins called Hamnet and Judith. We also know that in 1590 Shakespeare moved to London, without his family, to take on the job of one who 'struts and frets his hour upon the stage' as well as to write plays. He was a prominent member of the theatre company the Lord Chamberlain's Men (later the King's Men) who went on to 'achieve greatness'. The company built and occupied the Globe Theatre on the 'concave shores' of the River Thames from 1599 and over his career Shakespeare became the most popular playwright in England and was patronised by both Queen Elizabeth I and King James I. He succumbed to the 'fell sergeant, death' in 1616 on his fifty-second birthday.

Shakespeare's plays have remained popular for centuries – rarely a minute goes by without one of them being performed somewhere, whether it be a lisping school production of *Romeo and Juliet* or an elaborate star-studded RSC interpretation of *King Lear* – and no doubt they will continue to attract audiences 'tomorrow and tomorrow and tomorrow'. Shakespeare is also celebrated for his Sonnets but 'the play's the thing!' and it is for his unforgettable characters, his astonishing facility with language, his virtuoso mastery of blank verse and his dramatic versatility that he has 'grasp'd an immortality'.

A HANDFUL OF HAMLET TO LEARN BY HEART

Hamlet is probably Shakespeare's most famous play. It was written around 1600 and is the tragic story of a moody young Danish prince whose father has recently died. Hamlet is distressed by his mother's recent remarriage to his uncle Claudius and this isn't helped by the fact that at the start of the play his father's ghost pitches up to tell him that Claudius is responsible for his death. Over the course of the action Hamlet is tortured by this information and eventually decides to kill Claudius but accidentally ends up killing Polonius, the officious Lord Chamberlain, instead. As a result of this rather upsetting error, Polonius's daughter Ophelia goes mad and kills herself and his son Laertes challenges Hamlet to a duel. During the fight, Hamlet's mother drinks some fatal poison masquerading as wine that Claudius has intended for Hamlet. Before dying, Laertes reveals that Claudius is responsible for the poisoned wine and Hamlet stabs his uncle in revenge, before dying himself.

As you can see, the death toll is as high as any bloodthirsty Hollywood movie, but no glib summary can do justice to this exceptional work of art. If you actually see or read the play, you will find yourself

wholeheartedly caught up in the conflicts and struggles of the characters, and the ending will bring a tear to the eye of even the most jaded
of audience members. Here are Hamlet's famous musings on mortality
– the next time someone asks you if you are in a bad mood, try out this
little speech on them:

> I have of late, – but wherefore I know not, – lost all my mirth,
> forgone all custom of exercises; and indeed, it goes so heavily with
> my disposition that this goodly frame, the earth, seems to me a
> sterile promontory; this most excellent canopy, the air, look you,
> this brave o'erhanging firmament, this majestical roof fretted with
> golden fire, – why, it appears no other thing to me than a foul and
> pestilent congregation of vapours. What a piece of work is man!
> How noble in reason! how infinite in faculties! in form and
> moving, how express and admirable! in action, how like an angel!
> in apprehension, how like a god! the beauty of the world! the
> paragon of animals! And yet, to me, what is this quintessence of
> dust?

Act II, Scene 2, lines 287–98

**WILL'S WORDS:
PHRASES WE OWE TO SHAKESPEARE**

Shuffle off this mortal coil – *Hamlet*
Star-crossed lovers – *Romeo and Juliet*
One fell swoop – *Macbeth*
It was Greek to me – *Julius Caesar*
The green-eyed monster – *Othello*
Charmed life – *Macbeth*
Lay it on with a trowel – *As You Like It*
More in sorrow than in anger – *Hamlet*
That way madness lies – *King Lear*
The beast with two backs – *Othello*

ENGLISH TEST PAPER

1. **What do these words have in common?**

chimney	different	justice	luggage
monster	month	orange	pint
pizza	hospital	dictionary	promise
purple	silver	value	wasp
obvious	circus	galaxy	almond

2. **Spelling test**

   Underline the correct spelling of the words below:

   misspelt/mispelled/misspelled   millennium/milennium
   parallel/paralell   accommodate/acommodate
   cemetry/cemetery   wierd/weird
   friend/freind   calender/calendar
   liesure/leisure   daiquiri/daquiri
   drunkenness/drunkeness   liason/liaison
   rythm/rhythm   embarassment/embarrassment
   concience/conscience   fiery/firey
   arguement/argument   harass/harrass
   eighth/eigth   inoculate/innoculate

3. **Punctuate the following sentences:**

a) Foxes sometimes fight in the Browns garden as if staging a wrestling match but they always make up in the end

b) We always have been we are and I hope that we always shall be detested in France (Duke of Wellington)

c) I dont know what I said but I know what I think and well I assume its what I said (Donald Rumsfeld)

d) To lose one parent Mr Worthing may be regarded as a misfortune to lose both looks like carelessness (Oscar Wilde, *The Importance of Being Earnest*)

38

4. **Identify three different figures of speech used in the following sentences:**

Uriah, who was a bright spark, had his head buried in a book when we bumped into him in the park. 'Agnes!' he simpered. 'How impossibly beautiful you look today. It makes my life worth living to see you arrayed like a princess in all your seductive silks and satins.' 'Excuse Uriah,' I whispered to David, 'he's a bit of a fruitcake.'

5. **Identify the nouns, verbs and adverbs in the following sentence:**

As he walked slowly away from Brookfield School Mr Chipping thought fondly of his many years of service.

6. **Identify the correct sentence out of the following:**

a) 'The car, that was not environmentally friendly, was bought by my husband.'
b) 'The car, which was not environmentally friendly, was bought by my husband.'

7. **Is it Me, or I?**

Fill in the correct word in the following sentences:

a) Between you and ——, that new hairdresser is terrible.
b) Our boss was sure that Mildred and —— would both be successful in the promotion review.
c) It is —— alone who must take responsibility for the downturn in sales this month.
d) All the team, save ——, were good public speakers.

8. **Apostrophes**

Insert apostrophes as required in these sentences:

a) The only ladies gym in our town has had to close.

b) A mens working club has taken up the lease.
c) The three naughty girls homework was closely monitored.
d) Father returned to work yesterday after a few days at a gentlemens health resort.
e) The cars bumper was more damaged than the lorrys.

9. Insert the correct punctuation in the following sentences:

a) Good heavens she cried what do you think I meant to do eat the whole pie myself
b) Im so so sorry she wailed it wasnt my fault the jugs handle was broken
c) How queer it seems Alice said to herself to be going messages for a rabbit
d) Ladies prefer well cut silk lined dresses

10. Who, Whom or Whose?

Fill in the correct word, either 'who', 'whom' or 'whose', in the following sentences:

a) The boy —— stole the apple had to confess.
b) —— did you meet at the bus stop this morning?
c) To —— should I write for a new bus pass?
d) To —— does this bicycle belong?
e) The police kept an eye on the boys, —— they suspected of stealing the apples.

11. To hyphenate or not to hyphenate – that is the question!

Insert hyphens where appropriate in the following sentences:

a) My mother and father have gone to Skegness for a well earned rest.
b) The dentist's surgery was reached by an ill lit staircase.
c) The ball gown was sky blue in colour and reached her nicely shaped knees.
d) Sleeping cars are available on the night train to Edinburgh.

12. **Complete the following sentence, using either** *practise* **or** *practice*:

They say that —— makes perfect, but still I don't have time to —— guitar every day.

13. **Complete the following sentence, using either** *stationary* **or** *stationery*:

When the bus was finally ——, I jumped off and went to the —— shop to stock up on pencils.

14. **Complete the following sentence, using either** *passed* **or** *past*:

It was a very exciting cycle race. Tom quickly —— Stuart, and was first —— the post.

15. **A number of bees is called a swarm. Swarm is an example of a noun of assemblage. What are the corresponding nouns to describe a number of the following:**

a) crows
b) eggs
c) rooks and owls
d) monkeys
e) ferrets
f) badgers
g) cobblers

16. Verbal Reasoning

Can you answer the following riddles?

a) What relation is a child to its own father, if it is not its own father's son?
b) What goes uphill and downhill but never moves?
c) How many apples can you put in an empty barrel?
d) What is very light, but difficult to hold for very long?

17. What is synecdoche?

a) a popular dance often performed at children's parties
b) the offspring of a duck and an otter
c) a term for the rhetorical device of extreme exaggeration
d) a term for a rhetorical device where the part is used to represent the whole or vice versa.

18. Underline the example of litotes in the following sentence:

I was not overjoyed to hear that the light of my life, my innocent, fresh-faced sixteen-year-old daughter, was with child.

19. What is a hapax legomenon?

20. What is special about the following words:

Quack	Bang	Miaow
Slither	Click	Slurp

21. What is the etymology (where the word came from and how it developed) of the word 'gaudy'?

22. Literary couples

Match the classic couples from literature and then match them to the correct book:

Heathcliff	Scarlett O'Hara	*The Great Gatsby*
Mr Darcy	Daisy Buchanan	*Gone with the Wind*
Rhett Butler	Dolores Haze	*Lolita*
Aeneas	Beatrice	*Les Liaisons Dangereuses*
Count Vronsky	Madame de Tourvel	*The Divine Comedy*
Humbert Humbert	Catherine	*Anna Karenina*
Dante	Elizabeth Bennet	*Romeo and Juliet*
Jay Gatsby	Juliet	*The Aeneid*
Vicomte de Valmont	Anna Karenina	*Pride and Prejudice*
Romeo	Dido	*Wuthering Heights*

23. Famous first lines

Match these famous opening lines from great works of literature to the correct title and then match the title to the correct author:

'As Gregor Samsa awoke one morning from uneasy dreams he found himself transformed in his bed into a gigantic insect.'	*Moby-Dick*	J. M. Barrie
'It is a truth universally acknowledged, that a single man in possession of a good fortune, must be in want of a wife.'	*A Tale of Two Cities*	Franz Kafka
'Call me Ishmael.'	*Anna Karenina*	Charles Dickens
'Happy families are all alike; every unhappy family is unhappy in its own way.'	*Pride and Prejudice*	Anthony Burgess
'It was the best of times, it was the worst of times . . .'	*Metamorphosis*	George Orwell
'All children, except one, grow up.'	*Nineteen Eighty-four*	Leo Tolstoy
'It was a bright cold day in April, and the clocks were striking thirteen.'	*Peter Pan*	Herman Melville
'It was the afternoon of my eighty-first birthday, and I was in bed with my catamite when Ali announced that the archbishop had come to see me.'	*Earthly Powers*	Jane Austen

24. In 2008 which book won the coveted literary prize, the Best of the Bookers, celebrating the best of forty years of glorious winners?

a) *Life of Pi* by Yann Martel
b) *Possession* by A. S. Byatt
c) *Midnight's Children* by Salman Rushdie
d) *Lucky* by Jackie Collins

25. How many lines does a sonnet have?

26. What was Dickens's first job?

a) journalist
b) jam-maker
c) bottle washer
d) shoe-polish factory worker

27. In Milton's *Paradise Lost* he describes the punishment meted out by God upon snakes for their part in the fall of Adam and Eve. What was this punishment?

28. The line 'To swell the gourd, and plump the hazel shells' is the opening line of John Keats' evocative poem 'Ode to Autumn'. What metre is the poem written in?

29. How many feet does a tetrameter have?

30. What is a realis mood?

31. Which groundbreaking twentieth-century novel takes place over one day and is set entirely in Dublin?

32. According to John Milton's *Paradise Lost*, who do we have to blame for dreary April downpours?

33. Which heroine of a famous nineteenth-century novel has a particular fear of red wallpaper?

a) Dorothea Brooke from *Middlemarch*
b) Marianne Dashwood from *Sense and Sensibility*
c) Jane Eyre from *Jane Eyre*

34. Which of the following classic heroines has a pet cat called Dinah?

a) Scout Finch from *To Kill a Mockingbird*
b) Alice from *Alice's Adventures in Wonderland*
c) Maisie Farange from *What Maisie Knew*

35. Literary Conundrums: Who's Who?

a) Who is Marian Evans?
b) Who is Pip's mysterious benefactor in *Great Expectations*?
c) Who says the following to the man she eventually marries? 'I had not known you a month before I felt that you were the last man in the world whom I could ever be prevailed on to marry.'
d) Who is engaged to Natasha Rostov in *War and Peace* and who marries her?

36. Were you to run into some murderous supernatural creature of the night, who would you prefer to be on hand to help you out?

a) Mina Murray from *Dracula*
b) Elizabeth Lavenza from *Frankenstein*

37. Identify the classic novel from the newspaper headlines:

a) NANNY IN POSSESSED CHILDREN SHOCKER!
b) MAN SHIPWRECKED ON DESERT ISLAND FOR OVER 20 YEARS!
c) CANINE CONUNDRUM: FAMOUS DETECTIVE CALLED ON TO RID FAMILY OF ANCIENT CURSE!
c) TEENAGE GANG LEADER ON THE RUN IN BRIGHTON!

**38. How many people die violently during the course of
Shakespeare's play *Hamlet*?**

**39. The following quotations are from well-known
Shakespearean plays. Give the correct play, and if possible
the speaker, for each quote:**

a) 'Dost thou not see my baby at my breast
    That sucks the nurse asleep?'
b) 'A little more than kin, and less than kind.'
c) 'And gentlemen in England, now a-bed
    Shall think themselves accurs'd they were not here,
    And hold their manhoods cheap whiles any speaks
    That fought with us upon Saint Crispin's day.'
d) 'How sharper than a serpent's tooth it is
    To have a thankless child!'

**40. Name the Polish author who learned to speak French,
Russian and German before learning English (Hint: his
most famous novel was written in English and is set in
the Congo).**

2

MATHEMATICS

'**Mathematics** *n. pl.* the abstract science of number,
quantity, and space'
Oxford Concise English Dictionary

'If in other sciences we should arrive at certainty without
doubt and truth without error, it behoves us to place the
foundations of knowledge in mathematics'
ROGER BACON (1214–94)

For many of us, maths is remembered as the most hated of all school lessons. For some, nothing strikes fear into the soul as much as algebra or triggers traumatic tics quite like trigonometry. As most people have calculators on ubiquitous mobile phones, it would at first seem that the necessity of grasping the finer points of square roots or percentages is limited. But this shameful attitude is only for the idle or dim-witted.

It can be of great personal advantage to take an interest in mathematics: from ensuring your wage packet is correct, to calculating discounts in the January sales; from managing your household budget, to working out how many square metres of carpet you need for the living room. Mathematics is probably the most essential of the practical disciplines you learned at school and, if you take it slowly, it's not even as hard as you might remember.

On a higher level, maths is essential to unlocking the secrets of the

47

universe: physics, chemistry and biology all depend on mathematical methods, and its concepts also extend into architecture, art and even poetry. So, you see, mathematics can be beautiful – the purity of its logic and problem-solving make it a subject to revel in rather than revile – a star subject rather than a scary one.

This chapter will remind you of the mysteries of π and the glories of φ, the satisfaction of simplifying fractions and the aesthetic ramifications of the golden ratio, and much, much more. Take out your pencil and paper and turn over the page. You may begin.

ARITHMETIC

The word mathematics derives from the ancient Greek word for 'learning'. What most schoolchildren, labouring over their abacuses with sticky fingers, think of as maths is actually arithmetic: the art of counting. The symbols we use for numbers today are known as Hindu-Arabic numerals because, after being developed in India in the third century BCE, they were brought into use in Europe around 976 CE through the work of Arab mathematicians. Good mental arithmetic skills, such as those displayed by professional darts players and cricketers, are extremely useful in everyday life, not least for checking your change in the shops. Unfortunately, our numerical mental machinery seems to get rusty rather fast so you will probably need to practise your times tables and brush up on your division to get back up to speed again if you've been lazily turning to a calculator since your schooldays.

THE LAW OF AVERAGES:
MEAN, MEDIAN, MODE

There are three different ways of expressing averages: the **mean**, the **median** and the **mode**.

Let's assume that the total number of TVs owned by the members of your reading group is 30. The total number of people in the group is 16. To find the **mean** number of televisions per person divide the total number of TVs by the total number of members. This gives you the answer that there are 1.875 televisions per person in your group.

However, the mean can be misleading. It could give an inaccurate impression of the number of televisions most of your pals have if a new, nouveau riche chap who had 50 televisions in his palatial mansion suddenly joined your group. This would make the average number of televisions a shockingly vulgar 4.706. In this case, a more accurate reflection of your group's television ownership would be the median value. In order to get the **median** you arrange your individual observations in order of lowest to highest:

0, 0, 1, 2, 2, 2, 2, 2, **2**, 2, 2, 2, 2, 3, 3, 3, 50

Then you pick out the middle number, in this case 2. (If you end up
with an even number of observations – and thus two middle numbers –
then you find the median by calculating the mean of those two numbers
by adding them together and dividing them by two.)

The third 'm' of averages is the **mode**. To find the mode, display your
individual observations as you did to find the median and look for the
number that occurs most often.

0, 0, 1, 2, 2, 2, 2, 2, 2, 2, 2, 2, 2, 3, 3, 3, 50

In this case, the mode is clearly 2.

MINUS NUMBERS MINUS THE HASSLE: NEGATIVE AND POSITIVE NUMBERS

A positive number is not an annoying, chirpy, chin-up number, it is
simply a number that is greater than zero: 1, 2, 3, 4, etc. A negative
number is a number that is less than zero: -1, -2, -3, -4, etc. So, if your
auntie gives you £125 to spend on school uniforms for the kids and you
spend £145 on champagne and cakes then you will find that your bank
balance reads -£20.

Zero is the only number in the whole, vast universe that is neither
positive nor negative. Interestingly, in the ancient Babylonian system of
numbers, which dates back to the second millennium BCE, no character
for zero was invented until over a thousand years after other number
symbols were developed.

Adding negative numbers
The rule for adding negative numbers to negative numbers, or positive
numbers to positive numbers is: *When adding numbers of the same sign (i.e.*
+ or -), add their values together and give the result the same sign.

For example:

$$4 + 4 = 8$$
$$-4 + -4 = -8$$

However, if you add a negative number to a positive number, this is the same as subtracting the negative number from the positive number. So, 25 + -7 = 18 is the same as 25 - 7 = 18.

Let's say that you and your best friend have decided to buy a 1996 BMW convertible with all the money you have in your bank accounts. You have £2,500 but unfortunately your less economically minded friend is £700 into her overdraft (i.e. she has -£700). This means that between you you have £1,800 to spend on your honey-wagon.

The rule for adding negative and positive numbers together is: *When adding numbers of opposite signs, the first step is to ignore the signs and subtract the smaller number from the larger number. Then give the result the sign that was originally attached to the larger number.*

For example, if you want to calculate -36 + 4 the first step involves simply taking 4 (the smallest number) away from 36, which leaves 32. If you then look at the original calculation you'll see that the largest number (36) had a negative sign attached to it so your answer should be -32.

Subtracting negative numbers
Subtracting a negative number is the same as adding. For example, -25 - -7 = -18. This is the same as -25 + 7 = -18.

If your overdraft is -£15 and you reduce it by £5, this means you're adding £5 and you end up with a balance of -£10.

The rule here is: *Subtracting a number is the same as adding its opposite sign number.*

For example, subtracting 5 from 10 is the same as adding -5 to 10. The answer is 5. And subtracting -5 from 10 is the same as adding 5 to 10. The answer is 15. Sit up straight, ponder this awhile and you will soon see that it makes perfect sense.

Multiplying negative numbers
If you multiply a positive number by a negative number then the answer will always be a negative number. So 5 x -3 = -15.

If you multiply a negative number by a negative number the answer will always be a positive number. So -5 x -3 = 15.

If the signs are the same, the answer is positive.
If the signs are different, the answer is negative.

Dividing negative numbers
If you divide a positive number by a negative number, or a negative number by a positive number, then the answer will always be a negative number. So 12 ÷ -3 = -4.

If you divide a negative number by a negative number the answer will always be a positive number. So -12 ÷ -3 = 4.

All together, once again:

If the signs are the same, the answer is positive.
If the signs are different, the answer is negative.

THE ROOT OF ALL EVIL: SQUARES AND SQUARE ROOTS

Of course, your multiplication tables from 1 to 12 will be easily recalled, or *should* be after the time your parents and teachers spent drumming them into your skulls. If you find they are somewhat creaky it is a good idea to practise them in traffic jams. Repetition of them can also be used as a calming relaxation technique in stressful situations. If you are still struggling, after making a genuine effort, then you may use this helpful table (see opposite).

When you multiply a number by itself you get what is called its **square**. (Square numbers in this table are shown in brackets.)

4 squared means 4 x 4 and is written as 4^2. The superscript number next to the standard number tells you how many times to multiply the 4 by itself. $4^2 = 16$. (4 x 4 = 16).

(1)	2	3	4	5	6	7	8	9	10	11	12
2	(4)	6	8	10	12	14	16	18	20	22	24
3	6	(9)	12	15	18	21	24	27	30	33	36
4	8	12	(16)	20	24	28	32	36	40	44	48
5	10	15	20	(25)	30	35	40	45	50	55	60
6	12	18	24	30	(36)	42	48	54	60	66	72
7	14	21	28	35	42	(49)	56	63	70	77	84
8	16	24	32	40	48	56	(64)	72	80	88	96
9	18	27	36	45	54	63	72	(81)	90	99	108
10	20	30	40	50	60	70	80	90	(100)	110	120
11	22	33	44	55	66	77	88	99	110	(121)	132
12	24	36	48	60	72	84	96	108	120	132	(144)

Following on from this you can work out that 8^2 is 64, 13^2 is 169 and 23^2 is 529.

The ^{2} is also known as an index number or 'power'. So 4^2 can be called '4 to the power of 2' as well as 4 squared.

Remember: *The square of a number is the product of a number multiplied by itself.*

The definition of a **square root** is 'the number that, multiplied by itself, gives a specified number'. So the square root of 169 is the number that has been multiplied by itself to get 169. That is, 13. The square root of 16 is 4. This is written as $\sqrt{16}$. So $\sqrt{25}$ means 'the square root of 25', which is 5.

Every positive number has two square roots. If you multiply -5 x -5 you also get 25. So the square root of 25 can be 5 or -5.

SQUARE NUMBERS

An integer is a 'whole number' – e.g. 1, 2, 3, 4 rather than ½, 1.25, 2.5. 3.888, 4¼. 'Integer' is a Latin word meaning 'untouched' or 'whole'.

A **square number** is the specific term for the square of an integer. Square numbers are indicated in brackets in the multiplication table in the previous section.

4 is the square root of 16 and 16 is a square number because its square root is an integer.

THINKING OUTSIDE THE BOX: CUBES

4^3 means 4 cubed. This means 4 x 4 x 4, which equals 64.

The opposite of a cube number is a **cube root**, which is written as $\sqrt[3]{}$.

MILLIONS, BILLIONS AND TRILLIONS

Watch out when you're doing big business with our American cousins, as billions and trillions mean different things in traditional British usage and American usage. Nowadays most people use the American definitions. To add to the confusion, colloquially and hyperbolically, a billion or trillion can just mean 'a lot' – as in 'I ate a trillion cocktail sausages at last night's party'.

A million is a thousand thousands: 1,000,000. This can also be written as 10^6.

A billion is a thousand millions: 1,000,000,000. This can also be written as 10^9. (In traditional British usage a billion meant a million millions or 10^{12}.)

A trillion is a million millions: 1,000,000,000,000. This is also written as 10^{12}. (In traditional British usage a trillion meant a million million millions or 10^{18}.)

MAGIC NUMBERS:
INVESTIGATING PRIMES

A **prime number** is a number with two and only two factors. In other words, it is a positive whole number greater than 1 that can only be divided evenly by itself and 1.

All numbers are amazing, but prime numbers in particular are very special. Theoretical mathematicians have been getting excited about them for centuries. The famous ancient Greek mathematician Euclid (c.300 BCE) proved that the number of prime numbers is infinite. The intervals between primes get larger as the numbers get larger, and they appear in an irregular pattern. Mathematicians love a challenge, and, excitingly for them, no mathematical formula for generating primes has been discovered although computers are helping in the quest to come up with large primes. Cryptographers also love prime numbers and they are often used in secret codes.

The Electronic Frontier Foundation has offered a $100,000 prize to the first discoverer of a prime with at least 10 million digits.

Here is a table of all the prime numbers up to 1000:

2	3	5	7	11	13	17	19	23	29	31	37	41	43	47	53	59	61	67
71	73	79	83	89	97	101	103	107	109	113	127	131	137	139	149	151	157	163
167	173	179	181	191	193	197	199	211	223	227	229	233	239	241	251	257	263	269
271	277	281	283	293	307	311	313	317	331	337	347	349	353	359	367	373	379	383
389	397	401	409	419	421	431	433	439	443	449	457	461	463	467	479	487	491	499
503	509	521	523	541	547	557	563	569	571	577	587	593	599	601	607	613	617	619
631	641	643	647	653	659	661	673	677	683	691	701	709	719	727	733	739	743	751
757	761	769	773	787	797	809	811	821	823	827	829	839	853	857	859	863	877	881
883	887	907	911	919	929	937	941	947	953	967	971	977	983	991	997			

LONG MULTIPLICATION

To multiply two large numbers together, you can use your superior
intellect, a calculator or the time-honoured tradition of long multiplication. This is where you multiply the units, tens, hundreds, thousands,
etc. separately and then add the results together. Be warned however
that ways of teaching long multiplication vary. This is just one tried
and tested method. Following this technique, if you wanted to multiply
1743 by 2841 you would do it thus:

First, multiply 1743 by 1.

$$
\begin{array}{r}
1743 \\
2841 \ \times \\
\hline
1743
\end{array}
$$

Then multiply the 1743 by 4. Because the 4 is actually 40, you first need
to add a zero to the end of this row, directly under the 3.

$$
\begin{array}{r}
1743 \\
2841 \ \times \\
\hline
1743 \\
69720
\end{array}
$$

Then multiply the 1743 by 8. Because the 8 is actually 800, you need to
add two zeroes to the end of this row.

$$
\begin{array}{r}
1743 \\
2841 \ \times \\
\hline
1743 \\
69720 \\
1394400
\end{array}
$$

Then multiply the 1743 by 2. Because the 2 is actually 2000, you need to add three zeros to the end of this row.

$$
\begin{array}{r}
1743 \\
2841 \ \times \\
\hline
1743 \\
69720 \\
1394400 \\
3486000 \\
\end{array}
$$

Then add these values together to get the final sum:

$$
\begin{array}{r}
1743 \ + \\
69720 \ + \\
1394400 \ + \\
3486000 \ + \\
\hline
4951863 \ = \\
\end{array}
$$

Excellent work! You need never be stumped again when the carefully rote-learned times tables in your head are not adequate for your purposes.

FASCINATING FACTORS

A factor is a number that divides exactly into a larger number. For example, 4 is a factor of 20 because it divides into 20 exactly five times with no remainders. As with the factors contributing to divorce, global warming and ageing, there can often be more than one: 1, 2, 5 and 10 are also factors of 20.

LONG DIVISION

To divide a number by another number of more than one digit, use the method of long division. To those of you who shudder and come out in unsightly pink rashes when reminded of this magnificent exercise, rest assured that if you take it slowly and thoughtfully, step by step, you will find it child's play. First, there are a couple of swish and similar words that it's crucial you get the right way round:

The number you want to divide is called the **dividend**. The number you want to divide the dividend by is called the **divisor**.

Calmly lay out your working, as follows:

$$48 \overline{\smash{\big)}\ 655}$$

As with normal division, you try to work out how many times the divisor fits into the first figure of the dividend. 48 does not go into 6, so move along one place and work out how many times it goes into 65. The answer is 1. Write this above the 65. Then multiply this answer by the divisor and write this below the 65: 1 x 48 = 48.

$$48 \overline{\smash{\big)}\ \mathbf{65}5} \\ 48$$

Subtract this number from 65 and write the result below.

$$48 \overline{\smash{\big)}\ \mathbf{65}5} \\ -\mathbf{48} \\ \overline{\mathbf{17}}$$

Now bring the remaining figure in the dividend, the 5, down to the bottom row, next to the 17.

$$48 \overline{\smash{\big)}\ 655} \\ -48 \\ \overline{\mathbf{175}}$$

Next, divide 175 by 48. The answer is 3. Write the 3 on the top of the working, to the right of the 1.

$$
\begin{array}{r}
13 \\
48\,\overline{)655} \\
-48 \\
\hline
175
\end{array}
$$

Multiply the answer, 3, by the divisor and write this below the 175. 3 x 48 = 144.

$$
\begin{array}{r}
13 \\
48\,\overline{)655} \\
-48 \\
\hline
175 \\
144
\end{array}
$$

Subtract this number from 175 and write the result (31) below. Because 31 cannot be divided by 48, this is the remainder. The answer therefore, is found on the top and bottom of the working: 13, remainder 31. 48 goes into 655 thirteen times, with a remainder of 31.

$$
\begin{array}{r}
\mathbf{13} \\
48\,\overline{)655} \\
-48 \\
\hline
175 \\
-144 \\
\hline
\mathbf{31}
\end{array}
$$

Keep at it and with practice you will learn to love long division.

ANCIENT GREEK NUMBERS

It is surprisingly useful to know the ancient Greek prefixes for numbers. They turn up in geometry and many other places, including the definitions of poetic metre.

1 – *hen* or *mono*	3 – *tri*	5 – *penta*	7 – *hepta*	9 – *ennea*
2 – *dyo*	4 – *tetra*	6 – *hex*	8 – *okto*	10 – *deka*

THE SIGNIFICANCE OF SHAPES: GEOMETRY

Geometry is the branch of mathematics dealing with the size and shape of surfaces and solids and the position of points and lines on these surfaces and solids. Mother Nature, on close inspection, has organised the world around us with extraordinary regularity. In the sea, the sky, the rivers and the rainforests, you will often see the same shapes repeated, in honeycombs, ferns, rock formations and flower petals. And we humans are not complete fools, we know when to copy a good design. The significance of the shapes used in our technology and artistic endeavours stretches from the structure of a Stealth bomber, which uses trihedral planes to confuse radar, to patchwork quilts which please the eye with tessellating hexagons.

PROMINENT POLYGONS

A **polygon** is the term for a two-dimensional shape with any number of straight sides. The word comes from the ancient Greek '*poly*' meaning 'many' and '*gonos*' meaning 'angled'.

A **polyhedron** is the term for a three-dimensional solid whose faces are polygons. The word comes from the ancient Greek '*poly*' meaning 'many'

and '*hedra*' meaning 'base'. The shape shown below is a **pentahedron** – the Greek number for five is '*penta*' so this is a solid with five bases.

A **quadrilateral** is a polygon with four sides. The sum of all the angles in a quadrilateral is 360°. **Squares** and **rectangles** are both classic quadrilaterals. The word 'tessellation', which refers to the arrangement of polygons together without any gaps, is connected with the A-list quadrilateral – the square – and comes from the Latin word '*tessera*' meaning the small square tiles used in mosaics.

A **parallelogram** is a quadrilateral with two sets of straight parallel sides.

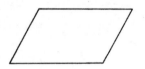

A **rhombus** is a parallelogram with oblique angles and equal sides.

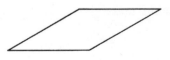

A **trapezium** is a quadrilateral with only one pair of parallel sides. However, in America, trapezium is used to describe a trapezoid and the word trapezoid is used to describe a trapezium, so be careful when

chatting casually in American bars about shapes or you could easily end
up feeling the wrath of an angered Yankee geometrist.

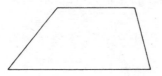

A **trapezoid** is a quadrilateral with no sides parallel. (But not in
America.)

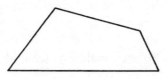

A **hexagon** is a polygon with six sides. The ancient Greeks believed that
bees had a natural sense of geometry because they pack their hives with
perfect hexagonal cells of wax. Only three regular polygons can be
efficiently packed like this: equilateral triangles, squares and hexagons,
and hexagonal cells offer a particularly sturdy and economical structure.

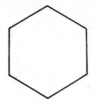

A **decagon** is a polygon with ten sides.

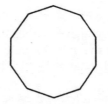

A **dodecagon** is a polygon with twelve sides. This shape is particularly popular in southern hemispherical mints, and many coins, including the Australian, Tongan, Fijian and Solomon Island fifty-cent pieces, are regular dodecagons.

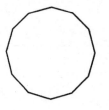

A **heptadecagon** is a polygon with seventeen sides.

An **icosagon** is a polygon with twenty sides.

A **googolgon** is a polygon with 10^{100} sides. Googol is an informal word for the number 10^{100}. Legend has it that the Internet search engine Google.com is named after the number googolplex (10^{googol}) as this is the largest named number and implies the multifarious things that can be found on the Internet.

WHAT'S YOUR ANGLE?

In the History chapter we will be learning about a different type of Angle (a member of a Germanic tribe which settled in England in the fifth century CE) but the ones we are mathematically concerned with are the spaces between two meeting lines or surfaces. The point where the two lines meet is called the **vertex**. The word angle comes from the Latin word '*angulus*' meaning corner.

Angles are usually measured in **degrees** from one line to the other line attached to the vertex. There are 360° in a complete circle and different sizes of angle have different names.

An **acute angle** measures less than 90°.

An angle of 90° is called a **right angle**.

An **obtuse angle** measures between 90° and 180°.

A **reflex angle** measures greater than 180°.

An **oblique angle** is an angle inclined at any other degree than a right angle. Acute, obtuse and reflex angles are all oblique.

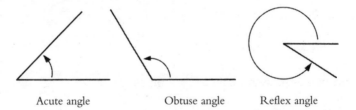

Acute angle   Obtuse angle   Reflex angle

Triangles can also be defined by their angles. A **right-angled triangle** contains one 90° angle, and the side opposite the right angle is called the **hypotenuse**. An **obtuse triangle** has one angle larger than 90°. An **acute triangle** has angles that are all smaller than 90°. An **oblique triangle** has no angles that are 90°.

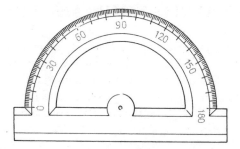

A protractor is a tool for measuring and drawing angles. The protractor doesn't seem as ubiquitous to handbags or manbags as it was to the pencil case. Let's change that. Buy yourself a new one and scratch the name of your favourite band on it in celebration of your new-found love of mathematics.

BORDER CONTROL: CALCULATING PERIMETERS AND CIRCUMFERENCES

The outside edge of a polygon is called its **perimeter**. The sum of the length of all the sides is the measurement of the perimeter.

The perimeter of a circle has a special name: the **circumference**. A circle is a round shape whose circumference is everywhere equidistant from its centre. The **diameter** of a circle is the measurement of a straight line that passes through the centre of a circle from one edge to the other. The **radius** is the measurement of a straight line, running from the centre of a circle to its circumference. The **diameter is equal to the radius x 2**. If you want to draw a circle with a diameter of 10cm, take your compass and set the arms to 5cm apart using your ruler.

π IN THE SKY

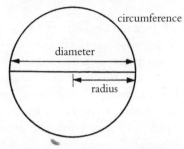

circumference

diameter

radius

The circumference of any circle is calculated by multiplying the length of the diameter by approximately 3.141592, otherwise known as pi. Pi is the sixteenth letter of the ancient Greek alphabet and is usually written as π. This formula is sometimes written out as a mathematical equation: c = πd. You can also calculate the area of any circle by multiplying the radius by itself and then by pi, using the formula πr^2 = area.

π

Since ancient Babylonian and Egyptian times pi has been very useful to mathematicians. Some people think that there is a reference to pi in the Bible's Book of Kings in a description of the construction of the great Temple of Solomon in Jerusalem – although it is slightly inaccurately expressed as 3 in this scenario. It is normally written as 3.141592 but actually stretches to an infinite number of decimal places. Pi is a mathematical and universal constant: in any circle, if you divide the circumference by the diameter, you will arrive at pi. This is the same formula as above, but written as

$$\pi = \frac{c}{d}$$

An easy way to remember pi to six decimal places is: 'How I wish I could calculate pi.' The number of letters in each word gives you pi.

AWE-INSPIRING ALGEBRA

Algebra is the branch of mathematics that uses letters and other symbols to represent numbers and quantities in formulae and equations. This may seem like making life more difficult than necessary – why use x and y instead of 2 and 3? – but algebra is essential when you don't know all the values of a calculation, or if those values are prone to fluctuation. Equations are everywhere, from the fields of computing, physics and chemistry, to the principles of architecture and engineering and even to methods of philosophical enquiry. As the famous equation maestro Albert Einstein once said: 'If **a** is a success in life, then $a = x + y + z$. Work is **x**; **y** is play; and **z** is keeping your mouth shut.'

THE MAGIC FORMULA: FORMULAE AND EQUATIONS

A formula is a mathematical rule expressed in symbols. Formulae can be applied to almost everything, and in recent years, psychologists have apparently even come up with the formula for happiness. Apparently our level of happiness $= P + (5E) + (3H)$, where P is personal characteristics, E is existence (health, financial stability and friendship) and H is Higher Order (self-esteem, ambition, etc.).

Formulae are expressed as equations. An equation is a mathematical statement which has an equals sign in it. All formulae are equations but not all equations are formulae, e.g. $2 + 4 = 6$ is an equation but not a formula, but the rule for finding the circumference of a circle $c = \pi d$ is a formula expressed as an equation.

Letters often stand in for unknown values in a formula. The arrangement of the formula expresses the relationship between the different values. You can replace the letters with any values you know to work out the other values in the formula.

In order to start fooling around with formulae, you need to embed in your grey matter that:

- Two letters or values written next to each other means that they should be multiplied, i.e. $c = \pi d$ means multiply π by d to get the value of c.

- If a formula contains brackets, this means that the calculation within the brackets should be performed first. For example: $c = x(2 + y)$. To calculate c, add 2 to y and then multiply this answer by x.

If you know that the formula for working out the circumference of a circle is $c = \pi d$, and you know that the diameter of your circle is 5cm, then you can work out the circumference as $c = \pi 5$. This means 'the circumference is equal to approximately 3.141592 x 5'. So, the circumference measures 15.70796cm. Easy-peasy.

You can also rearrange formulae to work out different unknown values. For example, if you know the circumference but you want to find out the diameter you would rearrange the formula to be $\frac{c}{\pi} = d$ with d as the subject of the formula instead of c.

You need to rearrange the formula step by step until you get the value you want to work out by itself on one side of the equals sign. In this case it means getting to the point where you have '= d' by itself. The rule for rearranging formulae like this is that whatever you do to the values on one side of the equals sign you have to do to the other side.

So to rework the formula above the steps would be:

$$c = \pi d$$

Divide both sides by π:

$$\frac{c}{\pi} = d$$

There you have it!

EQUALITY COUNTS:
WORKING OUT EQUATIONS

An equation is a mathematical way of stating that two expressions are equal. This is indicated by, obviously, the = sign, e.g. 18 + 7 = 25. In equation problems, a letter is used in place of an unknown value, e.g. 18 + x = 25. If you rework this formula, you will find that -18 from both sides of the formula gives you x = 7. Solving equations is a little like detective work, it's the art of uncovering missing numbers.

CALCULATING THE AREA
OF RECTANGLES AND TRIANGLES

Areas are expressed in square measurements such as cm² or m². The area of a rectangle is equal to the **base** multiplied by the **height**.

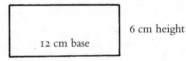

12 cm base

6 cm height

The area of this rectangle is 72 cm².

This rule can also be expressed by the mathematical formula A = (bh).

To calculate the area of a right-angled triangle, multiply the base by the height and divide the answer by 2. Remember, a right-angled triangle is half a rectangle (or half a square in the case of a right-angled triangle).

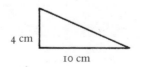

4 cm

10 cm

The area of this triangle is 20 cm².

This rule can also be expressed as the mathematical formula $A = \dfrac{(bh)}{2}$

TACKLING TRIG

Although they look pretty pedestrian, right-angled triangles are so prepossessing that they have their own branch of mathematics: **trigonometry** (which is named after the ancient Greek words for 'three-cornered' and 'measure').

To recap, a right-angled triangle has one angle of 90°. Of course, you'll remember that the side opposite the right angle is called the **hypotenuse**. Of the other two sides, the side adjoining the angle you are investigating is called the **adjacent** and the side opposite the angle you are looking at is called the **opposite**.

PYTHAGORAS' THEOREM

Pythagoras ($c.570$–490 BC) was a famous ancient Greek philosopher, mystic, mathematician, scientist and vegetarian. He invented a theorem: a mathematical formula used to calculate the length of any side of a right-angled triangle, as long as the lengths of the other two sides are known.

Pythagoras' theorem is expressed as:

In any right-angled triangle, the area of the **square** whose side is the hypotenuse (the side opposite the right angle) is equal to the sum of the areas of the squares whose sides are the two legs (the two sides other than the hypotenuse).

Or, in algebraic terms: $a^2 + b^2 = c^2$.

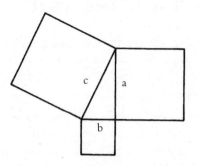

So if you have a right-angled triangle with one side of the right angle measuring 10cm and the other side measuring 5cm, this is how you work out the length of the missing side:

Multiply the length of the first side (10cm) by itself. $10^2 = 10 \times 10 = 100$cm

Multiply the length of the second side (5cm) by itself. $5^2 = 5 \times 5 = 25$cm

Add them together $= 125$cm. This is the length of the missing side squared (i.e. multiplied by itself).

So the length of the missing side is the square root of 125cm.

All calculators have a square-root button $\sqrt{}$. Key in 125 and press the button and you will get the length of the hypotenuse. In this case, it is 11.18cm.

If you happen to watch *The Wizard of Oz*, pay no attention to the Scarecrow's definition of Pythagoras' theorem, as it is wrong. He may just have received a brain from the Wizard, but clearly it is not a very good one and he needs to study this section with more diligence.

THE GOLDEN RATIO

A ratio is a way of expressing the relationship between two different amounts. For example, if you have 8 pairs of stilettos and 4 pairs of practical pumps, then the ratio of stilettos to pumps is 2:1; you have 2 pairs of stilettos for every 1 pair of pumps, which isn't very sensible, but will see you right at a variety of formal functions.

The **golden ratio**, also known as the **golden section** or the **divine proportion** is, like π, a very significant number in mathematics, as well as in the arts. It is also written 1: φ (which is the Greek letter '**phi**'). φ is normally written out in numerals as 1.61803 but actually stretches to an infinite number of decimal places. The mathematical formula for φ is:

$$\varphi = \frac{(1 + \sqrt{5})}{2}$$

A golden rectangle is a rectangle where the ratio of height to width is 1: φ. So if the height is 1cm, the width needs to be 1.61803cm to make a golden rectangle. Shapes constructed using the golden ratio are particularly pleasing to the human eye: the length and width of the Mona Lisa's face fits the golden ratio, for example. The golden ratio also occurs in nature, in the arrangement of leaves and petals, and the structure of shells. Nowadays, you can even get your teeth fixed so that the shape of each tooth adheres to the golden ratio.

MATHS HERO: THE FIBONACCI SEQUENCE

The Fibonacci sequence is named after Leonardo Fibonacci (*c.*1170–*c.*1240), a medieval Italian mathematician. It is a series of numbers in which each number is the sum of the two preceding numbers.

1, 1, 2, 3, 5, 8, 13, 21, 34, 55, 89, 144, 233, etc.

The Fibonacci sequence is special because the ratio of each successive pair of numbers is φ. For example, the ratio between 1 and 2 is 1:2, the ratio between 21 and 34 is 1:1.619, the ratio between 89 and 144 is 1:1.617. The further up the sequence you go the closer you get to an accurate expression of φ.

The design of one of the structures of Britain's top tourist attractions, the Eden Project in Cornwall, is based on the Fibonacci sequence, and it also features in Dan Brown's best-selling book *The Da Vinci Code*.

A PIECE OF THE ACTION: FRACTIONS

Fractions are a way of expressing quantities less than whole numbers. The easiest way to think of them is to imagine a pie, any kind of pie you like: steak and kidney, or blackberry and apple. As a fraction, a whole pie would be expressed as ⅟₁. If you take one pie and cut it into two equal pieces, each piece is half of the whole pie. This is expressed as ½. The top number is called the **numerator**, and the bottom number is called the **denominator**. The numerator tells us how many pieces we have, and the denominator tells us how many times we have split the whole pie. So ¾ means 3 pieces of a pie that has been cut into 4.

You can express the same fractions in different ways: ¾ is the same as ½. These are known as **equivalent fractions**. You should always use the simplest form of a fraction. If the numerator and denominator can both be divided by the same number then the fraction can be simplified. Any number that you can divide both sides of the fraction by is called a **common factor**. Keep going through steps to simplify the fraction until you can't find any other common factors.

²⁰⁰⁄₈₀₀ can be divided by the factor 100 to give ²⁄₈. The 2 and 8 both have a common factor of 2, so both can be divided by 2 to give ¼.

ADDING AND SUBTRACTING FRACTIONS

To add and subtract with different denominators, you first need to make both denominators the same, this is called finding the **common denominator**. The **lowest common denominator** is a term most properly used for the lowest common factor of the denominators of several fractions, but has also been extended to mean the least fetching common characteristic of a group of people. So if you want to add ³⁄₇ to ¹⁄₁₀, you need to find a denominator which 7 and 10 are both factors of. The easiest way to do this is to multiply the two denominators so, 7 x

10 = 70. You also have to multiply the numerators to match. So to get a denominator of 70, multiply both elements of the first fraction by 10, and both elements of the second fraction by 7.

$$10 \left(\tfrac{3}{7}\right) + 7 \left(\tfrac{4}{10}\right) = \tfrac{30}{70} + \tfrac{28}{70} = \tfrac{58}{70}$$

You can then simplify the answer down to $\tfrac{29}{35}$.

Fractions are subtracted using the same method.

MULTIPLYING AND DIVIDING FRACTIONS

To multiply fractions, multiply the numerators with each other and the denominators with each other and then simplify the answer.

$$\tfrac{4}{7} \times \tfrac{3}{8} = \tfrac{12}{56}$$
$$= \tfrac{6}{28}$$
$$= \tfrac{3}{14}$$

If you are multiplying a whole number by a fraction the whole number should be expressed as a fraction as well. e.g. $3 = \tfrac{3}{1}$. So $\tfrac{1}{4} \times 3 = \tfrac{1}{4} \times \tfrac{3}{1} = \tfrac{3}{4}$.

To divide a fraction you need to find the **reciprocal** of the divisor. A reciprocal is whatever you need to multiply a number by to get the answer 1. The reciprocal of 8 is $\tfrac{1}{8}$, and the reciprocal of $\tfrac{1}{8}$ is 8 (i.e. $\tfrac{8}{1}$). To find the reciprocal of a fraction, simply turn it upside down.

To divide a fraction, turn the divisor into its reciprocal and then multiply the first fraction by the reciprocal.

$$\tfrac{5}{7} \div \tfrac{10}{15}$$
$$\tfrac{5}{7} \times \tfrac{15}{10} = \tfrac{75}{70}$$

Obviously, $\tfrac{70}{70}$ is one whole, so the answer is $1\tfrac{5}{70}$ which simplifies to $1\tfrac{1}{14}$.

DECIMALS

Decimals are just different ways of expressing fractions. Most of us are familiar with the fact that 0.5 is the same as ½ and 0.25 is the same as ¼. To express fractions as a decimal, divide the numerator by the denominator. So, ½ = 0.5.

UNDERSTANDING PERCENTAGES

A percentage is a way of expressing a proportion.

1% means 1 unit out of 100 units; this can also be written as a fraction: $\frac{1}{100}$. If you have received 100 red roses from Claire's boyfriend Stupot and, in a fit of pique, Claire snatches 25 of your roses and stamps them into the ground, then you have lost 25% of your roses; or $\frac{25}{100}$.

To work out percentages, first write the percentage figure as a fraction. To calculate 30% of £80, first express the percentage as a fraction: $\frac{30}{100}$ or, simplified, $\frac{3}{10}$. Then multiply this by 80 expressed as $\frac{80}{1}$. $\frac{3}{10} \times \frac{80}{1} = \frac{240}{10}$. This simplifies to $\frac{24}{1}$ or 24. So 30% of £80 is £24.

If you are doing this on your calculator, just divide the number you want to find the percentage of by 100. This gives you the value of 1% of that number. Then multiply this by the percentage you want. So, for the above problem you would divide £80 by 100, which tells you that 0.8 (or 80p) is 1% of £80. So if you multiply 0.8 by 30 you get the value of 30% : £24.

You may also need to work out the relationship between two quantities as a percentage. So, in an IQ test, if you get 47 answers correct out of 70 questions, what percentage of the questions have you answered correctly? To work this out you should divide 47 by 70 and multiply that answer by 100.

$$47 \div 70 = 0.67. \quad 0.67 \times 100 = 67\%$$

This isn't a stunning result but with any luck, by the time you've finished this book, you'll be in the top 80%.

⚘ MATHEMATICS ⚘
TEST PAPER

1. Mental Maths

a) Chocolate bars are dearer than sherbet lemons, but cheaper than bubble gum. Which is the cheapest?

b) Florence has one brother, two sisters, a mother and a father, and two grandfathers. How many are there in the family?

c) Fifteen crows were in a tree. ⅕ flew away. How many crows remained in the tree?

d) What is the smallest number that can be divided by 3, 4, 6 and 8 without a remainder?

2. A prime number is:

a) the best number of all

b) a number greater than 5 that can only be divided by itself

c) a whole number greater than 1 that can only be divided by itself and 1

d) a whole number that cannot be divided by itself

3. Which of the following is *not* a prime number?

7, 11, 31, 47, 109, 224, 227, 571, 577, 827, 953

4. Calculating Area

Roger and Hal are having their kitchen redecorated.

a) They want to know how big their kitchen floor is. If their kitchen is 12m long and 8m wide, what is the area of their kitchen floor?

b) Hal needs to cover the skirting board with masking tape before painting the walls and wants to work out how much tape he will need. What is the measurement of the perimeter of the kitchen in metres?

c) Roger has chosen floor tiles which measure 50cm². (The length of each side is 50cm. This is equal to 0.25m² area per tile.) How many tiles does Roger need?

5. **What is the radius of a circle with an area of 24cm²? Give your answer to three decimal places.**

6. **Calculate the hypotenuse of a right-angled triangle with one side measuring 8cm and one side measuring 12cm.**

7. **The bill at your favourite gastropub comes to £80. There are five of you splitting the bill equally.**

a) What percentage of the bill should you pay?
b) How much should you pay?

8. **If you get 7 answers right out of 12 possible correct answers in the Maths section of *Homework for Grown-ups*, then what percentage have you got right?**

9. **How many sides does a icosagon have?**

10. **What is a denominator?**

a) the number you need to multiply a number by to get the answer 1
b) a number that sits at the bottom of a fraction
c) a number that sits on the top of a fraction

11. **If Jenny collects 2,234 bonus points on her loyalty card every week, how many will she have after a year of collecting?**

12. **If you have 378 guests coming to your daughter's wedding and 42 tables to seat them at, how many people will be seated at each table?**

13. What is an integer?

a) a clever mammal
b) a helpful person
c) a whole number
d) a whole apple

14. If you have afternoon tea with three of your friends and two of you eat four scones each and one of you eats one scone and your greediest friend eats five, what is the mean number of scones that has been eaten?

15. What is -27 multiplied by -6?

16. What number can be written as 6^2?

17. What is the square root of 4356?

18. What shape is a 50-pence coin?

19. What is a rhombus?

a) a type of Thai elephant
b) a parallelogram with oblique angles and equal sides
c) a quadrilateral with only one pair of parallel sides
d) a person of great standing in the mathematical community

20. Label the parts of the following diagram:

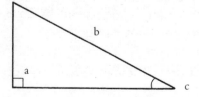

21. Work out the following formula:

   $c = 8(2 + 8)$

22. What are the two square roots of 144?

23. If you multiply a negative number and a negative number together, will your answer be positive or negative?

24. What is a radius?

25. What is special about these numbers? 1, 1, 2, 3, 5, 8, 13, 21, 34, 55.

26. What is 0.75 expressed as a fraction?

MENTAL ARITHMETIC – CALCULATORS MAY NOT BE USED

27. In a flower bed, there were more pink flowers than yellow ones, but fewer pink ones than red ones: of which colour were there the most flowers?

28. If Spike takes 40 steps to walk to the end of the playground, how many steps does he take to walk up and down the playground 6.5 times?

29. A painter was asked to paint the numbers on the doors of a terrace of 50 houses. How many noughts did he have to paint, how many ones and how many figure fives?

30. If the third day of January were a Tuesday, which day would the last day of January be?

31. A train arrived at Hackney Downs station at 4.05p.m. It was seven minutes late. What was the scheduled time of arrival?

32. What is two-twentieths of an hour?

33. There are 360° in a circle. Through how many degrees does the hour hand of a clock move between 1am and 4am?

34. What is 827 hours expressed as days and hours?

35. A group of Girl Guides do a sponsored walk:

a) Florence is sponsored £3.45 for each lap completed. She does 23 laps. How much does she raise?

b) Megan aims to raise £50. She is sponsored £3.25 for each lap. What is the smallest number of laps she must complete to reach her target amount for charity?

3

HOME ECONOMICS

'Home Economics *n.* the study of cookery and
household management'
Oxford Concise English Dictionary

'Home is a place not only of strong affections, but of entire unreserve;
it is life's undress rehearsal, its backroom, its dressing room'
HARRIET BEECHER STOWE (1811–96)

Once upon a time, Home Economics, along with its gentle sister subject
Needlework, was the sole domain of schoolgirls. Young gentlemen were
encouraged to spend their time running about sparring with each other
on games pitches rather than making a pineapple upside-down cake. Of
course, nowadays the life skills necessary to run a successful and efficient
household are absolute necessities for both genders. The modern-day
emphasis on avoiding waste for the sake of the environment harks back
to the days of 'making do and mending' and many of the lessons learned
in the golden era of the humble Home Economics class are more
relevant now than they have been for many years.

Even the government has decided that it is imperative that our obese,
nutritionally ignorant nation be taught how to cook properly so that we
can keep ourselves healthy. Beyond the creative joy of making delicious
dishes to stimulate our senses, food is part of all our lives, and its uses and
abuses are central to our fitness and happiness.

However, Home Economics is not simply about delicious nosh; it also
encompasses other life skills, from personal finance to first aid and, of
course, safety plans for nuclear attacks. These skills all fall within the
remit of the home and each of us should be proud to possess them.
Without them we'd all be throwing water on chip-pan fires, helplessly
watching our dining companions choke to death on our nutritious lentil
bake, or succumbing to food poisoning, caused by failing to observe the
correct rules for defrosting poultry. And all these risks lie in wait in our

kitchens, even discounting the threat of radio-active fallout. So roll up your sleeves and pull on your pinny: it's time to refresh your memory of how to make that potential deathtrap we call home-sweet-home a hearty, healthy, happy place to inhabit.

DAILY BREAD: HOW TO BAKE A LOVELY LOAF

550g strong white bread flour
7g easy-blend yeast (one sachet)
1 tbsp salt
300ml warm tap water
1 tbsp unsalted butter at room temperature

1. Mix 500g of the flour with the yeast, salt and 200ml of the water. Then mix in the butter. You should end up with what looks like shredded rags. Keep adding drips of water until you have a firm dough.
2. Knead the dough for 10 minutes on a surface you've dusted with the remaining flour. To knead, place the heel of your hand firmly into the middle of the ball of dough and push it away from you, stretching the dough out, then folding it back in on itself. Add a little flour if the dough is sticking to the surface or your hands too much. After 10 minutes you should find that the dough is nice and smooth.
3. Put the ball of dough into a large, greased bowl, rolling the dough until it's greased all over. Cover with cling film and put in a warm place for two hours.
4. Knead the dough again for a minute and then shape it on a baking tray. You can make whatever shape you like, and even tie it in knots or plaits if that tickles your fancy. Cover your creation with cling film and leave for half an hour until it's nearly doubled in size.
5. Preheat the oven to 220°C (gas mark 7). Dust the dough with flour and bake for 30 minutes. (When you've removed the bread from the tray, tap it on the bottom and see if it sounds hollow. If it doesn't, return it to the oven for a little longer.) Leave to cool on a wire rack.

HOW TO BOIL AN EGG

If you have successfully accomplished the bread-making recipe above then you might like to grill up some toast and make a feast of it by boiling yourself an egg. This simple meal should be within the grasp of even the most cack-handed chef and eggs are packed with a veritable alphabet of good things such as protein, vitamins A, B_2, D and E, iron, phosphorus and zinc.

1. Remove your egg from the fridge 15 minutes before you wish to cook it.
2. Take a small saucepan and fill with enough water to cover the egg by one centimetre. Bring this to a stable simmering point.
3. Lower the egg into the water gently and simmer for exactly 1 minute.
4. Remove the pan from the heat and put a lid on top of it. Leave the egg in the pan for 6 minutes for a runny yolk and 7 for a creamy yolk.

To hard-boil an egg, place it in a pan of cold water and bring to simmering point. Simmer for 7 minutes and then remove from pan and run under cold water for 2 minutes. Peel off the shell and enjoy.

CONVERSION TABLES

In the olden days people used to measure ingredients for recipes (and everything else) according to the imperial system. We have since moved on to the metric system, but many mothers, grandmothers and classic cookery books still use the romantically obscure ounces and pounds instead of the prosaic grams and kilograms, so it is useful to be able to convert between the two. Without this knowledge your valuable first editions of seminal works such as Elizabeth David's *French Country Food*, Mrs Beeton's *Book of Household Management* and Elaine Hallgarten's *Mince Matters* will be unintelligible to you.

In the important arena of weight measurements, 1oz is equal to 28g. Some people prefer to round the gram measurement down to 25g to make the maths easier, but for baking, you should use exact measurements as the slightest variations can turn your fairy cakes into rock cakes. You can use the table opposite to safeguard yourself against such vicious village fête humiliation.

ounces (oz)	exact grams (g)	rough grams (g)
1	28	25
2	56	50
3	84	75
4	112	100
5	140	125
6	168	150
7	196	175
8	224	200
9	252	225
10	280	250
11	308	275
12	336	300
13	364	325
14	392	350
15	420	375
16 (1 pound – 1lb)	448	400

For volume measurements you will find that measuring jugs will usually have both metric and imperial measurements on them. A rough guide follows in case you find yourself dealing with a less thorough measuring vessel.

fluid ounces (fl oz)	millilitres (ml)
2	60
3	90
5 (quarter of a pint – ¼ pt)	150
10 (half a pint – ½ pt)	300
15 (three-quarters of a pint – ¾ pt)	450
20 (one pint – 1 pt)	600
25 (one and a quarter pints – 1¼ pt)	750
35 (one and three-quarter pints – 1¾ pt)	1000 (1 litre – 1l)

It is also useful to know that a tablespoon is equal to roughly 15ml and a teaspoon to 5ml.

PINEAPPLE UPSIDE-DOWN CAKE

This is the perfect cake to impress your friends with: its topsy-turvy title makes it sound infinitely more difficult to craft than it actually is, and one whiff of its syrupy sweetness will transport all and sundry back to their childhood days.

300g unsalted butter, plus a little for greasing the tin
250g golden syrup
6 fresh or canned pineapple rings
10 glacé cherries
300g caster sugar
4 medium eggs, lightly beaten
300g self-raising flour
6–8 tbsp milk

1. Preheat the oven to 180°C (gas mark 4). Lavishly grease a deep 23cm cake tin and line it with baking parchment. Pour the golden syrup over the base of the tin, and heat it in the oven for 2 minutes. Lay the pineapple rings in an elegant circular pattern in the syrup, and place a tasteful glacé cherry inside each ring and in the spaces between them.

2. In a large mixing bowl, vigorously cream* the butter and sugar. Then slowly beat in the eggs until combined, and fold** in the flour slowly, spoonful by spoonful. As you are doing this, add the tablespoons of milk until you have a smooth mixture. Pour the batter over the pineapple, and bake until golden (approximately 35 minutes). To check it's ready, use the golden rule for cakes: stick a skewer into the middle of the cake and pull it out – if it comes out clean then the cake is ready. Resist the temptation to dive right in and leave to cool for half an hour.

3. Finally, and carefully, turn the cake upside down onto a plate. Cut into large slices and enjoy!

*The verb 'to cream' in cookery means to beat or blend ingredients until you have a light, creamy consistency.
** The verb 'to fold' means to mix lighter and heavier ingredients gently but decisively without taking the air out of the lighter ingredients. It is best to use a plastic spatula and cut down through the ingredients and then turn them over repeatedly until they are well mixed.

WEEKEND FEASTING:
PERFECTING YOUR ROASTING TIMES

There is a gargantuan difference between a desiccated, haggard old lump of beef and a sublimely juicy joint and, trust us, no one at the table will fail to notice if you've gone wrong. But whether you are frightened of undercooked meat or you are a bloodthirsty carnivore, there is still an optimum roasting time for every cut supplied by the butcher; stick to these and you cannot fail to impress. The best way to roast most meat involves cooking it at a high temperature to begin with (to seal in the delicious juices) and then lowering the temperature for the rest of the cooking time. Working out how long to cook the meat requires some simple maths involving its weight. Always take the meat out of the fridge 10 minutes before you begin cooking it, and always leave the meat to rest for at least 15 minutes once it's finished cooking.

Meat	Oven temperature for first 15 minutes of cooking	Oven temperature for rest of cooking time	Minutes per 500g of meat
Chicken	200°C (gas mark 6)	200°C (gas mark 6)	20 minutes + an extra 30 minutes added to the total cooking time. To check the chicken is done stick a skewer close to the leg and check the juices run clear, with no blood.
Lamb	250°C (gas mark 9)	200°C (gas mark 6)	12 minutes for rare meat or 20 minutes for well done.
Beef	250°C (gas mark 9)	180°C (gas mark 4)	15 minutes for rare, 25 minutes for well done.
Pork	200°C (gas mark 6)	180°C (gas mark 4)	30 minutes

THE HUMBLE PULSE: LENTIL BAKE

This is a simple, tasty recipe from that much admired oeuvre – 1970s Vegetarian Cooking. It is not beautiful or glamorous, it does not use swish ingredients (you'll find no pickled ortolan eggs, moon-dried tomatoes or kumquat coulis here), but it is an upstanding, honest and decent dish that requires very little effort. You can serve it alone or with salad or cooked vegetables. Serves 2-4.

200g red lentils	150g Cheddar cheese, grated
1 onion, chopped	1 egg, beaten
2 cloves garlic, finely chopped	4 tbsp plain yogurt
½ tsp dried chillies	small bunch parsley, chopped
1 red pepper, sliced	black pepper

1. Preheat the oven to 180°C (gas mark 4). Rinse and then boil the lentils with a vegetable stock cube (and a bay leaf if you have one handy) in a pan of water until tender (approximately 10 minutes).
2. Meanwhile, fry the onion, garlic, dried chillies and red pepper gently for around 7 minutes.
3. Drain the lentils and mix them with the onion, garlic, chillies and red pepper, 100g of the cheese, egg, yogurt and parsley (saving a sprinkle of parsley for serving).
4. Pour into a baking dish and top with the remaining grated cheese. Bake until the cheese is golden and bubbling (approximately 25 minutes).
5. Tuck in.

KEEP IT CLEAN:
TOP TIPS FOR FOOD HYGIENE

It is all very well larking about with fancy dinner parties and creating your own concoctions in the kitchen, but creativity in cookery is not all. As a cook you are not just an artist but also a scientist, and rigorous control of the basics is necessary to make your food enjoyable, both during and after the consumption of it. It is your duty to be responsible as well as remarkable.

It is imperative that you keep and cook food safely. The result of not paying scrupulous attention to cleanliness in the kitchen is the many-headed monster of food poisoning – an extremely nasty business that affects millions of people in the UK each year. Here are some basic and essential tips to avoid this unappetising fate:

- Always wash your hands before you begin cooking and after touching meat or fish.
- Make sure all surfaces and implements are spotlessly clean – a quick rinse under the tap or a swift wipe with a dirty dishcloth is not enough. Always wash with hot water and detergent.
- Use separate knives and chopping boards for preparing raw meat or fish and other ingredients.
- Make sure that meat and fish is properly defrosted before cooking.
- Only reheat food once, and check food is piping hot before eating.
- If you are keeping food that you have cooked, cool it as quickly as possible and store it in the fridge.
- Do not eat food that you find in the fridge that you can't remember putting there or anything that has changed colour or grown fur since you last laid eyes on it.

FIT FOR A QUEEN:
THE PERFECT VICTORIA SPONGE

The Victoria sponge is named after Queen Victoria (1837–1901), who is said to have enjoyed this satisfyingly moist yet celestially airy cake at afternoon tea. It is a perfect accompaniment to a pot of Earl Grey tea, and is best served on fine china on a sunny afternoon in a restrained yet mildly florally decorated drawing room while among friends and admirers.

175g margarine plus a little for greasing the cake tins
175g caster sugar
3 medium eggs, beaten
175g sieved self-raising flour
strawberry jam and whipped cream for the filling

1. Preheat the oven to 180°C (gas mark 4). If you have the option, do not use the fan function – cakes are traditional sorts and bake better in non-fan-assisted ovens.

2. Generously grease two 20cm sandwich cake tins and line with baking parchment.
3. In a mixing bowl, cream together the margarine and sugar until fluffy.
4. Beat in the eggs one by one, and add a tablespoon of flour along with the second egg.
5. Add the remaining flour and beat energetically until the mixture is smooth.
6. Divide the mixture equally between the prepared sandwich tins and bake in the preheated oven for 20-25 minutes until the cakes have risen and are firm to the touch. Do not open the oven door while the cakes are in the middle of cooking.
7. Leave to cool for a few minutes and then remove the cakes from the tins and place them on a wire rack to cool thoroughly. Once they are at room temperature, spread your filling over one sponge, right to the edges, and sandwich the second sponge on top. Dust the top with icing sugar and be sure to use a sharp knife when serving.

GREAT BRITISH DISHES:
TRADITIONAL SHEPHERD'S AND COTTAGE PIES

In previous decades British food had a reputation for being bland, unappetising and stodgy, but the rise in availability of good-quality ingredients has changed all that. More and more people are taking an active interest in food and experimenting with recipes from all over the world. However, on a drizzly winter's evening in Old Blighty there is a lot to be said for turning back to those old established dishes that kept our ancestors warm and well-fed. Two of these are variations on the same potato-based pie formula. Shepherd's Pie, made with lamb, was probably invented in the north of England or Scotland, where sheep-farming was prevalent, sometime in the eighteenth century. Its variation, using beef instead of lamb, is known as Cottage Pie.

SHEPHERD'S PIE

Serves 4.

450g minced lamb, broken up
700g potatoes, peeled
1 large onion, chopped
1 bay leaf
2 carrots, diced
25g plain flour

300ml lamb or beef stock
1 tbsp tomato purée
20g butter
4 tbsp milk
50g cheese
salt and pepper

a little olive oil for frying

1. Preheat the oven to 200°C (gas mark 6). In a large pan, fry the chopped onion, bay leaf and diced carrots in a little olive oil, then add the mince and cook for about 10 minutes.
2. Add the flour and seasoning and stir for a minute. Slowly stir in the tomato purée and the stock. Cook until the mixture thickens. Cover the pan and simmer on a low heat for 25 minutes.
3. At the same time, boil the potatoes for 20-25 minutes until tender.
4. Remove the bay leaf and place the mince in an ovenproof dish. Drain the potatoes and mash with the butter and milk. Spread the mashed potato on top of the mince mixture and top with the grated cheese. Bake for 15-20 minutes and serve piping hot with peas, broccoli or some other healthy green vegetable. Perfect for consuming while wearing thick woolly socks in front of an open fire.

WEIGHT WATCHER: THE BODY MASS INDEX

Whether you are skinny, slim, svelte, cherubic or a wee bit chubby doesn't really matter so long as you are not risking your health by being over- or underweight. The body mass index can be used to check if you are a healthy weight for your height, using standards set by the World Health Organisation. If you are outside the healthy spectrum for your height then you may need to change your diet, and possibly your exercise regime or lack of it, and should speak to your doctor about what steps to take.

To calculate your BMI, you need to know your height in metres and your weight in kilograms. Once you have this information use the following mathematical formula:

$$BMI = \frac{W \text{ (weight)}}{H^2 \text{ (height in metres, squared)}}$$

If your BMI is under 18.4 you are underweight. If it's between 18.5 and 24.9 then you are a healthy weight. If it's over 25 then you are overweight, and if it is over 30 you are clinically obese.

JACK SPRAT WOULD EAT NO FAT: DIETARY NUTRITION

Nutrients are the chemical compounds in food that your ingenious body can transform into the energy that allows you to run, dance, grow your hair, have children and make pineapple upside-down cake. The human body needs 5 essential nutrients, as well as water, in order to flourish and blossom:

carbohydrates   protein   lipids
vitamins   minerals

SWEETS FOR MY SWEET: CARBOHYDRATES

Carbohydrates have had a lot of bad press lately, but they are simply combinations of hydrogen, carbon and oxygen atoms that provide the most important and readily available source of energy to the human body and also the fibre that keeps your digestive system running smoothly.

There are two types of carb: **simple carbohydrates** which are types of sugar ranging from the evil white powder we sprinkle giddily into our tea, to fructose which makes fruit taste sweet. They are called simple because they are easy for the body to break down and use up quickly.

Complex carbohydrates, in contrast, take longer for our bodies to process and therefore keep us sated for longer – they are the starches and fibre found in wholegrains and vegetables.

PERSEVERANT PROTEIN

Proteins are constructed from one or more unbranched chains of amino acids. Amino acids are made from carbon, hydrogen, oxygen, nitrogen and a side group, e.g. sulphur. The side group is what differentiates one amino acid from another.

On a cellular level proteins are created by the body to maintain its structure: your skin, hair, nails and bones are all built of protein. They also act as transporters, as some proteins move about in bodily fluids and are involved in the transport of nutrients and other molecules. Antibodies are also proteins which contribute to the defensive force of our immune system. As you can see they have a very significant part to play in the wonder of you: in fact, 12-18 per cent of your body is made up of protein.

Meat, fish, eggs and dairy products are good sources of protein as they contain all the amino acids we need. Vegetarians have to combine different vegetables, seeds and pulses to ensure they provide themselves with the essential amino acids.

Amino Acids
There are 20 different amino acids which are split into 3 groups – **essential**, **conditionally essential** and **non-essential**. You probably have enough common sense to work out that some of them are more important for us to eat than others.

Essential: These are the 8 amino acids that we must eat because the body cannot make them in sufficient quantities: isoleucine, leucine, lysine, methionine, phenylalanine, threonine, tryptophan, valine.

Conditionally essential: These are the 2 amino acids children need so that they can grow: arginine, histidine.

Non-essential: These are the 10 amino acids that can be synthesised by the body in sufficient amounts to meet our needs and so do not have to be provided in the diet: alanine, asparagine, aspartic acid, cysteine, glutamic acid, glutamine, glycine, proline, serine, tyrosine.

LIPIDS

Lipid is the official dietary term for the fats found in food. They are made of hydrogen, carbon and oxygen and comprise 15 per cent of the healthy human body. People seem to spend a lot of time 'fighting the fat' in our fast-food, super-stressed world, but lipids do have positive functions. They store energy very effectively and are essential for cellular health, they are used in the production of hormones and in the absorption of certain vitamins and, of course, they provide a nice cushiony layer to break your fall if you trip while ice-skating or attempting to break-dance.

There are different types of lipids. The bad guys are **saturated fats**, which can cause a rise in cholesterol levels which isn't good news for your heart. Good lipids are **unsaturated fats** – both the monounsaturated and the polyunsaturated kinds – and **essential fatty acids** like linolenic acid (omega-3 fatty acid) and linoleic acid (omega-6 fatty acid), which cannot be made by the body itself and are important for cellular health, particularly that of nerve cells, and for processes such as inflammation and blood clotting. EFAs can be found in certain oily fish, vegetables, grains, nuts and seeds. Sources for the other lipids include meat, dairy, coconuts, vegetable oils, cakes and biscuits, but – STOP AND STEP AWAY FROM THE BISCUIT TIN – you should avoid making chocolate digestives your lipid source as biscuits are rammed with saturated fats. Why not try some lovely olives, pumpkin seeds or cod liver oil instead . . . ? Mmmm, delicious.

VITAL VITAMINS AND MANDATORY MINERALS

Our bodies only need vitamins and minerals in small quantities but they are essential to optimum health. Different vitamins and minerals are used for different biological processes; for example, vitamin A is needed for good eyesight in low light, vitamin K is needed to help our blood clot, calcium is needed to grow strong bones and zinc is important to help our body heal wounds. The difference between them is that vitamins are organic (which is a much bandied-about word with various meanings that in this context simply means they contain carbon) and minerals are inorganic.

There are thirteen different vitamins divided into two types: fat-soluble ones like vitamins A, D, E and K; and water-soluble ones like vitamins B_6, B_{12} and C. As you can see, vitamins are differentiated by letters and numbers although some of them are better known by their full names such as riboflavin (B_2), niacin (B_3) and folic acid (B_9). Fat-soluble vitamins are found in oily food like mackerel, liver and dairy products and are stored in the body, so you have to be careful not to eat too much of them. In contrast, water-soluble vitamins are found in fruit, vegetables and grains and are excreted in your urine if you eat too much of them – this also means you need to keep topping them up from your diet more often.

Minerals are found in all kinds of foods ranging from meat and fish to cereals and fruit. Some of the major minerals we need are calcium, iron, magnesium and potassium. Calcium is found particularly in dairy foods, iron in liver and beans, magnesium in leafy vegetables like spinach and potassium in bananas. Mixed up together all these foods would make a magnificent, if monstrously inedible, mineral milkshake.

BALANCING ACT:
HOW TO ORGANISE YOUR DIET

Perhaps when you look in the mirror you feel that your body is more of a sprawling hotel complex than a temple, but diet is one way to bring it to its lustrous, lissom, lively best.

The sensible Food Standards Agency recommends that each of us eats at least 5 portions of vegetables and fruit (approximately 400g) every day and makes complex carbohydrates (starchy foods – ideally the high-fibre wholegrain ones) the main focus of our meals. We should also eat moderate amounts of fish and lean meat to provide us with the protein, B vitamins and iron we need, and moderate amounts of milk and dairy foods (preferably low fat) to help keep our calcium, vitamin A and vitamin B levels healthy.

Sadly, we should only occasionally treat ourselves to foods high in fat, sugar and salt. If you want to take one simple step towards making your diet healthier, then it's best to cut out those villainous snack foods, crisps, fizzy drinks and biscuits, as these are all dripping with saturated fat, sugar and/or salt.

As a rough summary, one-third of your food each day should be fruit and veg, another third should be starchy carbs and the final third should be made up of the other food groups like fish, meat and dairy.

NUTRITIONAL DISEASES

Anorexia nervosa: an eating disorder which causes malnutrition as sufferers refuse to eat due to psychological problems.
Bulimia: an eating disorder which causes malnutrition as sufferers vomit up their food due to psychological problems.
Rickets: a childhood disease caused by inadequate absorption of vitamin D which leads to defects in bone growth, such as bow legs.
Kwashiorkor: a disease caused by lack of protein leading to swelling of the body, pot belly, discoloration of the hair and digestive difficulty.
Scurvy: a disease caused by lack of vitamin C – one of the oldest known nutritional diseases which often affected sailors on lengthy sea voyages without fresh fruit. British sailors would take limes on long trips in order to combat scurvy, which is where the national nickname 'Limey' comes from. Scurvy causes joint stiffness, bleeding gums and anaemia.

AVOIDING CONFLAGRATION: HOUSEHOLD FIRES

This is a very serious subject. Every year there are approximately 68,000 house fires in Britain, so don't assume that it won't happen to you. It is absolutely critical that you look around your house right this minute and think about how to reduce the risk of accidental fire and how you would cope should one begin. Here are some tips to help you:

Understand how fire works: three things need to be available to a fire for it to stay alight – oxygen, heat and fuel. If any of these elements are removed then the fire will go out.

Always fit smoke alarms and remember to check them regularly.

Think about your escape plan in the event of a fire. Buy fire-escape ladders or fire extinguishers for rooms high up in your house that would be difficult to escape from. Be aware that different types of fire extinguishers are required for different types of fire.

Take care with candles. If you are of a hippyish disposition and like to surround yourself with oil burners and candlelight, be sure to blow them out before you leave the room. It is best to avoid lighting candles of any kind before bed as there is a risk you will go to sleep without properly snuffing them out. Most household fires start at night. Always make sure that candles are placed away from any flammable (or inflammable – confusingly these words mean the same thing) objects.

Keep matches away from children. This is an obvious one. Keep them in the high-up or lockable cupboard with the plastic bags, bleach, sharp knives and medicines.

Buy a fire blanket for the kitchen. Check it has the British Standard Kitemark. Keep it near the cooker. If a fire starts cover it with the blanket. You should not use water or a fire extinguisher of the wrong type on electrical or oil fires, just the blanket. If safe to do so, you should also turn off the power source.

Don't deep-fry food. This is a health tip for your heart as much as a fire-safety tip. If you can't forsake your chip pan, be aware that they are the biggest cause of household fires in the country. Be very careful and never, ever leave the pan unattended. If it sets alight then **do not pour water on it.** This can produce an explosive fireball. If possible turn off the heat source and cover with a fire blanket.

Never smoke in bed. (Above and beyond all else it is a disgusting habit, and if you are in the need of some form of post-coital ritual, have a nice hot cup of tea instead. That way you only risk a light scalding rather than unconscious immolation.)

In the event of a fire, do not faff about. Leave the building immediately. If you are trapped, shut the door behind you in the safest room and seal off gaps with blankets or clothes. If there is smoke, cover your mouth with material and stay low to the floor where the air will be fresher. Call for help either by dialling 999 or by shouting out of the window.

BASIC FIRST AID

THE HEIMLICH MANOEUVRE

If a person is choking on their food and something is obstructing their airway you can help them by performing an action known as the Heimlich manouevre. Stand behind the person and wrap your arms around their waist. Form a fist and place the thumb side of it against the person's upper abdomen, above the belly button and below the ribcage. Grab your fist with your other hand and make a quick upward thrust. Repeat until the object blocking the airway is dislodged.

If a baby is choking, lie it down, face-up on a firm surface and then kneel or stand at the baby's feet. Alternatively, you can hold the child on your lap facing away from you. Place the middle and index fingers of both hands below its ribcage and above its belly button and press into the abdomen with a quick upward thrust – be very gentle and do not squeeze the ribcage. Repeat until the object is expelled.

DEALING WITH A CASUALTY

This is the essential process to follow should you be unfortunate enough to find yourself at the scene of an accident.

Danger: The first thing to do at the scene of an accident is to make sure you and any casualties are safe from further danger. Call for help if possible, and dial 999. Only move any casualties if it is absolutely necessary.

Response: When dealing with a casualty, first shout at them to see whether or not they are unconscious. If there is no response, check their pulse and breathing.

Airway: If the casualty is not breathing, you need to check that their airway is clear. Use your fingers to clear any vomit or broken teeth from their mouth. Turn the casualty onto their back, and open the airway by placing one hand on the casualty's forehead and gently tilting the head back, lifting the chin using two fingers only.

CPR: If the casualty is still not breathing, you need to begin CPR (cardiopulmonary resuscitation):

Compressions: For an adult, use a formula of 30 compressions to 2 rescue breaths. Place the heel of your hand in the centre of their chest. Place your other hand on top and interlock your fingers. Keeping your arms straight and your fingers off the chest, press down about 4 centimetres. Then release the pressure. Repeat this 30 times, at a rate of about 100 per minute.

Rescue breaths: Pinch the nose closed, take a deep breath, seal your lips around the casualty's mouth and blow into the mouth until the chest rises. Remove your mouth and allow the chest to fall. Repeat and begin compressions again. Continue CPR until help arrives or until the casualty begins to breathe normally.

Recovery position: Once the casualty is breathing normally, and if they have no other life-threatening conditions, move them into the recovery position. Turn the casualty onto their side, lift their chin forward to make sure their airway stays open. Check they are in a stable position, and monitor their breathing and pulse continuously.

TURN OFF THE LIGHTS: ENERGY-SAVING TIPS

Alas, with all our washing machines, microwaves, Ipods, stereos, juicers, plasma televisions and karaoke sets, modern human life exerts a great deal of stress on the environment. The natural resources of the world are finite and many of our home comforts cause increased carbon dioxide emissions that contribute to global warming. Mother Nature has been very generous to you and it behoves you to return the favour by becoming more energy-efficient.

• Always turn off electrical appliances when you have finished using

them. Leaving a computer monitor on all night uses the same amount of energy that a microwave needs to cook six suppers.
- Turn the thermostat in your home down by a few degrees. Wear a jumper if you get cold and put on some socks, or run round the block, instead of whingeing and using more heat energy.
- Never leave electrical appliances on standby. Turn them off completely.
- Use energy-saving light bulbs – these last longer so work out cheaper in the long run.
- When boiling the kettle, only boil as much water as you need – don't automatically fill the kettle.
- When boiling food on hobs, always use lids on your saucepans so you need less fuel to heat the food.
- Fix taps so that they don't drip and waste water.
- Wash your clothes at 30°C if they are not heavily soiled.
- Put half a brick or a full bottle of water into your lavatory cistern so that your loo uses less water every time it flushes.
- Make sure your house is properly insulated: use curtains and draught excluders to keep out draughts.

HOW TO MAKE A SAUSAGE-DOG DRAUGHT EXCLUDER

1. Take an old pair of tights – woolly ones are best – and cut off one of the legs.
2. Stuff the leg with material scraps, shredded old newspaper or old socks, and then sew up the open end.
3. Cut out some felt ears, legs and tail, and stick, or sew, onto the stuffed tube.
4. Glue on some googly eyes and you have a sausage-dog friend to lay in front of draughty doors to keep the wind at bay.

EVERYDAY ETIQUETTE: TABLE MANNERS

The very idea of table manners has been all but lost on many children and adults who rarely, if ever, sit down to a family meal around a table. But if someone has been kind enough to prepare a meal for you, the least you can do is make the experience of consuming it as pleasant as possible for your host and other guests. The simple courtesy of keeping your elbows off the table means that all diners have plenty of room and can see and speak to one another with greater ease than if everyone is hunched over like Neanderthals struggling over a carcass. It is definitely worth learning good table manners even if you occasionally abandon them when eating takeaway curry on the sofa in front of the television.

* Do not talk with your mouth full and do not eat with your mouth open. The sight of your mastication may be a source of disgust to your fellow guests.
* Do not put your elbows on the table.
* Never lick your plate.
* Put your napkin on your lap – do not tuck it into your collar. Never, ever blow your nose with it.
* Do not start eating until everyone has been served.
* Do not hold your knife like a pen. It is not a pen, it is a knife.
* Never put your knife in your mouth.
* The most appropriate way to eat peas is not to spoon them onto your fork, but to push them onto your fork, while it is facing down, with your knife.
* Do not wave your arms around or reach over people to grab the salt and pepper. Ask your neighbour to pass you things you need.
* When you have finished eating, leave your knife and fork together on your plate.
* If you are invited to a formal dinner, you may be startled by the array of cutlery you are presented with. It is important to use the correct utensils for the correct courses. With a formal place setting, work from the outside set in, i.e. use the knife and fork furthest away from your plate for eating your starter.
* Remember that table manners differ around the world. For example, in China it is perfectly acceptable to smoke and eat at the

same time and burp at the table; in Italy you should never touch your hair while you are eating; and in Korea you should not leave the table before the oldest person eating has finished their meal.

SPOTLESSLY CLEAN: CLOTHING-CARE SYMBOLS

In her 1938 book, *The Magic Key to Charm*, Eileen Ascroft takes great pains to point out that one of the key ingredients to appearing appealing and charming to your friends and acquaintances is to make sure that your clothes are spotlessly clean, fresh and pressed. That great labour-saving device the washing machine has made this almost effortless to achieve but it can also be an instrument of great destruction when used wrongly. Who among us has not put that beautiful lambswool twinset on a hot wash only to watch with horror as it comes out small enough to fit only your chihuahua? Make sure you can recognise the following symbols which appear on the labels of all mass-produced clothes. (If you are not wearing mass-produced clothes then you probably have a member of staff who can take care of your laundry concerns for you.)

Washing

Wash at 30°C

Wash at 40°C

Wash at 50°C

Wash at 60°C

Wash at 95°C

Cotton wash

Synthetic wash

Able to be chlorine-bleached

Do not bleach

May be tumble-dried

Tumble-dry – low heat

Tumble-dry – high heat

Do not tumble-dry

Drip-dry

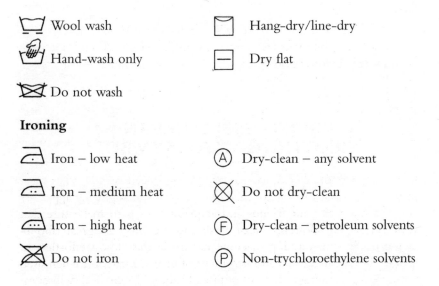

Wool wash | Hang-dry/line-dry
Hand-wash only | Dry flat
Do not wash |

Ironing

Iron – low heat | (A) Dry-clean – any solvent
Iron – medium heat | (X) Do not dry-clean
Iron – high heat | (F) Dry-clean – petroleum solvents
Do not iron | (P) Non-trychloroethylene solvents

HOW TO IRON A SHIRT

When you gaze upon your shirts on the hanger in your wardrobe you may think they look fine, but nothing sucks the aura of power and authority out of a person more than a slightly rumpled demeanour. Take pride in your own neatness and get out that iron. The best way to press a shirt to perfection is to iron each individual piece of it in the following order: collar, yoke (top back panel), cuffs, sleeves, back, front.

Finally, hang your masterpiece on a hanger and button it up before putting it gently back into your wardrobe.

If you need a mnemonic to help you get this process the right way round, remember this sentence: '**Celebrate Your Crispness, Striding Boldly Forwards**.'

KITCHEN CULTIVATION: INDOOR GARDENING

Certain plants, such as the versatile and hardy mint, flourish indoors so you don't need a garden to enjoy them. You can grow mint from seed or propagate a cutting from an existing mint plant, either from someone's garden or a supermarket. If you are growing it outside, plant it in the spring with plenty of space around the seeds. Mint doesn't need very rich soil or much watering except in very dry weather, but it does like to be in a sunny spot.

A RECIPE FOR MINT TEA

For a delicious and stimulating hot drink, pick some mint leaves (about 20 leaves will make enough tea for 2 people), ideally in the morning when the oils are most powerful. Place them in a teapot or mugs and pour hot water over them. Leave the tea to infuse for 5 minutes and then serve with a little honey if desired.

EATING SHOOTS AND LEAVES: SPROUTING SEEDS

Sprouted seeds are a delicious accompaniment to salads and are very high in vitamins. Mustard and cress are easy to grow on a sunny windowsill. Sprinkle mustard and cress seeds onto a layer of damp cotton wool in a bowl or tray, and in a few days you should see the seeds sprout and you can cut off the peppery shoots to use in salads or sandwiches. You can also sprout chickpeas, brown lentils, sunflower seeds or mung beans:

1. Rinse your seeds in a sieve.
2. Put the seeds in a jam jar and cover with a few centimetres of spring water.
3. Leave the jar in a warm place for 10-15 hours.
4. Pour off the remaining water and rinse the seeds then drain and return them to the jar.
5. Repeat this every morning for about 3-5 days until you see the seeds have sprouted and look ready to eat.

HOUSEHOLD BUDGETING

It is exceedingly slovenly and irresponsible not to be fully aware of where your hard-earned income goes, particularly if you are financially stretched by your responsibilities. It may be human nature to bury one's head in the sand to avoid bad news but it's only by taking control of your budget that you can properly free yourself from money worries.

A good first step to sorting out your worldly wealth is to use the following elementary table to keep a log of your income and expenditure. If you find it difficult to estimate what your monthly expenses are, keep all your receipts, cheque stubs and payslips for one month and use them to help you. In the right-hand column mark down your regular incomings or outgoings with a plus or minus sign next to them. After adding this column up, you will find the amount of money you should have left over at the end of each month to save for a rainy day (or an emergency such as the boiler breaking or a favoured football team changing their kit again). If you find that you end up with a minus number, look through the left-hand column to see which areas you might be able to cut back on.

Expense or income	Outgoings (-) or Incomings (+) per month
Salary/pension and/or benefits	
Interest on savings or investments	
Mortgage/rent	
Insurance payments – building, contents, medical, life, travel, motor	
Council tax	
Water bill	
Gas/oil bill	
Electricity bill	

Expense or income	Outgoings (–) or Incomings (+) per month
Phone bill (home, mobile and Internet)	
Household maintenance (including cleaning products, loo rolls, etc.)	
Education	
Food shopping	
Eating out (including drinks)	
Pets	
Cigarettes	
Travel (public transport or car/petrol and parking costs)	
Loan repayments (including credit card)	
Entertainment (including books, DVDs, fitness, cinema)	
TV licence and satellite subscription	
Clothes	
Presents	
Toiletries (including haircuts and manicures)	
Charity	
Health – dentist, massage, etc.	
TOTAL	

PRACTICAL PLUMBING:
HOW TO CLEAR A BLOCKED SINK

Sinks and plugholes often get blocked by hair and other rather unpleasant matter. To unblock a sink, you may be able simply to use your hands. You might want to wear an apron for this task as there is the vague possibility that you will be spattered with gunk. With a flannel in one hand, block off the overflow (you can also use wet tissue for this), then create a seal over the plughole with your other hand. Make sure there is some water in the sink. Pump your hand up and down to create a vacuum which should pull the matter up through the plughole. If your hand doesn't work, or for blocked loos, use a plunger.

DAPPER DRESSING:
HOW TO TIE A TIE

1.	2.	3.
Start with wide end of tie on your right and hanging down twice as far as the narrow end.	Cross wide end over narrow, and back underneath.	Continue around, passing wide end across front of narrow once more.

4.
Pass wide end up
through loop.

5.
Holding front of
knot loose with
index finger, pass
wide end down
through loop in
front.

6.
Remove finger
and tighten knot
carefully. Draw up
tight to collar by
holding narrow
end and sliding
knot up snugly.

HOW TO MAKE A BED
WITH HOSPITAL CORNERS

The joy of fresh linen stretched taut over a firm mattress can hardly be surpassed. It is always tempting to cut (hospital) corners and do things quickly and in a slapdash manner, but you should always try to aim for perfection. Here is the recipe for a perfectly made bed.

1. If you have an undersheet spread this over the mattress and smooth out.
2. Spread the bed sheet out over the undersheet and smooth down, leaving an equal edge hanging over all four sides of the bed.
3. Tuck in both the short ends of the sheet tightly.
4. Kneeling by one corner, take the corner of the loose end of the

sheet on one side and pull it towards you so that it is flat with the surface of the bed and then pull it towards the top of the bed, making a triangular fold.

5. Tuck the hanging edge under the mattress and then pull the triangular fold down over the mattress and tuck in so that the corner is neatly folded with a vertical line.

6. Repeat on the other three corners. The process should look like this:

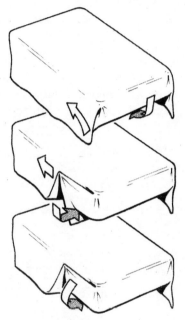

7. One corner at a time, take your duvet cover and gather it up so that the bottom opening is near the top two corners.

8. With one hand outside holding onto a top corner of the cover, push the top corner of the duvet in and grip with your outside hand.

9. Repeat with the other corner and then shake out the duvet cover over the duvet, keeping a tight grip on the top corners. Button or popper up the bottom and throw over the bed airily and neatly.

10. Put your pillows in their pillowcases and place them at the head of the bed.

11. Take off your shoes and get in for a well-earned snooze.

TOP TIPS:
HOW TO SUCCEED AT AN INTERVIEW

The economy of the home is obviously dependent upon the wages you bring into it so it's important to get the best job possible for your abilities and interests. These interview tips should help you make a good first impression on potential future employers.

DO wear clothes that are appropriate for the place you are being interviewed. i.e. a suit for a business interview but not for a waitressing job. Never wear wacky spectacles, socks or ties unless you are interviewing for the position of a children's entertainer.

DON'T express any extreme political or religious views during your interview. Do not be confrontational with your interviewer. Arm-wrestling is not an appropriate display of a go-getting attitude.

DO research the place you are being interviewed for properly beforehand. McDonald's is not a kilt-maker, Square Peg is not a laundry-supply retailer, Selfridges is not a refrigeration specialist and Microsoft has nothing to do with doll's-house upholstery.

DON'T whistle while the interviewer is asking you a question.

DO show enthusiasm and interest in the subject of your interview. Don't overdo it though; crying, emotional speeches, shouting and clapping will only frighten your interviewer.

DON'T avoid eye contact with the interviewer. It makes you look shady.

DO shake hands firmly and briefly with the interviewer. Do not use elaborate gang handshakes.

DON'T be nervous. Breathe deeply and slowly and imagine the interviewer naked to help yourself feel less intimidated. Be careful not to fall into a reverie, however.

HOW TO SURVIVE
A NUCLEAR ATTACK

In the event of a nuclear attack on the British Isles, there are various measures that individuals can take to increase their chances of survival. The first effect of a nuclear bomb is **heat and blast** which destroys everything around the centre of impact. This is followed by **fallout**, which is the fall of radioactive debris sucked up by the explosion. Even if you are far from the impact zone, **radioactive dust** can travel with the wind so you should be prepared to protect your home and family from it. Radioactive dust is very poisonous – it is invisible and odourless and can penetrate anything, although less of it penetrates dense material.

In the event of an attack, warnings will be broadcast on the radio and television and also possibly by local sirens and the police force. An attack-warning siren involves a rising and falling tone, three loud bangs indicate a fallout warning and a steady siren gives the all-clear.

You need to choose a place to shelter in the event of an attack. Pick a room in the centre of the house or underground if feasible – try to be as far away from the roof and exterior walls as possible. Prepare this room to house you and your family for at least fourteen days. Strengthen and add layers to all sides of the room including the floors and ceilings. Block up windows and chimneys and add extra layers of books, bricks and furniture against the walls. Build an inner refuge inside your fallout room. You can do this using doors, suitcases full of clothes, wardrobes, cupboards, tables and other solid furniture. It needs to be big enough for all of you to shelter inside.

You need to equip your fallout room with:

- Enough water to last everyone for fourteen days. Fill and seal bottles and any containers you have. Also fill the bath and all basins with water and cover them. The mains supply may be contaminated after an attack. Do not waste any water while you are in the fallout room.
- Enough food to last everyone for fourteen days. In preparation, keep tins (especially of fruit and vegetables) on hand in your store

cupboard at all times. Remember to bring a tin-opener and eating
implements into your fallout room.

- Thick clothing.
- Bedding.
- Torches, candles and matches.
- A clockwork radio. If you only have a battery radio, remember to
  bring batteries.
- A bucket with plastic bags, newspaper, disinfectant and loo roll to
  use as a toilet. Keep a bin to store waste in just outside the fallout
  room.
- Soap and towels.
- A first-aid kit.
- Paper and pencils.
- Books and toys for any children.
- A clock and a calendar.
- A fire extinguisher.

Before you enter your fallout room, make the rest of your house safe by
removing flammable items from near the windows (you can draw thick
curtains if you have them, however, to help protect against the blast),
blocking up windows and preparing buckets of water to douse any fires
that occur. Close all doors. Turn off all electrical appliances and the gas.

There will be a short period after the heat and blast before fallout
begins. This will be announced on the radio, TV and using sirens. In this
period you can go out of the fallout room to put out any fires in your
home. Then return to the inner refuge of your fallout room and stay
there without leaving for at least forty-eight hours. Listen to the radio
for advice.

If you have to leave the fallout room over the next fortnight then brush
off all dust and take off your shoes before re-entering the room. Do not
allow children out of the room. If someone dies then wrap them in a
sheet, attach identification to the body and move it quickly out of the
room.

❦ HOME ECONOMICS ❦ TEST PAPER

1. **How long would you roast a chicken weighing 1.5 kg for?**

2. **What is a lacto-ovo-vegetarian?**

a) a vegetarian who eats neither dairy products nor eggs
b) a vegetarian who eats both dairy products and eggs
c) a vegetarian who eats fish
d) a carnivore

3. **What is the first thing you should do at the scene of an accident?**

4. **Which of the following is inappropriate behaviour at an interview?**

a) shouting
b) showing knowledge of the company
c) maintaining eye contact
d) imagining the interviewer naked

5. **The Heimlich manoeuvre refers to:**

a) a Second World War incursion into Poland
b) a new type of German-engineered car
c) a way of helping a person who is choking

6. **Which of the following is not an acceptable thing to do at the table?**

a) masticating with your mouth closed
b) waiting until everyone else at the table has been served before starting to eat
c) blowing your nose with your napkin

7. What is the first thing you should do in the event of a nuclear attack?

8. What does this symbol mean:

9. How many grams are there in 13 ounces?

10. Name three food-hygiene procedures you should follow.

11. Where was Shepherd's Pie invented, and what is the handy way to remember the difference between a Shepherd's Pie and a Cottage Pie?

12. When ironing a shirt, which part should you always iron last?

13. How do you calculate your body mass index?

14. List the five essential nutrients the human body requires.

15. What is protein made of?

16. What are lipids for?

17. What proportion of your daily diet should be made up of complex carbohydrates?

18. What are the symptoms of the nutritional disease kwashiorkor?

19. What three things does a fire need to keep burning?

20. If your BMI, or body mass index is over 25, what should you do?

21. If you heard a rising and falling siren echoing through the streets, what would it be telling you?

22. What does the following symbol mean?

23. **Measurements:**

a) You need to give your daughter 15ml of cough medicine. How many teaspoonfuls should she take?
b) How much liquid in millilitres does a tablespoon hold?

24. **Following a recipe:**

a) In a recipe for a chocolate cake you are instructed 'to cream' the ingredients. What does this mean?
b) What should you do if you are told 'to fold' something in a recipe?

4

HISTORY

'**History** *n.* the study of past events, esp. human affairs'
Oxford Concise English Dictionary

'History is a distillation of rumour'
THOMAS CARLYLE (1795–1881)

Who could fail to be fascinated by the superb subject of History? Banish thoughts of dusty old tomes creaking on about the intricacies of the mechanics of ploughing, or the various permutations of obscure acts of Parliament. Far from being a dry and academic subject, History can move, bewitch, horrify and inspire. It is, after all, the story of the human race. The events of days of yore have the power to spark even the dullest imagination: monstrous monarchs, dastardly dictators, blood-thirsty battles, tip-top technology, oppression, religion, revolution, romance – all of these and more play a part in shaping world history. If you've ever wondered where a Becklespinax could be found, who won the Battle of Marathon, what the Magna Carta actually declared, what Mary Queen of Scots' big mistake was or what constituted the Warsaw Pact, then this is the chapter for you.

WORLD HISTORY TIMELINE

BCE
*c.*8000: Middle East – Walls of Jericho are built.
*c.*5000: Mexico – cultivation of maize established.

WHAT IS PREHISTORY?

Prehistory is the period for which no written records exist. Obviously it's hard to tell what actually went on without access to the diaries of Ugg the caveman or archived copies of the *Jurassic Times*, but this doubt is not just limited to prehistory. Events from all periods of the past are constantly being reassessed and argued about by different historians. It is rare indeed to find an uncontested interpretation of a historical event or process. A good historian knows that analytical skills are essential, and you must look very carefully at your sources. Ask yourself a series of telling questions: What is the source's context? Is there an agenda or bias? Is it primary or secondary evidence? An Iron Age tool is a **primary source**, a devastatingly insightful and perceptive article about Iron Age metalwork by a twentieth-century specialist is a **secondary source** and should be judged accordingly. The lack of records means that dates for events in prehistory are often doubtful and approximate.

THE GEOLOGICAL TIMESCALE

With our meagre threescore years and ten, it's a challenge for us to conceive of how long the Earth has been spinning, and how long she will spin after we're gone.

Scientists divide the history of the world into different time periods according to the geological timescale, which begins approximately 3.9 billion years ago and corresponds to the oldest rocks that have been dated. Archaeologists can date rocks by measuring the level of decay of certain types of carbon and radioactive elements in them.

The largest units of time on the scale are called **aeons**. Aeons are then divided into **eras**, which are in turn divided into **periods**, which are

---

c.4000: China – cultivation of rice established.
c.3100: Middle East – Sumerians develop cuneiform writing system.
c.2800: China – writing system developed.
c.2700–*c*.1300: Britain – Stonehenge constructed.
c.2575–*c*.2465: Egypt – Pyramids of Giza built.

divided into **epochs**, which are divided into **ages**, and ages are divided into **chrons**. Chrons are periods of time that last for a million years or fewer and ages can stretch for up to 10 million years.

There are three aeons: the **Archaean**, **Proterozoic** and **Phanerozoic**. The first two are called the **Precambrian** aeons and the **Phanerozoic** is divided into three eras – **Palaeozoic**, **Mesozoic** and **Cenozoic**, which are in turn divided into different periods. It is worth reading aloud the evocative names of the different periods, as they summon up mental images of rugged landscapes, wild forests and strange beasts, as well as making you aware of just how brief our hour upon the stage is.

AEONS	ERAS	PERIODS
Archaean and Proterozoic (Precambrian)		
Phanerozoic	Palaeozoic	Cambrian Ordovician Silurian Devonian Carboniferous Permian
	Mesozoic	Triassic Jurassic Cretaceous
	Cenozoic	Palaeogene Neogene

The easiest way to remember the order of the periods is to recite this sentence to yourself: '**Cats Often Sit Down Carefully, Perhaps Their Joints Creak Painfully and Noisily.**'

---

*c.*1270: **Middle East – Moses leads Israelite Exodus from Egypt to Canaan (Palestine).**
*c.*900: **Nigeria – Nok culture begins.**
814: **Africa – Phoenicians establish Carthage.**
776: **Greece – first recorded Olympic Games.**

DINOSAURS

Dinosaurs were giant reptiles that are always described as 'roaming'. They seem, however, to have galloped, cantered, sauntered and even thundered their way about. Their name comes from the ancient Greek word '*deinos*' meaning 'terrible' with '*sauros*' meaning 'lizard'.

Dinosaurs evolved in the Mesozoic era. The Mesozoic era is divided into three periods – the Triassic (227–205 million years ago), the Jurassic (205–144 million years ago) and the Cretaceous (144–65 million years ago). We know about dinosaurs from discoveries of their fossils, and around seven hundred species have been named. The most iconic dinosaurs – the ones we drew endlessly over our prep books when we were children – come from the Jurassic and Cretaceous periods. The British Isles were home to lesser known, but no less brilliantly monikered dinosaurs such as the Neovenator, the Lexovisaurus, the Megalosaurus and the Becklespinax.

There are various theories about why and how the dinosaurs died out: some scientists believe that a massive asteroid, or asteroids, crashed into the Earth, causing extreme weather conditions that killed them, others claim that different environmental changes were responsible.

Tyrannosaurus rex

563: India – birth of Siddhartha Gautama (Buddha).
509: Italy – Roman Republic established.
507: Greece – democracy established in Athens.
*c.*400: Mexico – settlement begins at Teotihuacán.
279: India – Asoka establishes first Indian Empire.

Stegosaurus

Velociraptor

Triceratops

Diplodocus

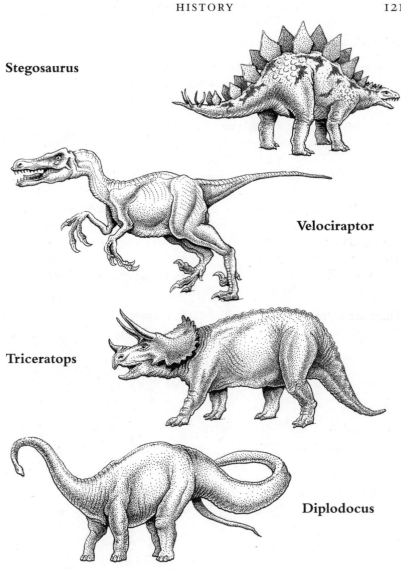

221: China – Qin dynasty unites China. Shi Huangdi becomes first
    Emperor of China.
*c.*200: Peru – Nazca Lines created.
51: Egypt – Cleopatra becomes queen.
44: Italy – Julius Caesar assassinated.

CARPE DIEM: OUR TIME ON EARTH

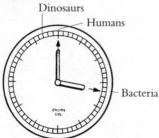

The 'terrible lizards' ruled the earth for 160 million years. Humans have existed for just over 3 million years so far.

If the 4.6 billion years of the Earth's existence were crammed into the last hour, then our first human ancestor appeared approximately two seconds ago, dinosaurs appeared approximately three minutes ago, and the first bacteria appeared approximately forty-three minutes ago.

EARLY MAN

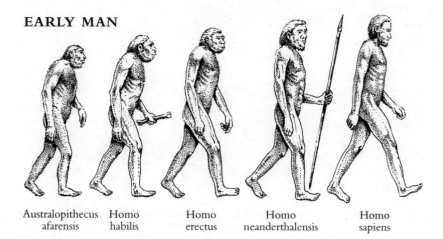

Australopithecus afarensis	Homo habilis	Homo erectus	Homo neanderthalensis	Homo sapiens

We human beings developed from primates millions of years ago. Modern humans are members of the species *Homo sapiens* that evolved 100,000 to 200,000 years ago. We are the only remaining human species, but at one time there were different hominins such as Neanderthal man (*Homo neanderthalensis*), who existed at the same time as early *Homo*

---

*c.*5: **Middle East – birth of Jesus.**

1st–5th centuries CE
*c.*58: **China – Buddhism reaches China from India.**
79: Italy – eruption of Vesuvius.

sapiens. It is generally held that we are related to these extinct hominins, and also to the apes, but it has never been conclusively established just exactly how.

INVASIONS OF BRITAIN

Our green and pleasant land has, over the course of its history, carried out more than its fair share of invasions – countries such as America, India and Iraq have fallen foul of our marauding nature – but it's also true to say that we've had some incursions ourselves.

1. WHAT DID THE ROMANS EVER DO FOR US?: THE ROMAN INVASION

The first recorded invasion of Britain was carried out by Julius Caesar in 55 BCE in order to punish the British for helping the indomitable Gauls stave off his conquest of their lands (modern-day France). Caesar was resisted by native Celtic tribes and forced to leave and try again a year later. Although this time he was successful, the Romans did not colonise Britain until the Emperor Claudius's invasion in 43 CE. Various tribal leaders continued to fight against Roman rule, the most serious rebellion coming in 61 CE, when brazen Boudicca, the queen of the Iceni tribe, fought back because of a territorial dispute with the colonisers. She efficiently burnt down Colchester (which was then the capital known as Camulodunum) and London before Roman troops managed to defeat her at the Battle of Watling Street. Rather than face capture, Boudicca killed herself by drinking poison. After Boudicca's revolt, the Romans maintained control of their British territories for the next 350 years and brought many new customs and technologies to Britain such as a system of law, towns, roads, shops, aqueducts and, best of all, baths and wine.

---

*c.*100: Hawaii – first settlers arrive.
*c.*100: China – invention of paper.
380: Christianity adopted by Roman Empire.
400: Easter Island – settlers arrive.
*c.*450s: Britain – Angles and Saxons settle.

ROMAN ROADS

Roman roads were designed to make the movement of troops around the country more efficient. They were so well planned that our modern roads are often built on top of them. The most famous Roman road is Watling Street which runs from Dover to London (and is now covered by the A2) and then from London to Wroxeter (now covered by the A5). So when you're next sitting in a traffic jam outside Oswestry, you can pass the time imagining the tramp of legionaries' feet as they travelled the same path as you, all those centuries ago.

2. THE ANGLO-SAXONS

The Roman Empire started to crumble in the fifth century CE, and the Romans finally withdrew from Britain in 410 CE. At the same time invaders from Angeln and Saxony in Germany arrived, as well as Jutes and Frisians from Denmark, Picts from the north of Britain and Scots from Ireland. The Anglo-Saxons spoke Old English which, over the passing of many years, has developed into the English language we speak today. The Anglo-Saxons originally ruled as separate tribes but eventually united into four separate kingdoms: Northumbria, Mercia, East Anglia and Wessex.

Anglo-Saxon articulation: some useful Old English words

man – human

wifman – woman

wer – man

modor – mother

faeder – father

dohtor – daughter

sunu – son

hors – horse

cu – cow

werwulf – werewolf

452: Europe – Attila the Hun invades.

6th–10th centuries CE
552: Japan – Buddhism introduced.
570: Mecca – birth of Muhammad.

3. THE VIKING INVASION

The Vikings were Scandinavian plunderers from Norway, Sweden and Denmark – the name 'Viking' is said by some to come from the Old English word *wicing* meaning 'pirate'. They attacked and settled in different parts of Europe between the eighth and eleventh centuries CE. From the end of the eighth century Viking ships began to stage raids on British territories and the invaders settled in various places. In 878 King Alfred defeated the invading Danes but agreed to establish the Danelaw in the north of Britain, where the Vikings were allowed to stay. In 1016 the Danish King Canute became ruler of most of England, as well as Denmark, Norway and part of Sweden. The Viking legacy is still visible today in various parts of Britain such as Toxteth and Orkney in the form of place names and family names such as Farmer, Fisher or Baxter.

4. THE NORMAN INVASIONS

Edward the Confessor was part of the Anglo-Saxon royal family that had been deposed by the Danes. After the death of King Canute's son, Harald Harefoot, and his half-brother, Hardicanute, Edward succeeded to the throne in 1042. When Edward died in 1066, disastrously he left no heir. On his deathbed, he bequeathed his kingdom to his brother-in-law Harold Godwinesone, the Earl of Wessex. However, there were conflicting claims to the throne from Tostig, Harold's own brother; the king of Norway, Harald Hardraade; and William of Normandy, who was Edward's cousin.

Harold was crowned Harold II in January 1066 but in that same year, rather inconveniently, all of his rivals attempted to invade. King Harold saw off the combined forces of Tostig and Harald Hardraade at the Battle of Stamford Bridge in Yorkshire on 25 September, but on 28 September William landed on the south coast and advanced his army to Hastings.

630: Mecca – Muhammad establishes Islam.
711: Spain – Moors take over Spain from Visigoths.
771: Europe – Charlemagne becomes king of the Franks. In 800 he
    becomes the first Holy Roman Emperor.
c.800: New Zealand – first settlers arrive.

On 14 October the Battle of Hastings saw William defeat Harold, who, according to the Bayeux Tapestry, was killed by an arrow to the eye. William I, now known as the Conqueror, was crowned in Westminster Abbey on Christmas Day 1066, and thus began the Norman lineage of English kings.

The Bayeux Tapestry

The Bayeux Tapestry is considered an astonishing work of art and craftsmanship, though Charles Dickens wasn't impressed, and slightly scathingly called it 'the work of very feeble amateurs'. In fact, the tapestry, like Dickens himself, employed sophisticated storytelling techniques that are still being used today – split-screen narration, dramatic tension and complex characterisation to name but a few. Constructed in the eleventh century, it stretches to seventy metres in length and contains 1,512 figures. It is the principal secondary source of information that we have about the Norman Conquest. A word of caution to all you historians though: this is by no means an unbiased source, given that it was commissioned by William the Conqueror's half-brother, Bishop Odo of Bayeux.

The tapestry itself has had a tumultuous history. During the 1789 French Revolution it was taken from the church where it hung to be used as a cover for military equipment and was only saved at the last moment by the local police commissioner; later on Napoleon used it for propaganda purposes; and during World War II the Nazis attempted to steal it away to Germany.

850: Zimbabwe – Bantu build city of Great Zimbabwe.
870: Iceland – Vikings settle.

11th–15th centuries CE
1062: Morocco – foundation of Marrakesh.

MONARCHS OF ENGLAND

House of Wessex
Egbert (802-39)
Ethelwulf (839-56)
Ethelbald (856-60)
Ethelbert (860-6)
Ethelred (866-71)
Alfred the Great (871-99)
Edward the Elder (899-924)
Athelstan (924–39)
Edmund the First (939–46)
Edred (946-55)
Edwy All-Fair (955-9)
Edgar the Peaceable (959-75)
Edward the Martyr (975-9)
Ethelred the Unready (979-1016)
Edmund II, Ironside (1016)

Danish Line
Canute the Great (1016-35)
Harald Harefoot (1035-40)
Hardicanute (1040-2)

House of Wessex, Restored
Edward the Confessor (1042-66)
Harold II (1066)

Norman Line
William I the Conqueror (1066-87)
William II Rufus (1087-1100)
Henry I Beauclerc (1100-35)

Stephen (1135-54)

Plantagenet, Angevin Line
Henry II Curtmantle (1154-89)
Richard I the Lionheart (1189-99)
John Lackland (1199-1216)
Henry III (1216-72)
Edward I Longshanks (1272-1307)
Edward II (1307-27)
Edward III (1327-77)
Richard II (1377-99)

Plantagenet, Lancastrian Line
Henry IV Bolingbroke (1399-1413)
Henry V (1413-22)
Henry VI (1422-61, 1470-1)

Plantagenet, Yorkist Line
Edward IV (1461-70, 1471-83)
Edward V (1483)
Richard III Crookback (1483-5)

House of Tudor
Henry VII (1485-1509)
Henry VIII (1509-47)
Edward VI (1547-53)
Lady Jane Grey (1553)
Mary I (1553-8)
Elizabeth I (1558-1603)

1066: Britain – William the Conqueror becomes king.
1096: Europe – first Crusade begins against Muslims in Palestine.
1113–50: Cambodia – construction of Angkor Wat.
1215: Britain – Magna Carta issued.
1218: Middle East – Genghis Khan conquers Persia.

MONARCHS OF GREAT BRITAIN

House of Stuart
James I (1603-25)
Charles I (1625-49)

Commonwealth (1649-60)

House of Stuart, Restored
Charles II (1660-85)
James II (1685-8)

House of Orange and Stuart
William III, Mary II (1689-1702)

House of Stuart
Anne (1702-14)

House of Brunswick, Hanover Line
George I (1714-27)
George II (1727-60)
George III (1760-1820)
George IV (1820-30)
William IV (1830-7)
Victoria (1837-1901)

House of Saxe-Coburg-Gotha
Edward VII (1901-10)

House of Windsor
George V (1910-36)
Edward VIII (1936)
George VI (1936-52)
Elizabeth II (1952-)

THE BIRTH OF DEMOCRACY?
THE MAGNA CARTA

In 1199 King John (1166-1216), also known rather spitefully as Lackland, succeeded his brother, the crusading King Richard I, 'the Lionheart' (a much more flattering nickname), to the throne of England. Civil unrest, rebellious barons, the failure of wars in France, excessive taxation and quarrels with the Pope made John an unpopular king and led to him signing the Magna Carta (or 'Great Paper') at Runnymede on 15 June 1215.

The Magna Carta's significance rests in the idea that the king's power could, for the first time, be constrained by a constitution or law rather than the monarch being solely answerable to himself. The Magna Carta has been influential in the development of ideas of democracy around the world.

1220: Peru – foundation of Inca civilisation.
1271: Italy – Marco Polo travels to China.
1297: Scotland – William Wallace takes back Scotland from English control.
1325: Mexico – Aztecs establish Tenochtitlán (Mexico City).

FRANCE VS. ENGLAND:
THE OLD RIVALRY
THE HUNDRED YEARS WAR (1337–1453)

The rivalry between England and France has stretched back nearly seven hundred years. As long ago as the Norman invasion, various territories in France were attached to the English throne and the succession of the two Crowns was linked. After the death without an heir of the French King Charles IV in 1328, the English King Edward III claimed the French Crown because of ties to the French royal family. A French assembly decided in favour of a different claimant, who became Phillip VI, who confiscated Edward's French territories in 1337, leading, unsurprisingly, to a bitter war. The Hundred Years War was brutal and gruelling and involved events such as the Battle of Agincourt and the rescue of Orleans by Joan of Arc. At the end of the war England had lost all of her territories in France apart from Calais.

THE BLACK DEATH

In the fourteenth century a plague pandemic wiped out between a quarter and third of Europe's population (approximately 25 million people). The plague was a disease passed to humans from fleas which lived on the black rat. The disease is thought to have originated in Asia and been brought to Europe in 1347 in an early instance of biological warfare, when Mongols attacking a town inhabited by Genoese merchants in the Crimea catapulted the dead bodies of plague victims over the town walls. The escaping Genoese brought the plague to Sicily from whence it spread its deadly grip across Europe.

1337: Europe – start of Hundred Years War between England and France.
1368: China – foundation of the Ming dynasty.
1378-1417: Europe – the Great Schism: Urban VI elected Pope in Rome and Clement VII in Avignon.

ARISTOCRATIC ACRIMONY:
THE WARS OF THE ROSES (1455-85)

The Wars of the Roses were fought between two sides of the Plantagenet royal family – the House of York and the House of Lancaster. The House of York was descended from the great King Edward III's fourth son, Edmund. The House of Lancaster was descended from Edward's third son, John of Gaunt. The House of Lancaster was represented by a red rose and the House of York by a white rose.

When Henry VI (of the House of Lancaster) lost his marbles in 1453, the powerful Earl of Warwick, known as the Kingmaker, helped Richard, Duke of York, become Protector of the Realm. After Henry's recovery and resumption of power in 1455, Richard found his influence severely curtailed and he took up arms against the king. This began a conflict that continued through the generations until Henry Tudor of the House of Lancaster defeated the Yorkist Richard III at the Battle of Bosworth Field on 22 August 1485. In 1486 Henry married Elizabeth of York in a move to unite the two sides of the family. He adopted as his symbol the Tudor rose, a perfect melding of the red and the white.

House of York   House of Lancaster   House of Tudor

1382-4: Britain – Wyclif translates the Bible into English.
1383: Middle East – Tamerlane conquers Persia.
1388: Britain – Chaucer writes *The Canterbury Tales*.
1400: Wales – Owen Glendower leads rebellion against the English.
1440: Germany – Gutenberg establishes printing using movable type.

DIVORCED, BEHEADED, DIED: HENRY VIII (1491-1547)

Henry VIII was one of the most important Tudor monarchs; however, he is not to be emulated or admired for his personal life. He is particularly remembered for his six wives: Catherine of Aragon, Anne Boleyn, Jane Seymour, Anne of Cleves, Catherine Howard and Catherine Parr. The easiest way to remember the fates each met is the rhyme:

Divorced, beheaded, died
Divorced, beheaded, survived.

To remember the order that these women entered into the dangerous state of matrimony with the king, think of this sentence where the first letters of the words correspond with the first letters of the unlucky ladies' titles or surnames: '**A Big Ship Came Hurrying Past**.'

Shortly after his accession to the throne in 1509 Henry married Catherine of Aragon, his dead brother Arthur's widow, as part of an alliance with Spain. She bore him six children, including two boys, but only one child survived, Mary. In 1527, desperate for a male heir and entranced by the bewitching Anne Boleyn, Henry asked the Pope to annul the marriage on the grounds that religious law meant he should never have married his brother's widow. Pope Clement VI refused as Catherine swore that the union was legitimate because she had never consummated her marriage with Arthur. The Pope was also loath to upset Catherine's nephew, the Holy Roman Emperor, Charles V.

Never one happily to accept not getting his own way, Henry married the pregnant Anne Boleyn without the Pope's permission in May 1533, and just four months later their daughter Elizabeth was born. Still furious with the Pope, in 1534 the king passed the Act of Supremacy which rejected papal intrusion into English religious affairs and made

---

1453: Constantinople (Istanbul) – Muhammad II, the Ottoman Emperor, conquers the Byzantine capital.
c.1461: Central America – peak of Aztec control.
1469: Spain – unification of Aragon and Castile through the marriage of Ferdinand and Isabella.

Henry the head of the Church of England, paving the way for the Reformation that was sweeping Europe to come to Britain.

Anne Boleyn also failed to bear Henry a son, and she was executed in 1536 after the king allowed her to be convicted of sexual misconduct and witchcraft. Henry married Jane Seymour eleven days after Anne's death, but the following year she died after giving birth to the future King Edward VI.

In January 1540 Henry married Anne of Cleves in order to form an alliance with the Protestant Duke of Cleves, her brother. The marriage was annulled on 9 July that same year when the alliance became less critical as the threat of an attack from Catholic powers diminished. Three weeks later he married Catherine Howard. After a short period of happiness, Henry was told of Catherine's previous affairs, which clearly did not amuse him. On 11 February 1542, the king made a law declaring that sexual misconduct by the queen constituted treason. Two days later Catherine was executed, the second of Henry's wives to lose her head on the block.

Catherine Parr married Henry on 12 July 1543. She took care of the three surviving children Henry had from his previous marriages – Mary, Elizabeth and Edward – and survived the king to marry again after his death. Good for her!

Henry VIII died on 28 January 1547. Legend has it that before Henry's marriage to Anne Boleyn, a Franciscan friar had predicted that if Henry went ahead with the illegal union, one day dogs would lick up his blood. As the body was being taken to the funeral, it is said to have split, because of his immense, diseased bulk, and a dog was seen licking his bodily fluids from the ground.

1478: Spain – Spanish Inquisition established.
1482: Ghana – Portuguese build settlements on Gold Coast.
1485: England – Battle of Bosworth Field. Henry VII defeats Richard III.
1485: South America – Inca conquest of parts of Chile, Peru and Argentina.

THREE QUEENS: BLOODY MARY, THE VIRGIN QUEEN AND MARY, QUEEN OF SCOTS

Mary I   Elizabeth I   Mary, Queen of Scots

Between 1553 and 1603 the fate of the British Isles was dominated by three women, and, happily for those students who struggle with names, two of them were called Mary.

After the death in 1553 of the fifteen-year-old King Edward VI, Henry VIII's only male heir, and the disastrous nine-day rule of Lady Jane Grey, Mary, Henry's eldest child and the daughter of Catherine of Aragon, came to the throne with much popular support. But the people's good-will soon turned to vitriol, in part because of her determination to make England a Catholic country once again. Her subjects rebelled against her, and she began a campaign to stamp out heresy and opposition, which led to three hundred Protestants being burnt at the stake. She was henceforth known as Bloody Mary.

Mary died childless and in 1558 the Crown passed to her half-sister, Elizabeth, the daughter of Anne Boleyn. Elizabeth was highly educated and a brilliant political strategist, and her reign is considered a golden age. She restored the Protestant Church of England, but rejected the

---

1492: Caribbean – Christopher Columbus lands in what he calls the West Indies.

16th–18th centuries
1502: America – first African slaves arrive.

extreme measures of religious control practised by her sister, saying that she did not want to 'make windows into men's souls . . . there is only one Jesus Christ and all the rest is a dispute over trifles'. Mary had brought disgrace to the Crown by losing Calais to the French, but Elizabeth's success against the Spanish Armada (led by Mary's widower, Philip II) restored national pride.

She further encouraged the love of her people through her patronage of the arts, and her endorsement of the cult of the Virgin Queen that grew up around her. Cleverly, she used her unmarried position to her political advantage by playing off various powerful international suitors against each other. However, she was loath to compromise her power by taking a husband: 'I will have here but one mistress, and no master.' Her decision not to marry left her vulnerable to plots from would-be successors, the most serious of which came from her cousin, Mary Stuart, Queen of Scots.

Mary Stuart returned to Scotland from France in 1561 after the death of her husband, King Francis II. In 1565 she married her second cousin, Lord Darnley. Even after the birth of their son, James, the relationship was turbulent, and when Darnley was murdered and Mary married the chief suspect three months later, her people turned against her. She was deposed in favour of her son, and imprisoned in Loch Leven Castle. She escaped and fled to England, where she was not a particularly welcome guest. She posed a threat to Elizabeth on two fronts: she was next in line to the throne, and she was a useful focus for Catholic plots. Elizabeth imprisoned her for nineteen years after plans for a Catholic uprising were discovered. Before her execution in 1587, she said to her executioner: 'I forgive you with all my heart, for now, I hope, you shall make an end of all my troubles.'

Elizabeth died childless in 1603, marking the end of the Tudor line and the beginning of the Stuart reign – she was succeeded by Mary, Queen of Scots' son, James VI of Scotland, who became James I of England.

---

*c.*1505: Germany – Peter Heinlein invents the watch.

1508: Italy – Michelangelo starts work on the Sistine Chapel.

1517: Germany – Martin Luther nails his *Ninety-Five Theses* to door of a church in Wittenberg starting the Reformation.

THE GREAT FIRE OF LONDON (1666)

In the early hours of Sunday 2 September 1666, baker Thomas Farynor awoke to the smell of burning from the shop below his living quarters on Pudding Lane. As the Farynor family fled across the rooftops (except for one maid, too frightened to move, who became the first victim of the fire), the alarm was raised. The ineffectual Mayor of London, Sir Thomas Bloodworth, was initially unmoved, remarking: 'A woman might piss it out.' In fact, the combination of a long, hot summer, a strong east wind and tightly packed overhanging timber housing meant that by the time demolitions of buildings were ordered to create fire-breaks and halt the flames, it was raging out of control. Samuel Pepys (1633–1703), watching the inferno from a boat on the river, described the scene as 'only one entire arch of fire from this to the other side of the bridge, and in a bow up the hill for an arch of above a mile long: it made me weep to see it'. London burned for five days; much of the medieval city was destroyed. By the time the dropping winds and fire-breaks had finally put out the flames, 13,200 houses, four-fifths of the City and 436 acres in total had been destroyed. Over 100,000 people were made homeless. Official figures put the number of dead at only four, but it's probable that the toll was much higher.

TURNING THE WHEELS OF HISTORY: SIX MAJOR REVOLUTIONS

1. THE GREAT REBELLION (1642–51)

Charles I (1625–49), son of James I, was a bit of a dandy and a fop, and became a deeply unpopular king who raised taxes to fund his art collections, rode roughshod over Parliament and failed to prevent civil wars breaking out in his territories. In 1641 Parliament issued a Grand Remonstrance outlining their grievances against the king, who then

1519-20: Mexico – Hernando Cortés captures the Aztec capital of Tenochtitlán.

1520: Istanbul – Suleiman the Magnificent becomes sultan of the Ottoman Empire.

marshalled an army of supporters. Forces loyal to Parliament rose against the royalists. The parliamentarians were known as **Roundheads** for their austere short haircuts which contrasted with the flowing locks of the royalists, also known as **Cavaliers**. In 1649, after nearly a decade of civil war, Charles was executed for high treason. Britain was declared a republic and named the Commonwealth, and Oliver Cromwell, a roundhead general, was appointed Lord Protector in 1653. After Cromwell's death in 1658 and the failure of his son to rule effectively as Lord Protector, Charles II (Charles I's exiled son) acceded to the throne in 1660, an event known as the **Restoration**.

(If you struggle to remember who's who out of the Cavaliers and Roundheads, think of the Cavalier King Charles spaniel – named after Charles II who loved this breed of dog – and its floppy, flowing ears that look like the Cavaliers' long lustrous locks.)

2. THE INDUSTRIAL REVOLUTION (1760–1830)

The Industrial Revolution changed the face of human history. Just try to imagine it: without the Industrial Revolution there would be no toasters, no IKEA, no London Underground. People used to work at home or on the land, but the domestic and agrarian systems that had been in place since primitive times were superseded over an astonishingly brief period which truly revolutionised Britain's economy.

The revolution began in Britain in the mid-eighteenth century and was characterised by the increased use of machines and organised labour working in factories. It particularly affected the textile, coal, iron and steel industries. One downside of this increased mechanisation and mass production is that now there is a chance you might turn up to a party wearing the same dress as someone else, but the upside is that women no longer have to choose between a career in childbirth or going slowly blind sewing shirts by candlelight for rich folk. The move to

1520: Europe – introduction of chocolate.
1534: England – Act of Supremacy declares Henry VIII head of the Church of England.
1542: Japan – Portuguese sailors arrive, initiating contact with the West.

factory work meant that more and more people started living in cities, which in turn necessitated an improvement in transport systems – chiefly to distribute manufactured goods and bring food to the workers. Gradually, industrial advances and inventions spread to the rest of the world.

The Luddites
The Luddites were a group of craftsmen who, between 1811 and 1816, carried out night raids to destroy the textile machinery that they believed was robbing them of their livelihoods. Nowadays, the term Luddite is used to describe a person who is opposed to technological advances, or someone who can't work out how to operate their DVD player.

---

3. *LIBERTÉ, ÉGALITÉ, FRATERNITÉ*: THE FRENCH REVOLUTION (1789–99)

The French Revolution was caused by the increasing disillusionment of the commons (the **Third Estate**) with the power of the monarchy and the other two elements of the French government – the nobility (the **Second Estate**) and the clergy (the **First Estate**). This unrest, along with bad harvests and ongoing economic problems, led to mounting political instability.

On 14 July 1789, a Parisian mob stormed the Bastille prison, a symbol of the monarchy's abuse of power and home to many political prisoners. The anniversary of this event is still celebrated with a public holiday in France today. The Third Estate then formed the National Constituent Assembly which established new laws and methods of government and did away with the *Ancien Régime*. On 21 January 1793, King Louis XVI was executed and his unpopular Austrian wife, Marie-Antoinette, met the same grisly fate nine months later.

1543: Poland – Nicolaus Copernicus announces that the Earth revolves around the sun instead of vice versa.
1583: North America – first English settlement in Newfoundland.
1586: Japan – Kabuki theatre begins.

The years of the revolution were characterised by internal conflicts and an aggressive foreign policy that led to war against other European powers. The most successful general leading France's expansionism was a little Corsican fellow called Napoleon Bonaparte, who, in 1799, staged a *coûp d'état* that ended the revolutionary period. Napoleon went on to become Emperor of France and its territories, until his defeat by the British and Prussians at Waterloo led to his exile to the rocky South Atlantic island of St Helena in 1815.

La Terreur

Between September 1793 and July 1794, the French revolutionary government, under leaders such as Maximilien François Marie Isidore de Robespierre, carried out a campaign of terror against those who opposed it. At least 300,000 people were arrested and 17,000 executed. The guillotine was the preferred method of execution – in 1789 a law decreed that all executions were to be carried out by 'means of a machine'. The guillotine gave the right to be killed by decapitation (considered to be the most painless method), previously only held by noblemen, to the common people. Lucky them.

1605: Spain – Miguel de Cervantes publishes first part of *Don Quixote*.
1605: England – Gunpowder Plot by Guy Fawkes to blow up
    Parliament foiled.
1611: England – King James Bible published.

THE FRENCH REPUBLICAN CALENDAR

Between 1793 and 1806, as part of the changes wrought by the French Revolution, France used a different calendar to the rest of Europe. The revolution aimed to establish a secular state and in order to avoid any Christian connotations a system was devised in which the twelve months of the calendar were named for weather or natural phenomena associated with the time of year. Given its bloody origins, the calendar retains an idyllic and pastoral beauty.

Gregorian calendar	Republican calendar	Translation
September/October	*Vendémiaire*	Vintage
October/November	*Brumaire*	Mist
November/December	*Frimaire*	Frost
December/January	*Nivôse*	Snow
January/February	*Pluviôse*	Rain
February/March	*Ventôse*	Wind
March/April	*Germinal*	Seed
April/May	*Floréal*	Flower
May/June	*Prairial*	Meadow
June/July	*Messidor*	Harvest
July/August	*Thermidor*	Heat
August/September	*Fructidor*	Fruit

Lobster thermidor is a hot dish of lobster cooked with wine, cream and cheese. It is thought to have been created in the late nineteenth century by a Parisian chef to celebrate the opening of a play about the French Revolution by Victorien Sardou called *Thermidor*.

1612: Germany – decimal point used in mathematics for the first time.
1613: Russia – Romanov dynasty founded.
1620: North America – Pilgrim Fathers land.
1625: Barbados – first English settlers.

4. MADE IN THE USA: THE AMERICAN REVOLUTION (1775–83)

After the Seven Years War (1756–63), which involved all the major European powers of the time and also extended to their colonies, Great Britain confirmed its position as the major player in North America. The peace treaty that ended the part of the war between France and Britain, the Treaty of Paris (1763), passed over all of France's colonial territories east of the Mississippi (except for New Orleans) to the British.

This war, however successful, had severely strained the British economy and to alleviate this the government imposed a series of unpopular taxes on their North American brethren. The Americans objected to these taxes as they did not feel that their concerns were properly recognised by Parliament in London – a cry went up rejecting 'taxation without representation'. These taxes led to conflicts between the Americans and the British governors and troops, such as the **Boston Massacre** (5 March 1770), where British soldiers opened fire on a crowd of Americans who were throwing snowballs at them, and the **Boston Tea Party** (16 September 1773), where rebel Americans, dressed up as Mohawk Indians, raided a British East India Company ship and threw the stock of tea onboard into the harbour.

Ultimately, the Americans decided to take a stand against the British and the Thirteen Colonies of the east coast formed the Continental Congress to represent their political and economic interests in 1774. The **Revolutionary War** began between the Americans and the British on 19 April 1775 in Concord and continued until the victory of American and French armies at Yorktown in 1781. The Thirteen Colonies were aided, particularly at sea, by France, who joined the war in 1778, and later by Spain and the Netherlands. The American Revolution officially ended on 3 September 1783 with the Peace of Paris in which Britain

---

1629: India – Shah Jahan starts building of Taj Mahal.
1633: Italy – Inquisition demands that Galileo retract his statement that the Earth revolves around the sun.
1642: Australia and New Zealand – Dutch explorer Abel Tasman discovers Tasmania and New Zealand.
1644: China – foundation of the Qing dynasty.

granted the Thirteen Colonies (which later became known as the United States) independence.

The Continental Congress had already declared the Thirteen Colonies independent from the British Crown on 4 July 1776 with the **Declaration of Independence** which was drawn up by Thomas Jefferson, Benjamin Franklin and other members of the Congress. The only colony not to approve the declaration was New York, which abstained. To commemorate the Declaration, 4 July is celebrated across America as Independence Day. In 1789, George Washington, who had fought as a general in the Revolutionary War, became the first President of the United States.

5. REVOLYUTSIA!: RUSSIAN REVOLUTION (1905–17)

The Russian Revolution was in fact a series of social and political upheavals rather than one stand-alone event. Tsar Nicholas II (a cousin of the British King George V), who reigned from 1894 to 1917, was the last of the tsars – ending the Romanov dynasty's 300-year rule. Nicholas's autocracy was deeply resented by an increasingly mobilised and vocal working class and in 1905, after peaceful, unarmed protesters hoping to petition their ruler for reform were shot on Bloody Sunday, growing public discontent forced the tsar to introduce his October Manifesto, which created a **Duma** (parliament) and Russia's first consti-tution. Initially, the Duma had no real power, but gradually the tsar's grip on his country became more and more tenuous. At the outbreak of World War I in 1914 he was barely hanging on to his throne.

War initially united Russia against the external enemy, but as the economy began to collapse and the death toll rose (in the first year of the conflict Russia lost two entire armies – over 250,000 men), public

---

1652: South Africa – Dutch found Cape Town.
1676: Denmark – Ole Rømer calculates the speed of light.
1682: England – Penny Post established in London.
1689: Ghana – Asante Empire founded.
1707: Britain – Treaty of Union.
1709: Italy – first piano made by Bartolomeo Cristofori.

protests began occurring with increasing frequency. On 22 February 1917 Nicholas left Petrograd (now St Petersburg) to visit troops at the front line. The following day, women gathered in the centre of Petrograd calling for bread and peace. The protest began quietly, but as male workers joined in, the crowd turned increasingly violent. The tsar sent a telegram ordering the military to stop the riots, and on 26 February troops opened fire on the crowds. However, the army's sympathy lay more with the rioting workers than the absent tsar and more than 80,000 soldiers mutinied and joined with the crowds against the police.

The Duma, united with the Petrograd Soviet of Workers' and Soldiers' Deputies, forced the tsar to abdicate and formed a Provisional Government. Wartime conditions worsened, and the Communist revolutionary leader Vladimir Ilich Lenin (1870–1924), aided by a German government looking to unsettle Russia further, returned to Petrograd in April 1917 and immediately began to work at seizing power for his Bolshevik Party. By the autumn, the Bolsheviks had achieved a majority in the Petrograd Soviet, and when Lenin called for a second revolution on 25 October government buildings were stormed at the Siege of the Winter Palace, with little resistance.

Lenin and the Bolsheviks instated an emergency dictatorship in Petrograd, but they only had real influence in the Russian heartland. Lenin's most pressing task was to get Russia out of the war. In order to accomplish this, Leon Trotsky, Lenin's lieutenant, was sent to the town of Brest-Litovsk in Poland in March 1918 and signed a treaty there that handed over large portions of Russia's territory to Germany. Anti-Bolsheviks were outraged and over the next few months joined forces with anti-Lenin leftists and for the next three years the Red Bolsheviks would fight a civil war against the White counter-revolutionary armies.

1775: North America – War of Independence starts, which continues until 1783.

1779: Hawaii – Captain Cook killed.

1787: Sierra Leone – British colony established.

1791: Canada – division of Canada into Anglophone and Francophone territories under the Constitutions Act.

Early victims of the war included the former Tsar Nicholas II and his family, all of whom were executed by members of the Bolshevik secret police at Yekaterinburg in July 1918. The White Russians were finally defeated in 1921, after the civil war had claimed the lives of around 100,000 people. In 1922 Russia was renamed the Union of Soviet Socialist Republics (USSR). Lenin led the USSR until he died in 1924, when a struggle for power began between Trotsky and the brilliant Party General Secretary, Joseph Stalin. Stalin emerged victorious and led the country until his death in 1953. Trotsky was exiled and after spells in Turkey and Norway he ended up in Mexico, where he lived for a time with the artist Diego Rivera (and, it is claimed, had an affair with Rivera's wife, Frida Kahlo). He was assassinated in 1940 by a member of Stalin's secret police who thrust an ice pick through his skull.

6. CHANGING CHINA:
THE CULTURAL REVOLUTION (1966–76)

For over 2,000 years China was ruled by a succession of emperors. In 1912, the Last Emperor, Xuantong, was forced to abdicate as a result of the republican and egalitarian Xinhai Revolution. After a period of civil war the Communist Party, led by Mao Tse-tung, took power and established the People's Republic of China in 1949. Between 1957 and 1960 Mao implemented the Great Leap Forward which sought to build rapidly a specifically Chinese form of communism by establishing communes, huge collective farms, and medical and educational programmes. In the last decade of his rule, Mao became determined to fully exert his authority, and to reinvigorate the revolutionary principles of the party. He established the Red Guard in 1966, which comprised paramilitary groups of students charged with rooting out and eradicating reactionary sentiment. They particularly persecuted the intelligentsia, and several

---

19th and 20th centuries CE

1801: Britain – Act of Union unites Great Britain (England, Scotland and Wales) with Ireland.

1810: Mexico – independence from Spain.

1821: Greece – War of Independence against Ottoman Empire until 1829.

hundred thousand people were executed. In 1968 Mao implemented the 'Down to the Countryside Movement', which involved sending young intellectuals to the countryside to be re-educated by living and working alongside the peasants; many died. After Mao's death in 1976, the Eleventh Party Congress officially ended the Cultural Revolution in August 1977.

THE CALAMITOUS DEATH OF ARCHDUKE FRANZ FERDINAND: STEPS TO THE FIRST WORLD WAR

The delicate balance of power and alliances that existed in Europe in the early twentieth century was catastrophically undone by a chain of events beginning on 28 June 1914 with the assassination of the Austro-Hungarian Archduke Franz Ferdinand by a nineteen-year-old Serbian nationalist called Gavrilo Princip. This led to Austria-Hungary declaring war against Serbia. In a horrific domino effect, Russia then mobilised in support of Serbia which led to Germany mobilising against Russia. France then mobilised against Germany and the Germans invaded Belgium, which the United Kingdom had promised to protect. The United Kingdom declared war on Germany on 4 August 1914.

The First World War would grow to involve many other nations around the globe and caused the deaths of 8,500,000 soldiers, a figure almost impossible to comprehend. Many died in brutal trench fighting in northern France and Belgium, and the war also caused huge civilian upheavals, mass destruction in Europe, and severe and long-lasting negative economic and political effects. At the outbreak of war in August many thought it would be over by Christmas, but in fact it stretched on for four years until Armistice Day, 11 November 1918.

1830: Algeria – French invasion.
1839: China – first Opium War between China and Britain begins.
1841: Hong Kong – occupied by British.
1845: Ireland – Great Famine, until 1851.

THE TREATY OF VERSAILLES

The Treaty of Versailles was signed on 28 June 1919 between Germany and the Allies at the end of the First World War. Woodrow Wilson, President of the United States; David Lloyd George, Prime Minister of the United Kingdom; Georges Clemenceau, Prime Minister of France; and Vittorio Orlando, Prime Minister of Italy, drew up the treaty, which asserted that:

- the Germans accepted the 'war guilt' of responsibility for the conflict and would pay reparations to Allied countries
- various contested German territories would be given to France, Belgium, Denmark and Poland
- all Germany's overseas territories would be handed over to the Allies
- the German Army would be restricted to 100,000 men
- military industry would be restricted and a demilitarised zone enforced in west Germany
- the collective security of the League of Nations member states would be guaranteed.

The Treaty of Versailles was hugely resented by the Germans as they felt it was far more punitive than the terms under which they had agreed to the armistice. The forerunner of the UN, the League of Nations, was also insufficiently powerful to uphold the treaty, particularly given America's absence. These factors combined to encourage the rise of Nazism and contribute to the start of the Second World War.

1848: Britain – Karl Marx and Friedrich Engels publish *The Communist Manifesto*.
1853: Crimea – Crimean War begins, which continues until 1856.
1857: India – Indian Mutiny begins and continues until 1858.
1861: USA – Civil War begins, which continues until 1865.
1863: Britain – beginning of construction of London Underground.

THE RIGHT HONOURABLE MEMBERS: PARLIAMENT

The word 'parliament' derives from the French word '*parlement*', which could be translated as talk, chat or powwow, and was first mentioned in 1236 to refer to the meetings of King Henry III's Great Council. At this time only bishops and barons could attend and only the king decided policy. Over the next hundred years two separate houses developed – the **House of Lords** to represent the nobility and clergy, and the **House of Commons** to represent the boroughs and towns. Parliament has been constantly evolving and, over time, the presence of the clergy diminished, and the power of the Commons grew.

Significantly, the **1689 Bill of Rights** established Parliament's authority over the monarch. The 1911 Parliament Act withdrew the power of the House of Lords to veto legislation passed by the House of Commons (so long as it had been approved by the Commons three times), and in 1999 the House of Lords Act barred the majority of hereditary peers from sitting and voting in the House of Lords.

We all know about the Upper House and Lower House, but did you know that the third part of Parliament is the Queen?

In general elections, every UK citizen over the age of eighteen can, and should, vote for their representative to become a Member of Parliament or MP. These MPs become members of the House of Commons and the political party with the most MPs forms the government. MPs debate and vote on political decisions, such as international resolutions, new laws and taxes. Members of the House of Lords are appointed by the Queen on the recommendation of the Prime Minister or the House of Lords Appointments Commission, and are no longer necessarily of noble birth. The Lords has no power over financial bills but can revise legislation passed by the Commons. As well as appointed peers, several archbishops, bishops and judges also sit in the Lords. The judges, or law lords, work for the House of Lords in its function as the Supreme Court of Appeal.

1865: Russia – first part of Leo Tolstoy's *War and Peace* published.
1867: Austria and Hungary – kingdom of Austria-Hungary established.

A PITHY POLITICAL GLOSSARY

These are a few curious but useful words that turn up in history books and in the political pages of newspapers frequently but are often skipped over by the ill-educated or lazy reader. Read, cogitate and try to gain a full understanding of the following terms.

Act: A written decree of Parliament.

Bill: A draft of a proposed act.

Black Rod: An officer of the House of Lords with administrative duties, who also leads the ceremony for the State Opening of Parliament. In an elaborate ritual, he calls the MPs from the House of Commons to hear the Queen's Speech in the House of Lords. The door is slammed in his face (an act symbolic of the Commons' independence from the House of Lords), and he must knock with his rod before they open the door to go with him to the Lords.

Cabinet: Appointed senior MPs of the governing party who decide policy. The **Shadow Cabinet** is comprised of the opposition party spokesmen.

Chartism: An 1830s movement for parliamentary reform, demanding among other things votes for all and fairer electoral districts.

Coalition: Coalition governments often occur in countries which use the proportional representation system. If no single party wins a majority in an election the members of all the different parties who have been voted in take on political posts in government.

Constituency: The UK is divided into 646 areas, called constituencies, each having an MP to represent it in Parliament.

Plurality system: The UK uses this electoral system whereby the electorate votes for an MP to represent their constituency. The party that returns the most MPs becomes the government. The UK system is also know as the **first-past-the-post** system.

Proportional representation: A system used by some countries whereby the electorate votes for a party rather than an MP. This means that each vote counts for part of a seat in a parliament and

---

1871: Tanzania – Henry Morton Stanley finds the explorer David Livingstone.

1875: USA – Alexander Graham Bell invents the telephone.

the parties are represented in the proportions that the electorate has voted for them.

Speaker: An MP who chairs all debates in the House of Commons.

Tory: In the seventeenth century the opposition to the Whig Party that supported traditional government and religion and the authority of the monarchy. It developed into the Conservative Party and is now a nickname for members of the party.

Whig: A member of the political party that after 1688 sought a constitutional rather than absolute monarchy and supported Parliament.

Whip: An MP or lord who is responsible for organising their party's members' votes. A **three-line whip** refers to the instruction given to a member to attend very important debates – the whip underlines important debates in their weekly notes three times.

WOMANKIND, ARISE!: THE SUFFRAGETTES

Suffrage is the right to vote in political elections. A suffragette was a member of the **Women's Social and Political Union** who campaigned for votes for women. Before 1832 only men who were large landowners could vote, but the 1832 Reform Act broadened the electorate by allowing people who held smaller properties to vote although it explicitly denied women's right to vote for the first time. The 1867 Act gave the vote to men working in towns and cities, and the 1884–5 Act extended the vote to agricultural workers. Neither of these acts made mention of half the population: women.

Mary Wollstonecraft and John Stuart Mill had campaigned for rights for women from the late eighteenth century, but the Reform Acts inspired the formation of official women's suffrage societies. In 1869 Parliament gave permission for women taxpayers to vote in local elections. However, the parliamentary vote was still denied them.

1876: Congo – king of Belgium, Leopold II, establishes Association of the Congo.

1876: USA – Custer's Last Stand. General Custer defeated at the Battle of Little Bighorn by the Sioux.

1879: South Africa – Zulu War against the British.

In Manchester in 1903, Emmeline Pankhurst founded the Women's
Social and Political Union, which started to use more militant methods
after petitions failed. The suffragettes staged public demonstrations,
marches and went on hunger strike when they were imprisoned. One
suffragette, Emily Wilding Davison, made the ultimate sacrifice for the
cause, by throwing herself in front of the king's horse at the Epsom
Derby in 1913. It was only when women's contribution to the war effort
brought the public firmly onside that women over the age of thirty were
finally given the right to vote in 1918. Ten years later the voting age was
lowered to twenty-one, the same as that for men.

Dates of women's suffrage around the world

1869 – Wyoming, USA
1893 – New Zealand
1902 – Australia
1906 – Finland
1913 – Norway
1917 – Russia
1918 – Canada and the United Kingdom
1919 – Austria, Czechoslovakia, Germany and Poland
1920 – Hungary and the United States
1922 – Burma
1929 – Ecuador
1930 – South Africa
1932 – Brazil, Thailand and Uruguay
1934 – Cuba and Turkey
1937 – Philippines
1944 – France
1945 – Italy
1947 – China
1949 – India
2005 – Kuwait

1879: Afghanistan – British occupation of Kabul.
1880: South Africa – first Boer War against the British.
1882: Vietnam – French conquer Hanoi.
1883: Indonesia – eruption of Mount Krakatoa.
1884: USA – first skyscraper built in Chicago.

SLAVERY AND
THE AMERICAN CIVIL WAR

A slave is defined as 'a person who is the legal property of another and is bound by absolute obedience'. The practice of enslaving defeated enemies and using them as servants and labour has existed since the beginning of human civilisation all over the world, but slavery plays a particularly important part in the history of the United States. The colonisation of the Americas led to huge numbers of African slaves being shipped in horrific conditions to work on sugar plantations in the Caribbean and tobacco and cotton plantations in the south of North America in the seventeenth, eighteenth and nineteenth centuries. Often 20 per cent of the slaves on-board these ships would die en route. These slaves were part of the trading cycle that went on between the colonies and Europe and Africa, and the economies of these colonial powers, and the United States, were hugely enriched by slave labour.

During the American Revolution, the cultural shift to an appreciation of the rights of all men to liberty led to the beginnings of the **abolitionist movement**. By 1804 all the northern states in the USA had freed their slaves. In Great Britain the MP William Wilberforce campaigned for an end to the slave trade, which came about in 1807. The USA ended their slave trade a year later. In 1833 the Slavery Abolition Act freed all slaves in the British Empire but it took longer in the USA where slavery was a key economic contributor to the southern states. In 1861 tensions over the northern states' plans to get rid of slavery led to the southern states of Alabama, Arkansas, Florida, Georgia, Louisiana, Mississippi, North Carolina, South Carolina, Tennessee, Texas and Virginia declaring themselves separate from the United States and establishing themselves as the **Confederate States of America**. This led to the **American Civil War** that ended with the Union (the North) forces' victory over the Confederacy in 1865, and the abolition of slavery throughout the USA.

1891: Russia – work begins on Trans-Siberian railway.
1896: Ethiopia – Italy recognises Ethiopian independence.
1898: France – Pierre and Marie Curie discover radium.
1903: USA – Orville and Wilbur Wright fly the first aeroplane.

THE SHADOW OF THE SWASTIKA: FACTORS CONTRIBUTING TO THE RISE OF THE NAZIS

- **Nazi Ideology:** The Nazi Party was formed by Adolf Hitler in 1919, when he took over control of the German Workers' Party and changed its name to the National Socialists (Nazis). Nazi ideology was attractive to many Germans because it claimed to protect the interests of the common man which, in its view, were under threat from Jews and Communists. It also aimed to build a strong Germany and overcome the humiliation imposed by the Treaty of Versailles. The Nazis expressed their views through powerful and emotive propaganda that used the whole range of media available to them. Hitler expressed his ideology in the 1920 **25-Point Party Programme** and in his 1925 book *Mein Kampf*.

- **The Treaty of Versailles:** The Nazi Party exploited resentment of the punitive Treaty of Versailles, which bankrupted Germany by demanding reparations and severely dented national pride. In contravention of the treaty, the Nazis also asserted that Germany's borders should be expanded to provide more living space for Germans (*Lebensraum*) and all German-speaking peoples should become part of Germany.

- **The Great Depression:** The worldwide rise in unemployment left millions in Germany destitute and searching for a strong party to lead them out of poverty. One of the founding principles of the Nazi Party was that Germany should work towards economic self-sufficiency (*autarky*).

- **Proportional Representation:** After the end of the First World War the kaiser was replaced by the democratic Weimar Republic. However, the system of proportional representation meant that the government was comprised of many small parties opposing one

---

1911: South Pole – Norwegian Roald Amundsen beats British Robert Falcon Scott's expedition to the South Pole.
1912: China – Republic of China established.
1912: Atlantic – *Titanic* sinks.

another, making it difficult to pass laws and weakening the government. The Nazi Party promoted the idea of a strong government
under the complete control of one leader, the **Führer**.

- **Article 48:** The constitution of the Weimar Republic also included
  a clause that meant that the president could issue laws without
  the consent of the rest of the government in emergency situations.
  In 1933, after the Nazis became a popular and a powerful force,
  President Hindenberg asked Hitler to become Chancellor. Hitler
  then used this clause to take absolute control of the government.

- **Civil Unrest:** The signing of the Treaty of Versailles and the
  deposition of the kaiser led to various rebellions that destabilised
  German society and put pressure on the Weimar government. The
  Nazis promised the security of a strong and effective government
  backed up by their paramilitary units, the **SA** and the **SS**.

- *The Protocols of the Learned Elders of Zion*: This was a fake book
  that circulated during the early twentieth century, which purported
  to reveal an international Jewish conspiracy to take over the world.
  The First World War was attributed to this conspiracy to destabilise
  Europe.

- **1923 Crisis:** In 1923 Germany missed a reparations payment due
  under the Treaty of Versailles and in response France invaded
  the Ruhr. At the same time there was a general strike and the
  government printed extra money to pay the workers, resulting in
  hyperinflation. This led to further uprising and instability, paving
  the way for the Nazis to gain popularity.

**1914: Europe – beginning of First World War, which continues until
1918.**
1916: Ireland – Easter Rising in Dublin.
1917: Russia – Russian Revolution.

FROM PLANTATION TO PEACE: KEY EVENTS OF THE ANGLO-IRISH CONFLICT

1171–5	After declaring sovereignty over Ireland, with the support of the Pope, Henry I of England conquers most of the island. He establishes a centre of power in Dublin but over the following centuries the English gradually lose territories back to the Irish.
1541	Henry VIII is declared King of Ireland by the Irish Parliament. He begins the practice of **'plantation'** whereby English settlers are given the lands of Irish rebels.
1607	**The Flight of the Earls**. Tyrone and other rebel earls flee to Rome. The plantation of Ulster (the province comprising the counties of Donegal, Tyrone, Derry, Armagh, Cavan and Fermanagh), mainly by settlers from Scotland, takes place.
1653	Irish Catholic rebellion crushed by Oliver Cromwell and more lands given to his supporters.
1690	**The Battle of the Boyne**. The Catholic king of Great Britain, James II, is defeated by the Protestant William of Orange in Britain in 1689 and then in Ireland at the Battle of the Boyne. William imposes anti-Catholic Penal Laws in Ireland. These laws limited Catholics' rights to own property and receive education and stayed in place until the eighteenth century.

1919: India – Mohandas Gandhi starts campaign of passive resistance against British rule.
1922: Italy – Benito Mussolini becomes prime minister.
1922: Turkey – Mustafa Kemal (Atatürk) deposes sultan and ends Ottoman Empire.

1704	**Test Act** passed. It decrees that only Protestant episcopalians can hold political office. Period of **Protestant ascendancy**.
1791	Formation of the **United Irishmen** a group determined to gain new rights for Catholics and parliamentary reform.
1801	**Act of Union**. Irish MPs (the majority Protestants) vote to abolish the Irish Parliament and join Great Britain (England and Scotland) to become the United Kingdom.
1845–9	**The Great Famine**. The Irish potato famine kills two million people. The lack of government aid from Britain increases resentment.
1867	Failed rebellion by the **Irish Republican Brotherhood** – also known as the **Fenians** after the mythological Irish band of warrior heroes the *Fianna Éireann*.
1870	Establishment of **Home Government Association** to campaign for Home Rule for the Irish.
1873	**Home Rule League** taken over by **Charles Stewart Parnell**.
1889	Fall from power of Parnell after being named as co-respondent in the divorce proceedings of his future wife, Kitty O'Shea.
1902	The Society of Gaels begins policy of '***Sinn Féin***' (ourselves alone), which involves passive resistance to British rule. The term would later become the

---

1922: Egypt – British archaeologist Howard Carter discovers Tutankhamen's tomb.
1924: Britain – first Labour government elected.
1926: Britain – John Logie Baird invents first working television.
1929: USA – Wall Street Crash.

name of the Roman Catholic political party that campaigned for a united and independent Ireland.

1905   **Ulster Unionist Party** established to resist Home Rule due to opposition by Ulster Protestants to the idea of being subsumed into a Catholic-majority, Dublin-ruled Ireland.

1912   Home Rule bill passed twice by House of Commons but rejected by House of Lords. Unionists lobby to exclude Ulster from Home Rule. Leader of the Ulster Unionists, Edward Carson, sets up the paramilitary **Ulster Volunteers Force** to resist Home Rule by force.

1913   **Paramilitary Irish Volunteers** established to oppose Ulster Volunteers Force.

1914   Home Rule bill passed but postponed until end of First World War. Irish soldiers fight for the British Army.

1916   **The Easter Rising**. Irish Republican Brotherhood stage a rebellion in Dublin which is put down by British troops. Fifteen of the leaders are executed.

1917   **Eamon de Valera**, surviving leader of the Easter Rising, is elected president of Sinn Fein and establishes a separate parliament in Ireland called the *Dáil Éireann*.

1919   **Irish Republican Army** replaces Irish Volunteers. **Irish War of Independence** begins.

1933: Germany – Hitler becomes Chancellor.
1936: Spain – Franco's rebellion leads to civil war, which continues until 1939.
1937: China – Chinese-Japanese War begins, which continues until 1945.

1920   British auxiliary police force, known as the **Black and Tans**, deployed in Ireland.

1921   **Anglo-Irish Treaty** ends the Irish War of Independence with the partition of Ireland into two self-governing states: **Northern Ireland** which remains part of the United Kingdom and the mainly Catholic **Irish Free State** which becomes a semi-independent dominion of the British Empire. Black and Tans withdrawn.

1922   **Irish Civil War** begins. Sinn Fein divides into one group supporting the Anglo-Irish Treaty, led by Michael Collins, and one group, led by Eamon de Valera, that rejects the treaty. Collins is killed in the fighting.

1923   End of the Irish Civil War with the victory of pro-treaty forces. The IRA continue to resist British control in Northern Ireland.

1927   Eamon de Valera establishes **Fianna Fáil** Party to call for the abolition of the oath of allegiance to British Crown.

1932   Fianna Fáil come to power in the Irish Free State.

1937   Irish Free State declares itself a sovereign state called **Ireland** or **Eire**.

1967   The **Northern Ireland Civil Rights Association** is established to campaign for equal treatment for Catholics in the predominantly Protestant Northern Ireland. Demonstrations lead to clashes between protestors and the Royal Ulster Constabulary that

---

1938: Hungary – Lazlo Biro invents the ballpoint pen.
1939: Europe – start of Second World War, which ends in 1945 with the atomic bombing of Hiroshima and Nagasaki in Japan.
1945: Vietnam – Ho Chi Minh announces Vietnamese independence beginning the conflict that will lead to the Vietnam War.

extend to conflict between the UVF and the IRA, beginning 'The Troubles'.

1969   The **Provisional IRA** is established as the Official IRA turns its back on violent methods.

1970   The Catholic non-violent Social Democratic and Labour Party is established. The Provisional IRA begins the **Long War**, a terrorist campaign that includes attacking British troops in Northern Ireland and violent activities in mainland Britain.

1972   **Bloody Sunday**: British troops kill fourteen Catholic protestors in Londonderry. During this year, 467 people are killed as part of the Troubles. **Home Rule in Northern Ireland ends** and government from London is reintroduced. **Bloody Friday**: the IRA set off 22 bombs in Belfast, killing nine people. Loyalist (Unionist) and Nationalist (Republican) violence continues.

1981   IRA Volunteer **Bobby Sands** dies on hunger strike in the Maze prison while protesting for the right to be treated as a prisoner of war rather than a civilian prisoner, leading to an intensification of IRA activity.

1984   **The Brighton Bombing**. The Grand Hotel in Brighton is bombed during the Conservative Party Conference, killing five people.

1985   The **Anglo-Irish Agreement** is signed. It states that Northern Ireland will remain part of the United Kingdom unless its citizens vote otherwise. It also gives the Republic of Ireland a consultative role in

---

1946: Greece – civil war between Communists and Royalists until 1949.

1947: India – partition divides India into India and Pakistan. Indian independence.

1948: Israel – State of Israel declared.

the government of Northern Ireland. Unionists stage protests.

1994   **Downing Street Declaration**. Peace talks between the British and Irish governments and the major political parties of Northern Ireland (except for Sinn Fein due to its terrorist links) lead to an IRA cease-fire. Combined Loyalist Military Command ceasefire also announced.

1996   IRA resumes its terrorist campaign due to stalling of peace talks on the issue of disarmament.

1997   IRA ceasefire reinstated. Sinn Fein are admitted to peace talks.

1998   **Good Friday Agreement** (also known as the Belfast Agreement). The **Northern Ireland Assembly** is set up, along with cross-border initiatives with the Republic of Ireland, and the Republic renounces its constitutional claim to Northern Ireland. A referendum in Northern Ireland and the Republic supports the agreement. Ulster Unionist David Trimble is elected head of the Northern Ireland Assembly. The Real IRA, a splinter group of the Provisional IRA who oppose the Agreement, set off a bomb at **Omagh** which kills twenty-nine people.

2001   IRA begin decommissioning weapons.

2002   Northern Ireland Assembly is suspended due to rows over decommissioning.

1948: South Africa – apartheid established.
1949: Belgium – NATO established.
1949: China – Mao Zedong establishes Communist People's Republic of China.
1950: Korea – Korean War begins, which continues until 1953.

2005	IRA declare an end to military action.

2007   **Home Rule reinstated** in Northern Ireland. **Operation Banner** (British Army's military operation since 1969) ended.

2008   Ian Paisley steps down as First Minister of Northern Ireland and is replaced by Peter Robinson.

WAR & WAR!: KEY MILITARY CONFLICTS

THE BATTLE OF MARATHON:
Graeco-Persian Wars (490 BCE)

Greek forces, led by Miltiades, resisted invasion by the Persians under King Darius I on the plain of Marathon in Northern Attica. Greatly outnumbered, the Athenians used superior military tactics to gain victory over the enemy. According to legend, a messenger was sent from Marathon to Athens (a distance of about twenty-five miles) to announce the Greek victory before dying of exhaustion. This is why the marathon races held around the world are so called.

THE BATTLE OF THERMOPYLAE:
Graeco-Persian Wars (480 BCE)

King Leonidas of Sparta led a small army of around 7,000 comprised of men from other Greek city states against the massive invading Persian army under King Xerxes at the pass of Thermopylae in central Greece.

1955: USA – Martin Luther King leads civil rights movement.
1956: USSR – first space satellite launched.
1959: Cuba – Cuban Revolution.
1961: Germany – construction of Berlin Wall.
1966: China – Cultural Revolution begins, continues until 1976.

They fought for two days until Leonidas ordered all but his royal guard – three hundred men – to retreat. The three hundred fought on to protect the Greeks' retreat, and have been immortalised as symbols of bravery ever since.

THE BATTLE OF YARMUK (August 636 CE)

After the death of the Prophet Muhammad in 632 CE in Medina, Muslim armies began to spread the Islamic faith. In 633 they moved north towards the Eastern Roman, or Byzantine, Empire and in 634 Abu Bakr, a close confidant of the late Prophet, called for war against the largely Christian Empire. At the Battle of Yarmuk an army of 25,000 Islamic men met a Byzantine army that numbered nearly 50,000. After six days the Islamic army was victorious and its power now reached out of the Arabian peninsula and into Syria and Palestine.

THE BATTLE OF BANNOCKBURN:
Scottish Wars of Independence (23–24 June 1314)

At the Battle of Bannockburn Robert the Bruce and a fearless Scots army took on Edward II's English army, which was more than twice its size at 18,000 men.

Bruce was careful to make use of the terrain: he adopted the circular formation for his pikemen that William Wallace, that other great Scottish hero, had pioneered some fifteen years earlier, and ensured that marshy ground protected his flanks. Edward, on the other hand, sent his archers on unprotected, and then commanded his whole force to charge full on into the Scottish front. The English knights became bogged down in the difficult ground and couldn't force a way past the pikemen.

The Scots were also strengthened by their common aim: to set their country free, and to avenge the wrongs they had suffered at the hands of the English. When the remaining English saw what they thought was a

1967: Middle East – Six Day War between Arab states and Israel.
1967: Nigeria – Republic of Biafra founded, continues until 1970.
1969: Moon – *Apollo 11* lands on the moon and Neil Armstrong walks on its surface.

second charge attacking from a nearby hill, they fled; in fact it was the 'small folk', the Scots reserves of yeomen, burgesses and artisans, less well armed or trained than the infantry, who had been kept out of sight until this point. Scottish victory was assured.

THE BATTLE OF AGINCOURT:
Hundred Years War (25 October 1415)

In 1415, as part of the Hundred Years War between Britain and France, King Henry V of England arrived in Normandy with some 10,000 men to take the town of Harfleur from the French. He succeeded, but his losses were heavy: about a third of his force perished. With his remaining troops Henry then set off along the north coast of France towards Calais, where French troops numbering 30,000 led by Constable d'Albret caught up with them at Agincourt. It seemed that the English, exhausted, weakened by dysentery and massively outnumbered, had not a hope in hell of surviving the battle. But brilliant military tactics and disastrous French procrastination led to a glorious victory by Henry V, and he went on to be recognised as heir to the French throne by the Treaty of Troyes in 1420.

THE SIEGE OF ORLEANS:
Hundred Years War (October 1428–May 1429)

Joan of Arc, or the Maid of Orleans, was a peasant girl born in 1412 who believed that visions of saints had visited her to urge her to save France from English domination. After persuading the French court to accept her help, she led French troops to victory at the siege of Orleans, when she was only seventeen. The French King Charles VII was crowned at Rheims in 1429, but in 1430 Joan was captured by the English at Compiègne and the next year burnt as a witch at Rouen. She was canonised by the Catholic Church in 1920.

1972: Northern Ireland – Bloody Sunday. Fourteen Catholic civil rights protestors are killed by British soldiers.
1973: Middle East – Yom Kippur War between Israel and Egypt with Syria.

THE DEFEAT OF THE SPANISH ARMADA:
The Anglo–Spanish War (1588)

In 1588 King Philip of Spain sent a huge fleet of Spanish ships to invade England in order to prevent the English from helping his unruly Protestant subjects in the Netherlands and to convert the country back to Catholicism. The Spanish Armada, though greater in size than Elizabeth I's navy, was no match for British naval officers' skills, their boats' manoeuvrability and the weather.

THE BATTLE OF WATERLOO:
Napoleonic Wars (18 June 1815)

At the Battle of Waterloo in Belgium, an allied army led by the Duke of Wellington from England and General Blücher from Prussia brought to an end twenty-three years of war with France (which had begun with the Revolutionary Wars of 1792 and continued with the Napoleonic Wars from 1803). This victory knocked Napoleon from his throne as emperor of the French. It had rained heavily on 17 June, and Napoleon decided to wait for the ground to dry – not knowing that at that moment French troops greatly outnumbered the allies and he was giving his opponents time to swell their numbers. In addition, he thought he had forced the Prussian army into a retreat. In fact, they were regrouping. In the end, as Wellington himself put it, it was 'a damned near-run thing', but the allies won and Napoleon was exiled to the island of St Helena where he died in 1821. Wellington returned home a hero and was made prime minister in 1828.

1974: USA – Watergate scandal. President Nixon resigns.
1975: End of Vietnam War.
1975: Cambodia – Khmer Rouge seize power.
1978: Britain – first test-tube baby born.
1979: Iran – shah is replaced by Ayatollah Khomeini's Islamic republican government.

HISTORY 163

THE BATTLE OF BALACLAVA:
Crimean War (25 October 1854)

This was a key but inconclusive battle during the Crimean War fought
between imperial Russia on one side and an alliance including Britain
and France on the other. Lord Raglan, the British commander-in-chief,
thought the Russians were retreating and sent the Light Brigade into
battle. In a disastrous tactical error, over 40 per cent of the brigade lost
their lives. Their bravery was immortalised by Tennyson in his famous
poem, 'The Charge of the Light Brigade':

> Cannon to right of them,
> Cannon to left of them,
> Cannon in front of them
> Volley'd & thunder'd;
> Storm'd at with shot and shell,
> Boldly they rode and well,
> Into the jaws of Death,
> Into the mouth of Hell
> Rode the six hundred.

Conditions in the Crimea were so cold that this campaign gave rise to
three new articles of clothing: the balaclava, cardigan and raglan coat.

THE BATTLE OF THE SOMME:
First World War (1 July–13 November 1916)

French and British troops, intending to lure the Germans from Verdun,
gathered troops at the Somme in July 1916. But what was meant to be an
incisive attack turned into one of the bloodiest episodes in the history of
warfare. After four months of attacking virtually impenetrable German
lines, over a million men had died: around 650,000 Germans, 195,000

1980: Middle East – Iran–Iraq War, which continues until 1988.
1982: Falkland (Malvinas) Islands – Falklands War between Argentina
    and Britain.
1983: France and USA – HIV identified.
1986: USSR – Chernobyl nuclear power station disaster.
1988: Palestine – Israel occupies Gaza Strip.

French and 420,000 British. The Battle of the Somme also saw the first use of the modern tank by the British.

GUERNICA:
Spanish Civil War (26 April 1937)

By 1937, Spain was in the grip of a fiercely fought civil war between right-wing Nationalist forces and left-wing Republican parties. On a worldwide scale, Spain was strategically crucial: if it fell to the Fascists backed by Germany and Italy, there would be one less country to halt the dangerous spread of Fascism through Europe. Britain and France were equally wary of Spain falling to Soviet-backed Republicans: Communism was seen as almost as great a threat to world peace as Fascism. The bombing of Guernica by the German Luftwaffe on 26 April 1937, in which a large number of civilians perished, outraged democracies across the world, but the Spanish Civil War went on to be won in March 1939 by right-wing General Franco who ruled until 1975. The events at Guernica were immortalised by Picasso in his deeply moving painting of the same name.

THE BATTLE OF BRITAIN:
Second World War (July–September 1940)

By the summer of 1940 the German forces had, using blitzkrieg (lightning war) tactics, taken northern France, Belgium and the Netherlands. It was Britain's turn next. By attacking the Royal Air Force over the Channel and then moving up towards London during the Blitz, the Germans hoped to pave the way for the land invasion of Britain. But the air raids failed, thanks to the battling of plucky spitfire pilots, and the Battle of Britain was seen as Hitler's first major defeat.

1990-1: Middle East – first Gulf War.
1991: Yugoslavia – civil war begins.
1991: USSR – dissolution of USSR.
1992-5: Bosnia and Herzegovina – Bosnian War.

PEARL HARBOR:
Second World War (7 December 1941)

An unprovoked and surprise attack by the Japanese on a US Navy base at Pearl Harbor, Hawaii, was the catalyst that brought the USA into World War II. The commander-in-chief, Isoroku Yamamoto, realised that Pearl Harbor was the only barrier to the complete Japanese conquest of all of South-East Asia and the Indonesian Archipelago. He sent a fleet by sea to a point around 275 miles from Hawaii and from there the attack was launched. On the morning of Sunday 7 December more than 2,300 Americans were killed, and the Japanese lost fewer than 100 men.

A BRIEF BACKGROUND TO
THE ARAB-ISRAELI CONFLICT

Growing Zionism in the nineteenth century called for a return of the Jews to their ancestral homeland in Israel. The Jews had first been dispersed from Israel in 586 BCE by the invading Babylonians and subsequently by the Romans in 70 CE. In the nineteenth century the biblical territory of Israel was actually part of Palestine, which in turn was part of the Ottoman Empire, and mainly inhabited by Arabs.

After the First World War and the collapse of the Ottoman Empire the British took control of Palestine. In 1917 Britain issued the **Balfour Declaration**, which promised an area of Palestine to the Jews to become Israel. It was in British interests to establish a friendly state in this area to help protect the Suez Canal and also to encourage popular opinion for their post-war policies in the United States and Russia, which both had large Jewish communities.

The later atrocities of the Second World War and the extermination of six million Jews at the hands of the Nazis led to worldwide sympathy for

1993: Netherlands – European Union established through Maastricht Treaty.
1994: South Africa – end of apartheid.
1994: Rwanda – massacre of Tutsis by Hutus.

the Zionist cause and in 1947 Palestine was divided into Jewish and Arab states. On 14 May 1948 David Ben-Gurion, first prime minister of Israel, declared Israeli independence. The Arab League Armies of Egypt, Syria, Lebanon, Iraq, Jordan, Saudi Arabia and Yemen immediately invaded. Since then, there have been repeated Arab-Israeli wars and the borders of Israel have grown, displacing and making refugees of many Palestinians.

A CHILLY CHAPTER: THE COLD WAR

The Cold War was a period of sustained animosity between the USA and the USSR stretching from the end of the Second World War to 1989.

*   **1940s:** During the Second World War the United States and the USSR had fought together as Allies against Hitler. After the end of the war in Europe, Winston Churchill, prime minister of the United Kingdom, Franklin D. Roosevelt, president of the United States and Joseph Stalin, the leader of the Soviet Union, divided up the battle-wearied territories of Europe into areas of influence at the **Yalta Conference** in 1945. The Soviet Union took control of Eastern Europe and the other Allied powers took responsibility for Western Europe. The USSR's installation of Communist governments in Eastern European territories led to the West's increased discomfort with the growth of Soviet power. In 1946 Winston Churchill claimed that Stalin had established an '**iron curtain**' across Eastern Europe. Between 1948 and 1951 the USA poured money into Western European economies in order to establish healthy capitalist democracies to stem the spread of Communism.

    Tensions between the two sides first erupted in the **Berlin Blockade** of 1948-9, where the USSR blocked access to the

1995-9: Serbia – Kosovo War.
1996: Afghanistan – Taliban capture Kabul.
1997: Hong Kong – Hong Kong returned to China by the British.
1998: Northern Ireland – Good Friday Agreement signed.

Western powers' territories in Berlin in response to what they saw as infringements of the post-war treaties. During the blockade, the Western countries of Belgium, Canada, Denmark, France, Iceland, Italy, Luxembourg, the Netherlands, Norway, Portugal, the United Kingdom and the United States formed the **North Atlantic Treaty Organization** in which they promised that they would defend one another from attack. NATO was designed to counteract the threat of the large Soviet presence in Europe. In the same year, the Communists came to power in China and allied with the Soviets. The USSR also tested its first atomic bomb, making it a nuclear power to match the USA.

* **1950s:** The **Korean War** between Communist North Korea and non-Communist South Korea broke out in 1950, and the USSR and the USA both involved themselves on the different sides until the armistice in 1953. In 1955 the **Communist bloc** countries of the Soviet Union, Czechoslovakia, Bulgaria, Albania, East Germany, Hungary, Poland and Romania signed the **Warsaw Pact**, which confirmed that Soviet military units would be stationed in all these countries. During the following years, the USSR would crush rebellions against its control in several countries in Eastern Europe. Simultaneously, the USA used the CIA to undermine pro-Communist governments in Asia, South America and the Middle East, and both the USA and the USSR competed in a nuclear arms race.

* **1960s:** The 1962 **Cuban Missile Crisis**, which brought the rival countries to the brink of war, was a result of the USSR establishing nuclear missile bases in Fidel Castro's Communist Cuba, too close for comfort for the USA. In 1964 the **Vietnam War** became another arena where the two powers battled, when USSR-backed Communist Vietcong fought US troops in support of the anti-Communist South Vietnamese. The Vietcong emerged victorious in 1975.

1999: Turkey – Izmir earthquake.

21st century CE
2001: USA – in New York, two planes fly into the World Trade Center, killing thousands.

•   **1970s and 1980s:** During the 1970s, Strategic Arms Limitation Talks
    – **SALT I** (1972) and **SALT II** (1979) – between the two super-
    powers led to some rapprochement. However, this was undermined
    by the Soviet invasion of Afghanistan in 1979 and tensions rose again
    during the 1980s when US President Ronald Reagan reinvigorated
    the arms race with his **Star Wars** programme and carried out anti-
    Communist interventions in various international hot spots such as
    Nicaragua. However, when Mikhail Gorbachev came to power in
    the USSR in 1985 he instigated a massive programme of economic
    restructuring (**perestroika**) to improve the Soviet Union's econom-
    ic position, which involved scaling back arms spending and led to
    better relations between the two powers. In 1989 both countries
    agreed to abandon their interventionist politics, and as a result many
    of the Communist bloc countries in Eastern Europe threw off their
    Communist governments, and the Berlin Wall that had divided
    Communist East Germany from West Germany since 1961 fell.

2003: Iraq – invasion of Iraq by US and coalition troops.
2004: Indian Ocean – a massive earthquake triggers a tsunami on
    Boxing Day, killing over 310,000 people.
2005: France – doctors carry out the first successful face transplant.
2006: Iraq – former president Saddam Hussein is executed in
    Baghdad.
2007: Scouting celebrates its hundredth birthday.

⟡ HISTORY ⟡
TEST PAPER

1. **Which of the following were first established in Britain by the Romans?**

microwaves	advertising	roads
aqueducts	pets	writing
sellotape	wine	law
potatoes	coins	baths
curtains	calendars	pigs
underfloor heating	cocktails	pens
giraffes	swords	peas

2. **Match the dates below to the following historical events:**

   1534, 1914, 1170, 1533, 1969, 1930, 1787, 1990, 1928, 1981, 1976, 1925, 1989, 1947, 1865, 1969, 1587, 1977, 1963, 1936, 1945, 1707, 1824, 1948, 1943, 1997, 1215, 1265, 1959, 1919

   1. ——— Neil Armstrong and Buzz Aldrin land on the moon
   2. ——— The first Woodstock Festival
   3. ——— Henry VIII marries Anne Boleyn
   4. ——— First World Cup final played in Uruguay
   5. ——— Death of John F. Kennedy
   6. ——— Signing of the Magna Carta
   7. ——— American Constitution signed
   8. ——— Outbreak of the Vietnam War
   9. ——— Marriage of Prince Charles and Lady Diana Spencer
   10. ——— Concorde's first commercial flight
   11. ——— Death of Lord Byron
   12. ——— Treaty of Versailles signed
   13. ——— Israel declares independence
   14. ——— Publication of *Mein Kampf*
   15. ——— Fall of the Berlin Wall
   16. ——— Birth of Dante Alighieri

17. ——— Partition of India
18. ——— Birth of Mick Jagger
19. ——— Passing of the Act of Supremacy
20. ——— Death of Mother Teresa
21. ——— Abolition of slavery in the United States
22. ——— Mary, Queen of Scots executed
23. ——— Death of Elvis Presley
24. ——— Abdication of Edward VIII
25. ——— The atom bomb is dropped on Hiroshima
26. ——— *Titanic* sinks
27. ——— Resignation of Margaret Thatcher
28. ——— Universal suffrage for all adults over 21 years of age
29. ——— Archduke Franz Ferdinand shot
30. ——— Thomas à Becket assassinated

3. **Who was the first king of England?**

4. **Is *Mein Kampf* a primary or secondary source?**

5. **A Luddite is:**

a) a small but harmless tapeworm
b) a person in favour of suffrage for women
c) a craftsman opposed to the Industrial Revolution

6. **The French Republican month Ventôse corresponds to which of our Gregorian months?**

7. **What is the Warsaw Pact?**

8. **Which is longer: an aeon, an era or a period?**

9. **What is Anglo-Saxon for 'werewolf'?**

10. **What rose is the symbol of the House of York?**

11. **Tsar Nicholas II was the last in line of which Russian dynasty?**

12. **Which of the following was not one of the Thirteen Colonies?**

a) Rhode island
b) Texas
c) New Jersey
d) Georgia

13. **In what year did Kuwait achieve women's suffrage?**

14. **Who was the first British prime minister?**

15. **In what year did the Great Famine, which would eventually wipe out two million people, begin in Ireland?**

16. **When was the first tank used in military conflict?**

17. **When was the Berlin Wall built?**

18. **What is prehistory?**

19. **Put the following periods of the geological timescale in the correct order:**

a) Ordovician
b) Jurassic
c) Paleogene
d) Devonian

20. **What was the Danelaw?**

21. **Who won the Battle of Hastings in 1066?**

22. **Who commissioned the Bayeux Tapestry?**

23. **What was King John's nickname?**

24. **What was the significance of the Magna Carta?**

25. In which long-lasting war did Joan of Arc fight?

26. Who was Henry VIII's third wife?

27. Why is Mary I known as Bloody Mary?

28. When was the Battle of Waterloo?

29. What was good about the guillotine?

30. Who was the last tsar of Russia?

31. What does the hammer and sickle symbol of Communist Russia stand for?

32. What was the Down to the Countryside Movement?

33. What was Gavrilo Princip's contribution to history?

34. Who are the law lords?

35. Name the three elements that make up the British Parliament.

36. What does *Sinn Féin* mean?

❦ 5 ❦

SCIENCE

'**Science** *n.* a branch of knowledge conducted on objective
principles involving the systematized observation of and experiment
with phenomena, esp. concerned with the material and
functions of the physical universe'
Oxford Concise English Dictionary

'Science offers the best answers to the meaning of life.
Science offers the privilege of understanding before you die
why you were ever born in the first place'
RICHARD DAWKINS (1941-)

Many people seem to take pride in the fact that they have an inferior
understanding of the principles of physics and are brazenly unashamed
of yawning at the glories of the periodic table. These very same people
are cluttering up our casualty departments with their stomach aches,
purely because they do not understand the process of their own digestive
tracts! A basic knowledge of science is the only way to understand the
world around you and your place in it.

Did you know that everything in the universe is made of combinations
of only a hundred or so basic elements? And that you, in all your unique
splendour, are 90 per cent composed of only four of these elements:
hydrogen, oxygen, carbon and nitrogen? And that both the workmanlike
graphite in your pencil and the dazzling diamonds in your necklace are
simply carbon?

Did you know that whales can communicate over immense distances
because sound waves travel faster in water than through the air? Or that
you go wrinkly in the bath because the outer layer of your skin can
absorb water and expand but the inner layer can't? All these mysteries
and more will be revealed in this chapter.

PHYSICS

AMAZING ATOMS

Let's start at the beginning: everything in the universe is made of matter and energy. It's amazing but true that all matter, from your mug to your Auntie Maude, can be broken down into smaller and smaller parts. Matter exists in one of three states: **liquid**, **gas** or **solid**, and each of these can be broken down into their pure component parts – the **elements**.

The water in your glass, for example, is a liquid that can be divided into individual water molecules. These molecules can be further dismantled into atoms of the **elements** hydrogen and oxygen. There are 118 named different types of atom in the world (94 of which are found in nature) and substances that are made entirely of one type of atom are called elements. Therefore, if you are paying attention, you will have deduced that there are 118 different elements. Everything around you is made of a combination of these elements.

Atoms are the minuscule building blocks that make up everything around us – they are so tiny that you could fit about 10 trillion of them onto the head of a pin. Scientists once thought that atoms were the smallest units of matter but they have since discovered even tinier fellows inside these atoms. These are the subatomic particles: **protons**, **neutrons** and **electrons**. It may seem hard to believe but protons and neutrons are actually composed of even tinier parts called **quarks**. Quantum physics – the branch of physics people seem to be most terrified of – is the study of subatomic particles.

The next time you are struggling to remember the parts of an atom, be it to fill in a crossword answer or to write a stiff letter to your electricity supplier, just remember what you are probably holding in your hand: a pen – **p(roton) e(lectron) n(eutron)**.

THE ANATOMY OF AN ATOM

An atom of helium

Interestingly, atoms are predominantly composed of empty space. The protons and neutrons are held in the nucleus of the atom and the electrons are constantly moving in orbit in paths – known as **shells** – in the empty space around the atom's nucleus.

Protons and electrons are charged – that is, because of the natural phenomenon of **electromagnetic force**, they attract particles of the opposite charge and repel particles of the same charge. Protons have a **positive (+) electrical charge** and electrons have a **negative (-) electrical charge**. Neutrons have no charge. When an atom is in balance there are an equal number of protons and electrons (which are attracted to each other because of their opposite charges). This equality means the atom as a whole has a neutral charge. The number of protons in an atom determines what type of element it is. A hydrogen atom, for example, has just one proton, and an atom of oxygen has eight.

FRIGHTENING LIGHTNING: STATIC ELECTRICITY

Sometimes electrons from the outer shells of atoms rub off onto other atoms. The atoms that have lost an electron become positively charged and the atoms that have gained electrons become negatively charged. Just as with subatomic particles, atoms with opposite charges are attracted to each other and atoms with the same charge are repulsed by each other.

When you brush your hair with vim and vigour your hairbrush picks up electrons from your tresses leaving strands of your hair positively charged. This is an example of **static electricity** (static electricity simply means electricity that doesn't flow in a current). Because all your strands of hair are positively charged they move away from each other, causing your hair to stand on end messily, leaving you looking like the Wreck of the *Hesperus*.

Lightning is a natural form of static electricity. It's caused by ice drops and air movements in clouds causing electrons to jump to different atoms and create charges. These charges are attracted to other, differently charged clouds or the ground, or, if you're particularly unlucky, the tip of your umbrella. Thirty people a year are struck by lightning in Great Britain thanks to static electricity. However, static electricity also allows us to make photocopies, so it's not all bad news.

PHYSICS HERO:
BENJAMIN FRANKLIN (1706–90)

Benjamin Franklin was an extraordinary man: a famous American statesman and an inventor who is credited with great advances in our understanding of electricity. He initially carried out experiments using a Leyden jar, which was an early form of capacitor (a device for storing an electrical charge). He discovered that some substances, like metal, conduct electricity (they allow electrons to move through them very easily) and some substances stop the flow, like rubber and fabric. Substances that allow the free flow of electrons are called **conductors** and those that prevent the flow are called **insulators**.

Franklin used these principles to prepare his most famous experiment which aimed to prove that lightning was electricity. In 1752 he demonstrated his theory by flying a kite with a metal tip into storm clouds and observing that this produced electrical sparks from a key hung from the end of the kite string.

Franklin was also the first person to come up with the concept of positive and negative electrical charges and, as if this was not enough for one man, he invented the lightning rod – along with bifocals, a special type of stove and the glass harmonica. He even found time to write the Declaration of Independence.

MAGNETIC ATTRACTION

As electrons spin round the nucleus of the atom, they create a small magnetic field. In most substances the combination of atoms includes electrons spinning in both directions, so the magnetic field is cancelled out. However, in magnets all the atoms have electrons spinning in the same direction creating a magnetic field with two poles: north-seeking and south-seeking. **Like poles** repel each other and **opposite poles** attract. Some elements, such as nickel, cobalt and iron, are naturally magnetic. On a grand scale, our planet's magnetic fields are created by the movement of the Earth's outer core around the inner core. Magnets can be used to help create electricity as their force can move electrons from one atom to another. The ancient Greeks, Romans and Chinese realised that certain stones, called lodestones, magically seemed to attract iron and always ended up pointing in the same direction if allowed to move freely. The Chinese were the first to use lodestones to help navigation as they knew they would always point in a north or south direction. These stones were examples of naturally occurring magnetite, a type of iron.

FARADAY'S FIND: ELECTROMAGNETIC INDUCTION

In 1831 Newington Butts' most famous son, the British scientist Michael Faraday, was the first person to create an electric current from a magnetic field, a process called **electromagnetic induction**. Electromagnetic induction is used in power generators all over the world to produce electricity; magnets are moved in relation to coils of wire to allow the magnetic field to work on the electrons in the wire, causing a current. In generators, either a coil of wire rotates in a magnetic field or a magnet is spun inside a coil of wire. When the magnet in the coil moves (or the coil moves in relation to the magnet) the current changes direction as the opposite poles of the magnet pass the wire. The greater the number of coils in the wire the greater the current. The movement of the magnet or wire is powered by mechanical force: for example, wind turbines use the rotation of the sails to cause the movement between the magnet and the wire.

ELECTRICITY ON THE MOVE: ELECTRIC CURRENT

Current is the movement of electrical charges. Electromagnetic force dictates that electrons are negatively charged and are therefore attracted to positively charged particles, and repulsed from their own kind. An electric current is created by building up lots of electrons at one end of a circuit and particles of a positive charge at the other end. This causes the electrons to move round the circuit in an attempt to flee their fellow electrons and move towards the seductive positive charge.

There are two types of current: **DC** (direct current) where the charge moves in one direction round a circuit, and **AC** (alternating current) where the charge moves back and forth in alternate directions. The mains supply is an alternating current and batteries provide a direct current. Physics-loving Australian rockers AC/DC are named after electrical appliances that can work using both varieties of current.

HOW DOES A LIGHT BULB WORK?

In your home, the electrical wiring (usually made of copper because it is an extremely good conductor) creates an **electrical circuit**. A light switch works by completing or breaking a circuit of wires so that current either flows from the power source through the circuit, and any appliances such as light bulbs that are part of the circuit, or not. In official physics-speak, appliances on a circuit are referred to as **loads**.

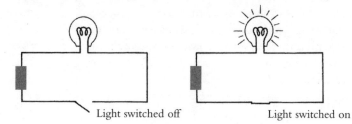

Light switched off   Light switched on

When a light switch is turned on, the electricity flows around the circuit and through the wires in the light bulb. The tiny coiled wire in the middle of the bulb is called the **filament**. The filament is made of tungsten, a metal that can withstand great heat. The flow of electricity through the filament causes it to heat up to a very high temperature which makes the tungsten glow, emitting light. The bulb is filled with argon, an inert gas which prevents the oxygen in the air coming into contact with the hot tungsten. If the two met, the bulb would burst into flames. The first light bulb was invented by the American scientist Thomas Edison, also known as 'The Wizard of Menlo Park', in 1879.

INIMITABLE ISAAC: NEWTON'S LAWS OF MOTION

Sir Isaac Newton (1642–1727) is one of the shining stars of Britain's intellectual history. He was the first scientist to be knighted and his ideas on colour, gravity, calculus and motion changed the face of science forever. (He also invented the catflap.) However, his most famous work is

Principia Mathematica (1687), in which he describes his three laws of motion and his theory of gravity.

- **The first law of motion** – the law of inertia: An object in motion will stay in motion until it is acted upon by an outside **force**. If you set a baby in a pram in motion, it would stay in motion forever if the frictional forces of air resistance, rough ground and busybody passers-by didn't work to slow it to a stop.

- **The second law of motion** – the force acting on an object is equal to its **mass** multiplied by its **acceleration**. Written as an equation this is: **F = ma**. Force is usually measured in newtons (N), mass in kilograms (kg), and acceleration in metres per second squared (m/s²).

- **The third law of motion** – the action reaction law: For every action there is an equal and opposite reaction.

FORCE, SPEED, VELOCITY, ACCELERATION AND DRAG

Force is the term for a push or a pull. Earth's gravity is a force which pulls us down at approximately 10 newtons per kilogram of our mass.

Friction is the force exerted by the resistance of one object moving over another.

Speed is the rate at which a body moves. Light can travel at nearly 300,000km per second in the right circumstances. This is called the **speed of light**. However, light can only reach this speed in a vacuum, and travels more slowly when it has to pass through substances such as air, water or objects.

Velocity is the speed and direction of a moving body.

Acceleration is the rate at which the speed changes in a moving body.

Drag is the resistive force exerted on a moving body by its environment.

Terminal velocity occurs when the resistive forces and the gravitational forces on a falling object are in balance. It is the moment at which a falling body ceases to accelerate. A feather has a lower terminal velocity than a brick and a cat has a lower terminal velocity than a person.

GRAPPLING WITH GRAVITY

In 1666 Newton was forced by the plague to return from Cambridge University to his manor house in Lincolnshire and it was here that he developed his most famous theory. The story of an apple hitting Newton on the head while he snoozed under a tree is a wonderful English myth: nobody knows exactly what happened to make Newton connect the fall of an apple from a tree with the moon's orbit around the Earth.

Newton's relative, John Conduitt explained the story thus: '. . . while he was musing in the garden it came into his thought that the power of gravity (which brought an apple from the tree to the ground) was not limited to a certain distance from the earth but that this power must extend much farther than was usually thought. Why not as high as the moon said he to himself & if so that must influence her motion . . .'

Newton developed his law of gravity from observing the fact that an apple accelerates as it falls to the ground. According to his own second law of motion this means that a force is acting upon the mass of the apple to cause the acceleration. This force is gravity. Newton realised that this force could extend as far as the moon and that gravity would there-fore explain the moon's orbit around the Earth.

Every mass in the universe exerts a pull on every other mass. The larger the mass, the larger the gravitational pull. The Earth has a greater gravi-tational pull than the moon and this is how it holds its pale cousin in orbit around itself.

MASS, WEIGHT AND DENSITY

Mass is the quantity of matter that an object contains: it is not the same as weight. Weight changes depending on the force of gravitational pull, but mass doesn't. On the moon, which has weaker gravitational pull, we would weigh less.

Weight is the force experienced by a body as a result of gravity.

Density is a measure of how tightly packed matter is in a substance. It can be calculated by dividing the mass of an object by its volume.

$$D = M/V$$

EXCELLENT EINSTEIN: THE THEORIES OF RELATIVITY

Newton's law of gravity was only superseded over two hundred years later, by Einstein's general theory of relativity. Albert Einstein (1879–1955) is the most famous physicist in the world – he is a household name even though few people are familiar with his complex ideas, his **special theory of relativity** (1905) and his **general theory of relativity** (1915). These theories did not prove Newton wrong: they simply proved that Newton's laws were incomplete, and that different rules applied to objects in extreme circumstances, such as particles travelling near the speed of light, or to objects in very strong fields of gravity.

THE SPECIAL THEORY OF RELATIVITY

Einstein's special theory of relativity states that time is NOT constant and unvarying. People had always thought that time passed in a regular way wherever you were in the universe and whatever you were doing. Einstein showed that the faster an object travelled the slower time would run. His theory showed that time was relative rather than absolute, and that the speed of light is the only constant.

An additional paper that followed Einstein's special theory of relativity contained his famous equation: $E = MC^2$. $E = MC^2$ means energy = mass multiplied by the speed of light squared.

The central concept of $E = MC^2$ is astonishingly counter-intuitive. It tells us that matter (mass) and energy are interchangeable. Amazingly, this means that a lemon and a beam of light are essentially just different forms of the same thing. The sun, for example, is converting its mass into light energy all the time. Four million tonnes of sun disappear every second to make sunlight. Because the speed of light squared is such a large number, Einstein's equation shows that even a small amount of mass can potentially be converted into a huge amount of energy. The atomic bomb is a horrific example of $E = MC^2$ in action.

THE GENERAL THEORY OF RELATIVITY

Einstein's general theory of relativity changed the way we think about gravity. Newton's laws explained how gravity works on Earth but didn't explain why gravity exists or how it might work in more extreme environments. Einstein proposed that space and time are bent by the presence of large bodies such as planets and the resulting curvature of space and time causes the effect we experience as gravity.

BLACK HOLES

A black hole is an astronomical body whose gravitational pull is so massive that not even light can escape. Once light has passed the **event horizon**, which is the gravitational boundary enclosing a black hole, it will never be seen again. Black holes can be created by the death of a star: when the star dies and collapses in on itself, the huge weight of matter falling in from all sides compresses to a point of zero volume and infinite density called the **singularity**.

HOT STUFF:
THE LAWS OF THERMODYNAMICS

Thermodynamics is the science of heat and energy. Heat is energy that flows from warmer to cooler temperatures. The molecules of hot things bounce around more wildly than the molecules of cold things and heat travels through hot, bouncy molecules bumping into cooler molecules and setting them bouncing as well.

Thermodynamics deals with the exchange and transfer of energy with the area around it. This may sound rather dry but it has incredible and mind-bending implications. The laws of thermodynamics were formulated during the Industrial Revolution when scientists began investigating the energy efficiency of the new machines that were used in factories. They were attempting to create a machine that used the energy it inevitably wasted as heat to continue to power itself.

Unfortunately, they found this impossible but they did find these amazing laws instead. The first and second laws of thermodynamics are the really juicy ones and you should take some time to ponder them.

- The **zeroth law of thermodynamics** seems obvious but is a key principle of thermodynamics. It states that if object A is in **thermal equilibrium** with object B and object B is in thermal equilibrium with object C, then object C is also in thermal equilibrium with object A.

  For example, if Molesworth's cup of tea is the same temperature as Gillibrand's cup of tea and Gillibrand's cup of tea is the same temperature as Fotherington-Thomas's cup, then Fotherington-Thomas's cup of tea is also the same temperature as Molesworth's.

  Thermal equilibrium is when no heat moves between one object and another. Heat moves between objects when they are at different temperatures, but cool does not move. It's easy to remember this as cool people tend not to move much, choosing instead to lean moodily against a wall chewing a match and staring into the middle distance. If you put ice into a glass of lemonade the ice doesn't send its coldness into the lemonade, the lemonade sends its heat into the ice in order to try to achieve thermal equilibrium. This reduces the temperature of the lemonade and melts the ice. This law allows us to measure heat in the form of temperature.

- The **first law of thermodynamics** (also known as the law of conservation of energy) states that the change in a system's internal energy is equal to the difference between heat added to the system from its surroundings, and work done by the system on its surroundings.

  In thermodynamics the part of the universe under consideration is referred to as the **system** and everything around it is referred to as the **surroundings**. In physics, **work** means the exertion of force overcoming resistance or producing molecular change. On Monday mornings you may also feel that your work is the exertion of force overcoming resistance.

  One way of visualising this law is to think about what happens when you boil a pot of water. If you heat a pot of water on a stove, you are adding heat energy to the system of the pot of water and the temperature and energy of the water will rise. The system also releases energy and works on the environment around it – the boiling water will cause the air around the pot to heat up as well. The change in energy of the pot of water is equal to the energy added by the stove, minus the work done on the air around the pot.

This law is unbelievably important: it shows that **energy is never truly lost**. It can neither be created nor destroyed – it can only be converted from one form to another.

The reason that this law is so thrilling is that the universe is the ultimate closed system and therefore nothing in it is ever lost or truly destroyed. A **closed system** is a system that is isolated from its surroundings by a boundary that admits no transfer of matter. The amount of energy in the universe has not changed since the Big Bang that created it. So even when you shuffle off your mortal coil, the energy that animates you now will always exist, as will all your atoms. In fact, you are made of atoms and energy that were produced by the Big Bang and the resulting stellar formations; you are all stars.

- The **second law of thermodynamics** (also known as the law of increased entropy) states that it is impossible to completely and efficiently convert heat into work: some energy will always be dispersed in the transfer and become unusable. A steam train's furnace uses coal to heat water to make steam to drive the engine. However, not all of the heat energy in the coal goes towards powering the engine – much is lost uselessly heating up the engine itself, the air around it and the poor stoker, slaving away with his shovel. **Entropy** means unusable, disordered energy: the less usable energy there is in a system the more disorder and chaos increase. This law means that, in a closed system, the amount of useful energy decreases over time.

Everything moves towards entropy: even if you scrupulously tidy your bedroom it will not take the hint and become more and more tidy over time, it will tend to entropy, and become more and more untidy. Nothing can be totally energy-efficient.

The second law of thermodynamics also states that heat energy will only naturally travel from an object of a higher temperature to an object of lower temperature. Heat is headed in only one direction – towards an area that is cooler. Your supper is only going to get colder as it sits in the kitchen waiting for you to lay the table.

• The **third law of thermodynamics** states that it is impossible to reduce the temperature of a system to **absolute zero** in a finite number of steps.

This law deals with the relationship between entropy and temperature. The only point where entropy would stop happening is at the theoretical temperature known as absolute zero, where all molecular movement stops. This is impossible to achieve as absolute zero is unreachable.

The easiest way to remember the three laws is to recall the novelist and scientist C. P. Snow's quick summary:

1. **You cannot win (you cannot get something for nothing because matter and energy are conserved).**
2. **You cannot break even (you cannot return to the same energy state because entropy always increases).**
3. **You cannot get out of the game (because absolute zero is unattainable).**

HOT AND COLD: TAKING THE TEMPERATURE

Heat can be measured according to different scales: Fahrenheit is the system still used by grandmas in the UK and by everyone in the United States; Celsius (which was called centigrade) is a metric system used today in the UK and the rest of Europe. In the Celsius system pure water freezes at 0°C and boils at 100°C. (In the Fahrenheit system water freezes at 32°F and boils at 212°F.). When people say 'It was 100° in the shade!' they are using the Fahrenheit scale: 100°F is 37.7°C.

Celsius	Fahrenheit
0	32
5	41
10	50
15	59
20	68
25	77
30	86
35	95
40	104
45	113
50	122
55	131
60	140
65	149
70	158
75	167
80	176
85	185
90	194
95	203
100	212

Scientists are special people and so use a different temperature scale called the Kelvin system which is based on the concept of absolute zero. Temperature is actually a measure of molecular movement: as we have seen, the molecules of hot things move around a lot and molecules move more and more slowly the colder they are. The point at which molecules stop moving altogether is called absolute zero. Absolute zero is -273.15° Celsius and -459.67° Fahrenheit. Absolute zero is a hypothetical temperature as it is impossible to create it: this is as cold as it doesn't get. The Kelvin scale is named after the Northern Irish scientist who invented it: William Thompson, First Baron Kelvin (1824–1907).

FEELING ENERGETIC?:
THE TYPES OF ENERGY

Kinetic energy is also called movement energy. All moving objects have kinetic energy. The greater the mass of an object and the greater the speed of its movement, the more kinetic energy it has. An elephant thundering towards you across the savannah has more kinetic energy than a snail.

Nuclear energy is the energy stored in the nuclei of atoms.

Electrical energy is the energy of electrical charges.

Sound energy is the energy released when objects vibrate.

Elastic potential energy is the energy stored when an elastic object is compressed or stretched.

Thermal energy (heat) is energy that flows from warmer to cooler temperatures.

Chemical energy is the energy stored in the chemical bonds that hold different atoms together to create substances. Energy is released when chemical bonds are made. This kind of energy is found in batteries, in scones, cabbage, potatoes and lollipops (all food in fact), and in coal, gas and oils.

Magnetic energy is the energy held in magnets.

Gravitational potential energy is the energy held in an object that has been raised against the force of gravity. If you pick a rock up from the ground you are investing it with gravitational potential energy.

Radiant energy is light (also known as electromagnetic energy).

You can remember the types of energy by keeping the following phrase in mind:

Katie **N**ever **E**ats **S**cones **E**ven **T**hough **C**harlie **M**akes **G**reat **R**ecipes.

Types of energy can change. The electric energy passing through a light bulb creates both heat energy and light energy. Interestingly, in creating light, conventional light bulbs actually disperse more energy as heat than as light.

FEEL THE HEAT: HEAT TRANSFER

Ever in search of colder climes, heat travels in three different ways:

1. Convection

Heat moves by convection in substances that expand when they are heated, such as water and air.

When water is heated in a kettle, the water molecules that are closest to the heat source get hot first. Water expands when heated and becomes less dense. Heat makes the molecules bounce around and this creates more space between them, reducing the density. The less dense water rises above the cooler, denser water which then ends up closest to the heat source. As this water heats up it also moves, causing a pattern of circulation known as a **convection current**. In the end, all the water will be heated through convection.

2. Conduction

If one is foolish enough to leave a metal poker resting in an open fire, the end of the poker in the fire will heat up, and then gradually the whole poker will become hot, and even the end furthest from the fire will give you a nasty burn if you pick it up. The metal molecules near the heat source begin to move about vigorously because of the heat from the fire, and they then bump into the molecules further up the poker causing them to bounce around. This process, called conduction, continues until the whole poker is hot. Substances have different molecular structures, so some are more heat-conductive than others. Silver is the most thermally (and electrically) conductive metal in the world.

3. Radiation

Conduction and convection both move heat through the molecules of substances. Thermal radiation uses electromagnetic waves rather than molecules. In thermal radiation a hot object gives out these waves and they are absorbed by a cooler object.

Every single object radiates heat: you are radiating it right now. If some-one sinister and technologically equipped was tracking you at night using thermal imaging equipment, they would be able to see you because of the infrared heat you are radiating. Matt, dark surfaces absorb radiant heat more effectively than reflective, light objects. If you wear a white T-shirt on a sunny day you will feel less hot than if you wear a black T-shirt. The sun transfers its heat to the Earth through the vacuum of space (where there are no molecules) using radiation. When you use a toaster you are also using thermal radiation to toast your bread.

HEAT EXPANSION

The addition of heat to a gas, liquid or solid can cause an expansion of its volume, in the same process that decreases its density. The same amount of heat will cause a greater expansion in gases than liquids and in liquids than solids. The reduction of heat causes contraction (water is an exception to this rule as it actually expands as it becomes ice). If you take away enough heat from a gas, it will turn into a liquid, and with an even greater reduction liquids can turn into solids. This is why if you cool steam it will turn into water and then eventually into ice. Bridges and other structures are built with special expansion joints which expand and contract with the air temperature to prevent them from buckling or collapsing.

GOOD VIBRATIONS: LIGHT AND SOUND WAVES

Light and sound travel in waves. Waves are vibrations that carry energy from one place to another. **Sound waves** are vibrations that travel through particles, moving energy through the particles without actually moving the particles themselves. **Light waves** are electromagnetic waves that don't need to travel through particles; instead, they are vibrations in electrical or magnetic fields.

Waves in the sea and light waves are **transverse waves**. In transverse waves the vibrations of the wave move at right angles to the forward movement of the wave.

Sound waves are a different type of wave called a **longitudinal wave**. In longitudinal waves the vibrations of the wave move in the same direction as the forward movement of the wave.

Both types of waves are measured according to their **amplitude**, **wavelength** and **frequency**.

The amplitude of a wave is the maximum measurement of a vibration from its point of equilibrium. The greater the amplitude of a sound wave, the louder the sound. The wavelength is the measurement between the same points on two successive waves, e.g. the crests. The frequency is the number of waves that occur per second. Sound waves' frequencies are measured in hertz (Hz). The higher the frequency the higher the pitch of the sound. Humans can pick up sound waves of between about 15 hertz and about 20,000 hertz, and dogs can hear as high as 40,000 hertz. This is why some dog whistles are inaudible to the human ear. Bats use sound waves to 'see' in the dark by emitting high-pitched sound waves which hit objects and bounce back to them, allowing them to judge distances and shapes using a process called **echolocation**.

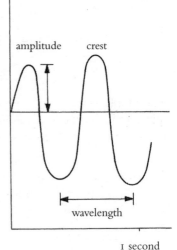

LET THERE BE LIGHT!

What we call light is actually just part of the **electromagnetic (EM) radiation spectrum**. Visible light is in the middle of the entire EM spectrum which also contains radio waves, microwaves, infrared rays, ultraviolet rays, X-rays and gamma rays. EM has no mass – it is a form of energy delivered in small amounts called **photons**. In a very bright, intense beam of light, the photons will be very closely packed together and carry more energy; in a dimmer beam of light, there will be fewer photons carrying less energy. The further away you get from the light source, the more the photons are spread out and the less intense the light becomes.

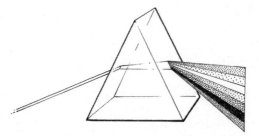

The visible light we can see is called **white light**. White light can be split into its component colours, which all have different wavelengths, by refracting it through a prism.

When light hits an object and bounces off it this is called **reflection**. A red rose appears red to us because all the colours in white light apart from red are being absorbed by the rose, and the red rays are being reflected back into our eyes.

When light moves from one substance to another – for example, from the air into a prism and back into the air – it bends. This bending is called **refraction**. The amount of refraction depends on the wavelength of the light.

The series of colours created by refracting white light is called the **spectrum**. The order of colours in the spectrum is red, orange, yellow, green, blue, indigo, violet. Violet rays are the shortest light waves we can see, and red are the longest. A rainbow is a natural spectrum caused by white light being refracted by raindrops. The easiest way to remember the order of the colours is to keep in mind the sentence: 'Richard Of York Gave Battle In Vain.'

WHY IS THE SKY BLUE?

The sky appears blue during the day because of a process known as **Rayleigh scattering**. This occurs because the gas molecules present in the Earth's atmosphere absorb and scatter the shorter waves of light coming to us from the sun – which are blue – more effectively than they scatter light from the red end of the spectrum. This means that the sky appears blue because more of the blue light is reaching us than the other colours in the spectrum.

The sky changes colour at sunset because as our part of the Earth turns away from the sun its light has to travel further to reach us and by the time it gets to us most of the shorter blue rays have been scattered away leaving only the longer yellow and red rays. This effect is intensified on cloudy or polluted days as the more particles there are in the atmosphere for the sunlight to bump into, the more the rays will scatter.

CHEMISTRY

'**Chemistry** *n*. the study of the elements and the compounds they
form and the reactions they undergo'
Oxford Concise English Dictionary

'The meeting of two personalities is like the contact of two chemical
substances: if there is any reaction, both are transformed'
CARL GUSTAV JUNG (1875–1961)

ELEMENTS, MY DEAR WATSON

It's time to take out your white coat, fire up your Bunsen burner and put
on your dashing safety goggles – let's start with the basics of chemistry.
All **liquids**, **gases** and **solids** in the universe can be broken down into
their pure component parts – these are called the elements. This means
every single thing, from ping-pong balls to pachyderms, from acorns
to aeroplanes, from milk to mustard gas, is made of the hundred or so
different elements in our universe. That essential defining characteristic
of our world, water, is made up of just a combination of the two
elements: hydrogen and oxygen.

Elements can never be changed into other elements through chemical
reactions – despite good old Roger Bacon's best efforts, alchemy is
impossible and you can never change lead into gold. Elements can be
broken down into individual atoms of the same type; if you are lucky
enough to find a lump of pure gold and take it back to the lab to break
it down into its individual atoms, you'll find that all the atoms will be
identical atoms of gold. The densest elements in the world are osmium
and iridium – surprisingly, often found in the nibs of fountain pens.

As we discovered in our Physics lesson, atoms are made up of protons
and neutrons with electrons arranged in shells of different levels which
spin, like orbits, around the nucleus. An atom's **atomic number** is the

number of protons it holds in its nucleus, and all of the atoms of an element share an identical atomic number.

A **molecule** is a combination of two or more atoms together. If a molecule is made up of the same type of atom then it is an element. If the molecule is made up of two or more different types of atoms that are chemically bonded then it is a **compound**. Salt, that essential culinary necessity and oceanic mainstay, is a chemical compound of sodium and chlorine atoms.

Small molecular changes can have far-reaching effects: carbon dioxide (which chemists refer to using the abbreviation CO_2) is a gas benignly present in the air around us all the time, but without that second oxygen atom CO_2 becomes CO – carbon monoxide – which is lethal to us humans. Other common compounds that we see around us are water (H_2O), salt ($NaCl$) and, if you are the Queen, rubies (Al_2O_3Cr). Once different atoms have chemically bonded together in compounds, it is very difficult to separate them from each other and compounds can have very different properties and appearances to the separate atoms they are composed of.

BREATHING SPACE: THE COMPOSITION OF AIR

When you stand on a clifftop and take a deep breath of health-giving fresh air, you should be aware that the combination of elements you are sucking into your lungs is perfectly calibrated to support life on Earth. Air is, for the main part, comprised of nitrogen and oxygen. It is approximately 78 per cent nitrogen and 21 per cent oxygen. The final per cent is made up of water vapour and a few other gases.

THE PERIODIC TABLE

We all remember those hours spent gazing at the poster of the periodic table on the wall of the science laboratory, and some of us might even remember trying to learn it off by heart – but it's easier to check back to this section the next time someone asks you the atomic number of praseodymium over cocktails.

The periodic table was first devised by a Russian chemist called Dmitri Mendeleev (who also invented his own brand of vodka) in 1870 as a way of organising the different elements that had been discovered. Since then more have been added as scientists have created new elements using nuclear experiments.

The periodic table is organised as a grid. **Metals** are on the left and **non-metals** are on the right. Each square in the grid shows the atomic number of the element and an abbreviation of the element's name. The atomic weight of the element is listed under the abbreviation. Each row running from left to right is called a **period**. All elements in the same period have the same number of atomic shells. The first row of the table is made up of elements which have atoms with one shell, all the elements in the second row have two atomic shells, and so on. The maximum number of shells that any atom we have discovered has is 7, so this is the bottom row of the table.

The columns of each table are called **groups**. They run from top to bottom. As a general rule every element in each group has the same number of electrons in its outer shell. However, as you might expect from such a multilayered diagram it's not quite that simple throughout the whole table. Hydrogen, helium and the transition metals have special qualities that mean that they don't follow this rule rigidly. In fact the transition metals, which sit in the 3rd to the 12th columns in the table below, can have up to 32 electrons in their outer shells and so should be treated as separate. This means that the 13th column is actually the group of elements with 3 electrons in their outer shells, and the final column, the noble gases, are the elements with 8. Some versions of the table don't actually give the transition metals group numbers so the remaining columns simply run from 1 to 8. All clear? Good.

THE PERIODIC TABLE

1 H 1.0079								
3 Li 6.941	4 Be 9.0122							
11 Na 22.990	12 Mg 24.305							
19 K 39.098	20 Ca 40.078	21 Sc 44.956	22 Ti 47.867	23 V 50.942	24 Cr 51.996	25 Mn 54.938	26 Fe 55.845	27 Co 58.933
37 Rb 85.468	38 Sr 87.62	39 Y 88.906	40 Zr 91.224	41 Nb 92.906	42 Mo 95.96	43 Tc –	44 Ru 101.07	45 Rh 102.91
55 Cs 132.91	56 Ba 137.33	57–71	72 Hf 178.49	73 Ta 180.95	74 W 183.84	75 Re 186.21	76 Os 190.23	77 Ir 192.22
87 Fr –	88 Ra –	89–103	104 Rf –	105 Db –	106 Sg –	107 Bh –	108 Hs –	109 Mt –

57 La 138.91	58 Ce 140.12	59 Pr 140.91	60 Nd 144.24	61 Pm –	62 Sm 150.36
89 Ac –	90 Th 232.04	91 Pa 231.04	92 U 238.03	93 Np –	94 Pu –

					2 He 4.0026

5 B 10.811	6 C 12.011	7 N 14.007	8 O 15.999	9 F 18.998	10 Ne 20.180
13 Al 26.982	14 Si 28.086	15 P 30.974	16 S 32.065	17 Cl 35.453	18 Ar 39.948

28 Ni 58.693	29 Cu 63.546	30 Zn 65.38	31 Ga 69.723	32 Ge 72.64	33 As 74.922	34 Se 78.96	35 Br 79.904	36 Kr 83.798
46 Pd 106.42	47 Ag 107.87	48 Cd 112.41	49 In 114.82	50 Sn 118.71	51 Sb 121.76	52 Te 127.60	53 I 126.90	54 Xe 131.29
78 Pt 195.08	79 Au 196.97	80 Hg 200.59	81 Tl 204.38	82 Pb 207.2	83 Bi 208.98	84 Po -	85 At -	86 Rn -
110 Ds -	111 Rg -							

63 Eu 151.96	64 Gd 157.25	65 Tb 158.93	66 Dy 162.50	67 Ho 164.93	68 Er 167.26	69 Tm 168.93	70 Yb 173.05	71 Lu 174.97
95 Am -	96 Cm -	97 Bk -	98 Cf -	99 Es -	100 Fm -	101 Md -	102 No -	103 Lr -

1. Hydrogen – the most abundant element in our universe
2. Helium
3. Lithium
4. Beryllium
5. Boron
6. Carbon
7. Nitrogen
8. Oxygen
9. Fluorine
10. Neon
11. Sodium
12. Magnesium
13. Aluminium
14. Silicon
15. Phosphorus
16. Sulphur
17. Chlorine
18. Argon
19. Potassium
20. Calcium
21. Scandium
22. Titanium
23. Vanadium
24. Chromium
25. Manganese
26. Iron
27. Cobalt
28. Nickel
29. Copper
30. Zinc
31. Galium
32. Germanium
33. Arsenic
34. Selenium
35. Bromine
36. Krypton – a rare gas used in special light bulbs (nothing to do with Superman)
37. Rubidium
38. Strontium
39. Yttrium
40. Zirconium
41. Niobium
42. Molybdenum
43. Technetium
44. Ruthenium
45. Rhodium
46. Palladium
47. Silver
48. Cadmium
49. Indium
50. Tin
51. Atimony
52. Tellurium
53. Iodine
54. Xenon
55. Caesium
56. Barium
57. Lanthanum – a rare earth element used in cigarette lighter flints
58. Cerium
59. Praseodymium
60. Neodymium
61. Promethium
62. Samarium
63. Europium
64. Gadolinium
65. Terbium
66. Dysprosium
67. Holmium
68. Erbium
69. Thulium
70. Ytterbium

71. Lutetium
72. Hafnium
73. Tantalum – a metal used for diverse purposes from electrical capacitors to pins for broken bones
74. Tungsten
75. Rhenium
76. Osmium
77. Iridium
78. Platinum
79. Gold
80. Mercury
81. Thallium
82. Lead
83. Bismuth
84. Polonium
85. Astatine
86. Radon
87. Francium
88. Radium
89. Actinium
90. Thorium
91. Protactinium
92. Uranium
93. Neptunium
94. Plutonium
95. Americium
96. Curium
97. Berkelium

98. Californium
99. Einsteinium
100. Fermium
101. Mendelevium (Mendelevium is a radioactive rare earth metal named after Dmitri Mendeleev who invented the periodic table)
102. Nobelium
103. Laurencium
104. Rutherfordium
105. Dubnium
106. Seaborgium
107. Bohrium
108. Hassium
109. Meitnerium
110. Darmstadtium
111. Roentgenium

Seven other elements have also been reported but have not yet been added to the official table:
112. Ununbium
113. Ununtrium
114. Ununquadium
115. Ununpentium
116. Ununhexium
117. Ununseptium
118. Ununoctium

TEST YOUR METAL:
THE METALS AND NON-METALS

Metal elements are like members of the same family with similar characteristics: they appear shiny, they conduct heat and electricity well and they are malleable.

Non-metal elements also have key, less positive-sounding, characteristics: they are dull, conduct heat and electricity badly and are brittle.

STRENGTH IN NUMBERS: ATOMIC BONDING

The evidence is all around us that the teeny tiny atoms don't just float free – they are bound together to create different substances. As you'll remember from our introduction to the elements, molecules made of different types of atom bonded together are called compounds. There are different ways in which atoms choose to bond together:

Covalent bonds: Remember how atoms have shells of orbiting electrons? In some cases an atom's outer shell has room for extra electrons, and it will fill this if it possibly can by teaming up with another atom so that they can share electrons between the two of them. Molecules containing covalently bonded atoms are made up of atoms sharing electrons which forge a link between them. It is possible for atoms of different or the same element to covalently bond – two atoms of oxygen bond to create O_2. Covalent bonding occurs only between non-metal atoms.

Ionic bonds: An **ion** is an atom that has lost one or more of its electrons or gained an extra one or more. Because electrons are negatively charged, if an atom gains an electron it becomes negatively charged and if it loses an electron it becomes positively charged – so ions have charges. Some elements are more careless than others and are more likely to lose electrons and some are more likely to gain them. Ionic bonds occur between positively and negatively charged ions. The force of electrostatic attraction that rules that substances with different electrical charges are attracted to one another draws these differently charged ions together. The salt you sprinkle on your food in an effort to jazz up your hopeless meat loaf is made of ionically bonded sodium and chloride. Ionic compounds create lattice patterns of different ions and because of this they often form crystals. They have high melting points and high boiling points.

Metallic bonds: These bonds occur in metal atoms which generously allow their outer-shell electrons to move about freely and to be shared among other metal atoms. Because of this freedom, metals are good conductors of heat and electricity.

AN INTRODUCTION TO ISOTOPES

Atomic number: The atomic number of an element is the number of protons in the nucleus of each of the atoms of that element. Every element has a different atomic number, as you can see from the periodic table earlier in this chapter.

Nucleons: Nucleons are an atom's protons and neutrons, which are situated in its nucleus.

Mass number: The mass number of an element is the number of nucleons in an element's atom's nucleus.

Isotopes: Isotopes are different forms of atoms of the same element which have differing numbers of neutrons. They have the same atomic number as the standard form of the element but a different mass number. The atomic number (the number of protons in an atom) is fixed – an atom of carbon can't have 7 instead of 6 protons or it would be an atom of nitrogen instead. However, the number of neutrons in an atom can vary. Atoms of hydrogen can have 0, 1, or 2 neutrons. These different forms of the hydrogen atom are called the isotopes of hydrogen. Obviously, an isotope of hydrogen with 3 neutrons will have a greater atomic mass than an isotope with 0 so isotopes can all have different atomic masses.

CHANGES OF STATE:
SOLIDS, LIQUIDS AND GASES

All matter exists as either a solid, liquid or gas. However, just when you think you've got a handle on the fact that a bar stool is a solid, beer is a liquid and methane is a gas, we have to let you know that, subject to the right environmental circumstances, all of these things can change form.

If you cool water to 0°C it changes from a liquid to a solid – ice – as it freezes. As the polar bears are well aware, at temperatures above 0°C, ice melts and changes from a solid to a liquid. If you boil water, it will begin to evaporate and turn into water vapour (water in its gaseous form). The change from a solid to a gas, missing out the liquid phase, is called **sublimation**. Dry ice is solid carbon dioxide that sublimes directly into gaseous carbon dioxide.

BROWNIAN MOTION

Brownian motion is the name given to the random fluctuation pattern of tiny particles suspended in a gas or fluid, even if the gas or fluid appears to be totally still. It is named after the Scottish botanist Robert Brown, who, in the 1820s, while studying pollen under a microscope, observed that pollen particles suspended in fluid seemed to jump in zig-zags. In fact, the pollen particles were being buffeted by water molecules which were moving because of the effect of the liquid's temperature. Albert Einstein made the theory famous in his own studies in 1905 and it has since given rise to mathematical models which can be used to predict other apparently random patterns, such as fluctuations in the stock market.

WARNING!:
CHEMICAL HAZARD SYMBOLS

HARMFUL
Substances that may involve limited health risks.

IRRITANT
A non-corrosive substance, that may cause inflammation or lesions through contact with the skin or eyes. Your bottles of household cleaning fluids are likely to display this symbol.

FLAMMABLE
A substance that catches fire easily. If marked Highly Flammable the substance may be spontaneously flammable in air. Methane and hydrogen gases are both highly flammable. The famous *Hindenburg* airship disaster of 1937 was caused by the hydrogen in the balloon catching alight.

OXIDISING
A substance that produces a reaction giving off great heat when in contact with other substances. Chlorine and ozone are both oxidising materials.

CORROSIVE
A substance that can destroy living tissues on contact. Hydrochloric acid and ammonia are both corrosive.

EXPLOSIVE
A substance that may explode when heated or subjected to shock or friction. Nitroglycerine is an explosive material used in dynamite.

TOXIC
A substance that can cause health problems or death if ingested, inhaled or taken in through the skin. Arsenic and hydrogen cyanide are both extremely toxic.

DANGEROUS TO THE ENVIRONMENT.
A substance that may harm the environment (particularly the aquatic environment). Some agricultural pesticides and painting materials such as turpentine are dangerous to the environment.

CRAZY CHROMATOGRAPHY

If you didn't do this wonderfully psychedelic experiment at school then you've missed out. Luckily, it's one of the least dangerous chemical experiments that you can carry out in the comfort of your own home, so set aside that hydrochloric acid and get out a tube of Smarties instead.

When different substances are mixed together but not bonded to form compounds, you have what is called a **mixture**. The different colours of Smarties are made up of different dyes mixed together. Chromatography will separate out the dyes so that you can see which pigments have been used to colour each Smartie.

Apparatus
3 saucers
3 coffee filters or blotting paper
3 different-coloured Smarties (you'll get the best effects if you include a
    brown one)
a glass of water

Method
Cut your coffee filters or blotting paper into 3 circles and place them on
    the saucers.
Place one Smartie in the middle of each piece of paper.
Drip some water onto each Smartie until there is a circle of damp
    around each sweet about 5cm in diameter.
Leave for 30 minutes.

Conclusion
After half an hour, haloes of colours should have appeared around each Smartie, showing which inks have been used in the dye mixture for each colour. The different inks in the dye mixture have different levels of solubility in water and so move at different rates through the paper when dissolved in water and this is why you can see them separated out in rings.

Before solvent (water) is added:

After solvent has worked on Smartie:

THE pH SCALE:
ACIDS, BASES AND ALKALIS

In films, villains often threaten to submerge the hero in a vat of acid, but what many people don't know is that alkalis can be just as deadly and some acids and alkalis are perfectly harmless. No swashbuckler worth his salt is ever going to be worried by a bath of lemon juice.

Acids are substances with a high concentration of hydrogen ions. They are usually corrosive and measure less than 7 on the **pH scale**. The pH scale is a specific measuring scale used for establishing the acidity or alkalinity of a substance – 0 is the most acidic point on the pH scale and 14 is the most alkaline. Substances which are neutral have a pH of 7. Substances that react with acids to neutralise them are called **bases**. Bases which can be dissolved in water are called **alkalis** and have a pH of more than 7. Alkalis can be just as corrosive as acids. You can make a neutral solution by mixing the right amount of an acid and base.

• If you mix an acid and a base and neutralise the acid then salt and water are produced.

• If you mix an acid and a metal carbonate then salt, water and carbon dioxide are produced.

• If you mix an acid and a reactive metal together then salt and hydrogen are produced.

Definition	pH	Examples of solutions that match this pH
Acid	0	battery acid
	1	stomach acid
	2	lemon juice, vinegar
	3	orange juice
	4	tomato juice, beer
	5	black coffee
	6	milk
Neutral	7	pure water
Alkali	8	sea water
	9	baking soda, soap
	10	milk of magnesia
	11	ammonia
	12	bleach
	13	oven cleaner
	14	drain cleaner

There is a special type of paper called **litmus paper** which can be used to indicate the acidity and alkalinity of solutions. Red litmus paper stays red in acids and neutral solutions but turns blue in alkalis. Blue litmus paper stays blue in alkaline or neutral solutions but turns red in acids.

If you boil up some red cabbage and save the purple water that is left in the pan, you can use this as your own indicator solution. The cabbage water stays purple when mixed with neutral substances but will go redder when mixed with acids and greeny yellow when mixed with alkalis.

PROTECTIVE JACKET REQUIRED: CHEMICAL REACTIONS

The term 'chemical reaction' conjures up images of a mad scientist's laboratory – full of strange smoking liquids, mucilaginous test tubes and blackened cauldrons – but in fact these reactions take place all around us every day and can be as simple as frying an egg.

When certain elements and compounds are combined with other elements and compounds entirely new substances can be produced. This interaction is called a chemical reaction. The substances you start with are called **reactants** and the substances that are created are called **products**. A substance that helps a chemical reaction occur faster without undergoing any change itself is called a **catalyst**. Chemical reactions are normally permanent. There are different types of chemical reaction:

- An **exothermic reaction** gives out heat.
- An **endothermic reaction** causes a drop in temperature or requires a heat source to occur.
- **Thermal decomposition** uses heat to cause compounds to break down.
- **Electrolysis** is a reaction in which compounds are broken down with the use of electricity.
- **Neutralisation** is when an acid and base react to make a salt or neutral solution.
- **Oxidation** is when a substance gains oxygen.

- **Reduction** is when a substance loses oxygen.
- **Displacement** is when a more reactive element displaces or pushes out a less reactive element from its compound.

Rust is formed by oxidation that occurs when iron, oxygen and water are in contact for a long period of time. When your car rusts pitifully in the garage because you have become environmentally conscious and started to cycle everywhere, the oxygen atoms and water in the air combine with the iron atoms in your car and change into hydrated iron oxide, which is a fancy name for rust.

BIOLOGY

'Our body is a machine for living. It is organised for that, it is its
nature. Let life go on in it unhindered and let it defend itself, it will
do more than if you paralyse it by encumbering it with remedies'
LEO TOLSTOY (1828–1910)

PHILANDERING FLORA:
THE ANATOMY OF A FLOWER

When you skip through fields of poppies, pluck golden apples from trees
and blow dandelion clocks, you are not simply gallivanting through
nature's riches, but actually fulfilling the devious designs of the plants
that surround you and assisting them in their tireless pursuit of spreading their seed.

Some plants have just one sex but to the right you will see an
illustration of a flower which has both male and female parts. The male
part, the **stamen**, produces pollen, which is the plant equivalent of
sperm. This either self-fertilises the same plant by coming into contact
with its female part, the **stigma**, or cross-fertilises a different plant of the
same species by being carried by insects, the wind or your turn-ups to
another plant's stigma. This is called **pollination**.

Petals are often brightly coloured in order to attract insects so that they
are lured into the plant and covered in pollen which they carry to other
plants. The pollen is transferred from the stigma to the ovary where it
fertilises the plant's egg. Once the plant is fertilised the ovary begins to
develop into a fruit containing seeds. The petals fall off the flower and
the fruit grows into a juicy orange, plum, tomato, rosehip or suchlike.

When the fruit is ripe it disperses the seeds so that they fall to the ground, **germinate** and begin to grow new plants. Seeds are dispersed in many ingenious ways – sometimes the fruit bursts, sometimes the seeds get stuck to our clothes or to animals' fur, sometimes they are blown away by the wind, and sometimes the fruit is eaten by birds or animals and the seeds are excreted.

Once the seed has reached the ground, if the supply of heat, moisture and nutrients are adequate, then it will germinate. The plant embryo held inside the seed will start to grow and burst out of the seed, creating roots and stems that will one day become a new adult plant and begin the process again.

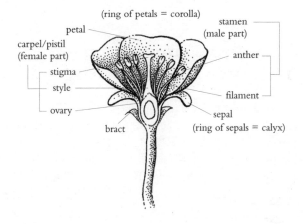

A FANTASTIC FASCINATING FLOWER FACT

The face of a daisy is not just one flower but a cluster of tiny flowers, or florets – the yellow florets are **disc florets** and the white florets are **ray florets**.

LEAVES

Leaves are the means by which plants nourish themselves through the process of **photosynthesis**. Photosynthesis requires light, so leaves are arranged on the plant's stem in order to catch the most light possible.

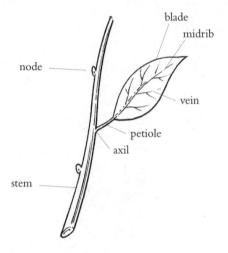

Looking at a plant's leaves is one of the most useful ways of identifying it, as different species have different shapes and arrangements of leaves. It is often more helpful to look at a plant's humble, dowdy leaves rather than its gaudy, showgirl flowers.

COMMON LEAF SHAPES

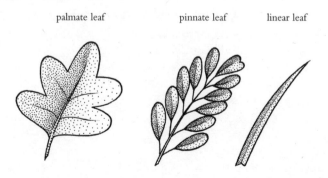

palmate leaf   pinnate leaf   linear leaf

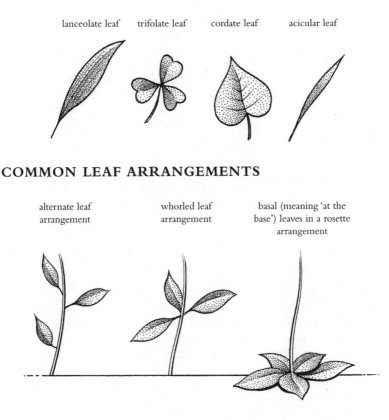

lanceolate leaf   trifolate leaf   cordate leaf   acicular leaf

COMMON LEAF ARRANGEMENTS

alternate leaf   whorled leaf   basal (meaning 'at the
arrangement   arrangement   base') leaves in a rosette
                                              arrangement

ONES AND TWOS:
MONOCOTYLEDONS AND DICOTYLEDONS

Flowering plants (**angiosperms**) are divided into two groups called **monocotyledons** and **dicotyledons**. Cotyledon means 'seed leaf' and most monocotyledons have one seed leaf when the plant is an embryo and . . . wait for it . . . dicotyledons have two seed leaves. There are other distinguishing characteristics that help you to differentiate a mono-cotyledon from a dicotyledon. Monocotyledons typically have parallel leaf veins, are primarily herbaceous and have flower parts arranged in sets of three, whereas dicotyledons typically have leaf veins in netted arrangements, are primarily woody and have flower parts arranged in sets of four or five. Grasses, lilies and irises are monocotyledons, and magnolias, roses and geraniums are dicotyledons.

So if someone sends you lilies, your thank-you note should read 'In utmost gratitude for the marvellous monocotyledons.' If, more predictably, you should receive roses you should respond: 'Thank you for the delightful dicotyledons.'

THERE'S NO BUSINESS LIKE PHOTOSYNTHESIS

Photosynthesis is the process by which plants change energy from light into glucose to feed themselves. Plants, and photosynthesis, are key elements of life on Earth. This is so important, we'll say it again: **Plants, and photosynthesis, are key elements of life on Earth**. Plants provide the basic food that keeps all living things alive. The process of photosynthesis, happily for us O_2-loving creatures, also produces oxygen as a by-product. Without photosynthesis there would be no oxygen and no food and our world would be a dismal, deathly desert.

Photosynthesis occurs in the leaves of green plants when carbon dioxide in the air and water from the soil are changed by the plant's **chlorophyll** as well as light energy from the sun into glucose and oxygen. Chlorophyll is the extraordinary green chemical inside leaves' cells, which interacts with light to rearrange the molecules of carbon dioxide and water absorbed by the plant into glucose and oxygen molecules. Plants, like all living things, also respire, taking in oxygen and giving out carbon dioxide, but they use less oxygen than they produce and use more carbon dioxide than they produce so in the end plants contribute oxygen to the atmosphere.

The glucose produced by photosynthesis is transported around the plant via its circulatory system to help it grow. This system is made up of tubes called **phloem**, which are living permeable cells which transport the glucose, and **xylem**, which are tubes made of dead and impermeable cells which transport water and minerals from the roots up the plant to help photosynthesis.

WHAT IS OSMOSIS?

The word osmosis comes from the Greek word '*osmos*' meaning to push. If you have two solutions separated by a semipermeable membrane which contain different concentrations of water molecules, then water molecules will naturally move through the membrane from the higher concentration to the lower: this is osmosis. In plants, osmosis is crucial for the transfer of water from the soil into the plants' root cells, whence it can be carried around the plant to contribute to photosynthesis. This happens because the water in the soil has a higher concentration of water molecules than the water in the root cells (which is mixed with salts, sugars and other chemicals), so the water molecules from the soil move into the root cells. The transfer of water through the plants' cells also helps to keep the plant upright as its cells fill with water and become **turgid**. Plant cells without enough water are referred to as **flaccid**.

REVOLUTIONARY EVOLUTION: CHARLES DARWIN (1809–82)

Charles Robert Darwin was the British naturalist who developed the theories of **evolution** and **natural selection** that explain how we got where we are today. He hypothesised that all life on Earth evolved over millions of years from a few common ancestors.

When he was twenty-two years old, Darwin wanted to be a naturalist aboard the HMS *Beagle* on a British science expedition around the world. Like many young people he had to argue with his father about going travelling, as Darwin Sr was much set on the idea of Charles settling down as a doctor or vicar rather than gadding about all over the place. Eventually, however, he relented and Charles was given permission to take the assignment, which lasted five years. After overcoming strength-sapping seasickness, he enthusiastically began collecting and cataloguing thousands of specimens of the various plants and animals he discovered at each of the places the ship visited, including Brazil, Argentina, Tierra del Fuego, Chile, the Galapagos Islands, Tahiti, New Zealand, Australia and South Africa.

In South America, Darwin found fossils of extinct animals that were similar to modern species. On the Galapagos Islands in the Pacific Ocean, he noticed many variations among plants and animals of the same general type as those on mainland South America. Upon his return to London, Darwin conducted thorough research of his notes and specimens. Out of this study grew several related theories:

- Evolution did occur. This means that species developed and changed form from earlier descendants.
- Evolutionary change was gradual, requiring thousands to millions of years.
- The primary mechanism for evolution was a process called **natural selection**, which is popularly known as the theory of 'survival of the fittest'. Natural selection is the term for the process by which individuals within certain species have traits that help them flourish in their particular environments leading to them surviving longer than their rivals, therefore producing more offspring endowed with these favourable traits.
- The millions of species alive today arose from a single original life form through a branching process called **speciation**.

Darwin set forth these theories in his *On the Origin of Species* (1859), which sold out on the first day of publication and went on to become a huge best-seller. It was denounced by the Church as sacrilegious, as it claimed that humans were descended from animals rather than created by God in His own image. However, eventually Darwin's ideas became mainstream. After publication of *On the Origin of Species*, Darwin continued to write on botany, geology and zoology until his death in 1882. He is buried in Westminster Abbey.

WHO DO YOU THINK YOU ARE?: THE CLASSIFICATION OF LIVING THINGS

When surveying the multicoloured, multi-limbed, multi-eyed multitude of flora and fauna in our world, it is soothing to know that animals and plants can be neatly filed into different categories which group them together with other similar creatures.

The Swedish biologist Carolus Linnaeus (1707–78) was the first to formalise the rules for categorising living things. Every living creature now has a **kingdom**, a **phylum** (named from the ancient Greek word for 'tribe'), a **class**, an **order**, a **family**, a **genus** and a **species**. Yes, even you have a kingdom of your own!

Human beings are part of the Animal kingdom, and our phylum is Chordata (our subphylum is Vertebrata which puts us alongside other **vertebrates** – animals with a backbone). Our class is Mammalia, which puts us in a club with all the other mammals. Our order is Primate, our family is Hominidae, our genus is *Homo* and our species name is *Homo sapiens*. We are the only surviving species of the *Homo* genus. The genus *canis*, in contrast, includes different species of dogs, wolves, coyotes and jackals.

The easiest way to remember the different elements of biological taxonomy is to use the following mnemonic: **K**ing **P**hilip **C**uts **O**pen **F**ive **G**reen **S**nakes

An octopus's family tree would read as follows:

> Kingdom: animal
> Phylum: mollusc
> Class: Cephalopod
> Order: Octopoda

There are many different families, geni and species of octopuses. Our favourite is the gorgeous greater blue-ringed octopus. His family is Octopodidae, his genus is *Hapalochlaena* and his species name is *lunulata*. He lives in Australia and is only tiny but he's a clever little chap and very, very poisonous.

HOW DO BIRDS FLY?

When the sparrow in your garden flits from tree to tree, or the vultures circle overhead as you gasp for water in the Sahara, they are not simply borne aloft by fortuitous aeolian gusts but are using sophisticated aerodynamics to achieve flight.

The bones and feathers of flying birds are light and strong and the feathers are arranged on the wings in the perfect shape to enable flight. The bird flaps its wings to create thrust for take-off. It is driven forward and upward and this begins the flow of air over the wings. The curved shape of the wing provides a surface area on the top of the wings that is larger than that of the bottom. This means that when air hits the front of the wing it has to travel faster over the top of the wing than the air below. This creates low pressure above the wing and high pressure below the wing resulting in lift. Lift and forward propulsion, with steering from the tail feathers, allow controllable flight.

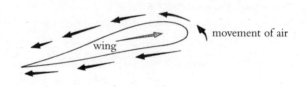

A cross-section of a bird's wing

Diagram of a bird's wing

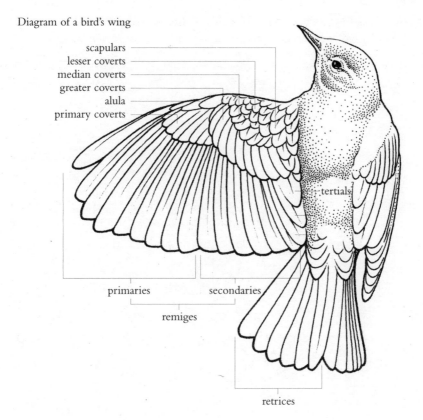

scapulars
lesser coverts
median coverts
greater coverts
alula
primary coverts

tertials

primaries   secondaries

remiges

retrices

DISSECTION OF A FROG

Take a deep breath – it's now time to look at the intimate workings of *Rana temporaria*. Although it is unlikely that you will ever be called upon to carry out this kind of fatal inspection in the wild, these poor muculent martyrs often find themselves crucified on grimy, biro-etched workbenches being pored over by snotty fifth-formers in the interests of greater anatomical knowledge. Only medical students ever get to study the insides of human beings, so the dissection of frogs is actually a privileged insight into the way that skeletons, blood systems, nerves and digestive systems fit together to provide the miraculous means for life.

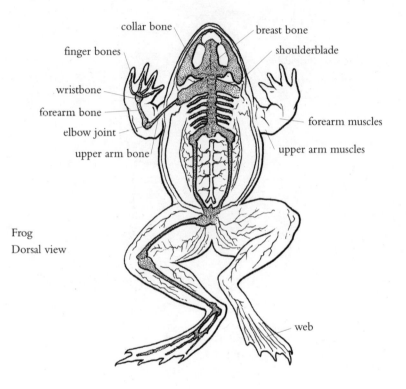

Frog
Dorsal view

DEM BONES: THE HUMAN SKELETON

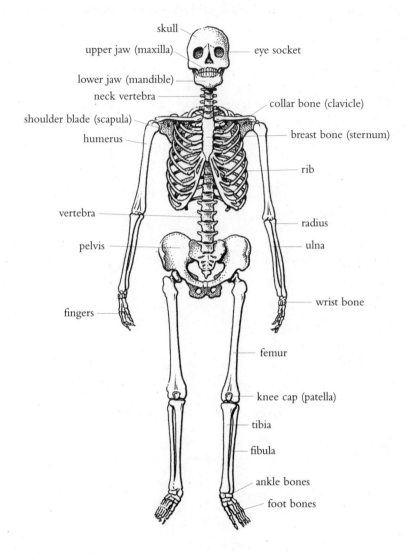

skull

upper jaw (maxilla)

eye socket

lower jaw (mandible)

neck vertebra

collar bone (clavicle)

shoulder blade (scapula)

humerus

breast bone (sternum)

rib

vertebra

radius

pelvis

ulna

wrist bone

fingers

femur

knee cap (patella)

tibia

fibula

ankle bones

foot bones

Humans have an internal skeleton (**endoskeleton**) that supports and protects the organs and tissue. Some animals, such as insects, have exterior skeletons (**exoskeletons**) rather than an internal structure. Even more exotically, some creatures, such as jellyfish, starfish and worms, have a skeleton made of a fluid-filled cavity known as a **hydrostatic skeleton**.

The human skeleton is made up of bones which in turn are mainly made of a protein called **collagen** and the mineral **calcium phosphate**. The outside of a bone is rigid and hard, but the inside is filled with soft marrow which produces blood cells. Bones fit together at joints where they are articulated in arrangements such as hinges or ball-and-socket joints to allow for movement.

ORGANISING ORGANS

Organs are the groups of tissues that carry out particular functions to keep your body in perfect working order.

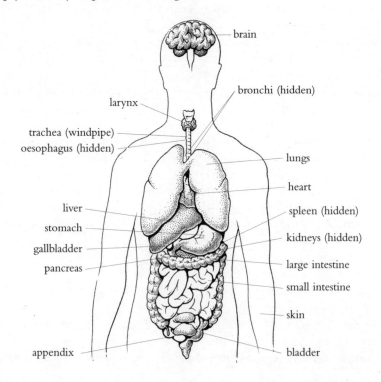

brain

bronchi (hidden)

larynx

trachea (windpipe)

oesophagus (hidden)

lungs

heart

liver

spleen (hidden)

stomach

kidneys (hidden)

gallbladder

pancreas

large intestine

small intestine

skin

appendix

bladder

Brain: This is the organ that controls the mind and body.

Larynx: This is the voice box. It contains the vocal cords which allow you to sing in the shower and shout at your children. It also protects the airway.

Bronchi: These are the tubes that connect the nose and mouth to the lungs via the windpipe, allowing you to breathe.

Lungs: We each have two lungs and they are responsible for oxygen transfer from the air to the blood.

Heart: The heart is the organ that pumps blood around the body.

Liver: The liver is responsible for regulating the toxic materials that all of us take in, particularly during a night on the town.

Gall bladder: This little fellow stores the yellowy-green bile made by the liver, which is used to help digest food.

Spleen: This organ is part of the immune system and is involved in the destruction of old red blood cells.

Stomach: This is where your supper ends up, after you've greedily stuffed it down your oesophagus, and is the start of its journey through the digestive system.

Pancreas: This is a gland which helps digestion and a special part of it, poetically named the **islets of Langerhans**, secretes the hormone insulin which regulates blood sugar.

Small intestine: This is about five metres long and is broken down into three parts: the **duodenum**, the **jejunum** and the **ileum**. It is responsible for absorbing the nutrients from food.

Large intestine: This is approximately one and a half metres long and is responsible for absorbing excess water and carrying the waste products left after all the goodness has been taken from your food.

Kidneys: These two neat organs filter the blood and get rid of excess water and waste that travels to the bladder whence it is excreted as urine.

Appendix: Nobody knows what this little cul-de-sac in our gut is for; biologists think it may be a relic from our previous ancestors who ate much tougher, more fibrous food than us.

Genitals: These are your reproductive organs.

Skin: Skin covers and protects all of the body. It is the largest organ you have.

THE LONELY HUNTER: HOW THE HEART WORKS

Nobody is foolish enough to believe that if someone wins, breaks or steals your heart, the organ beating in your breast is in any way affected. Although the heart has historically been romantically linked with the experience of falling in love, most of the physical symptoms of this temporary insanity actually take place in other parts of your body (e.g. dilation of pupils, butterflies in your gut, sweaty palms, the urge to yawn and drape your arm stealthily over your beloved's shoulder in the cinema . . .). However, it is true that the heart is essential for love, in that it is essential to our survival. And although its true form doesn't often grace valentine cards, it is actually far more intricate and beautiful than its frivolous caricature.

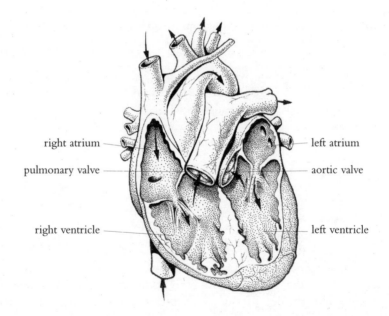

right atrium

pulmonary valve

right ventricle

left atrium

aortic valve

left ventricle

The heart is an organ made of muscle that is responsible for pumping blood through the arboreal web of your blood system by repeated, rhythmic contractions. Blood takes oxygen and food to all your organs and limbs enabling them to function. The heart is about the size of a man's fist and is normally on the left side of your chest, unless you are dextracardial, in which case it is on the right. It is divided into four chambers: the right side receives the blood that has travelled round the body, and needs to collect more oxygen from the lungs and get rid of the carbon dioxide it has taken on from the tissues; the left side takes the blood from the lungs and pumps it round the body.

Blood is bright red when it is full of oxygen and bluish when it has fed that oxygen to your organs and limbs. This is why your veins are blue. **Haemoglobin** is the protein present in red blood cells that carries oxygen and causes these colour changes.

The heart fills and allows the blood to flow into its chambers and then pumps it out – this is what causes the heartbeat and the pulse. When you exert yourself running for the bus, or get yourself in a state about falling house prices, your heart beats faster in order to supply your muscles and organs with more oxygen to help them do their jobs.

The healthy average resting heart rate is around 70 beats per minute. Amazingly, in his prime, tennis star Björn Borg was reputed to have a resting heart rate of 35 beats per minute.

THE BLOOD SYSTEM

Some animals, such as insects and invertebrates, have circulatory systems that are **open**, where the blood flows freely around the organs; earthworms don't even have hearts. Human beings and other mammals have **closed circulatory systems** that comprise a network of branching tubes called blood vessels. There are different types of blood vessels: **arteries** carry the oxygen-filled blood from the heart and branch repeatedly into smaller arteries called **arterioles**; these in turn branch into a network of tiny **capillaries** which run between the cells of the tissues and close to the organs which the blood feeds; capillaries join together to form **veins** that carry the blood back to the heart.

Blood circulation carries out various functions: the blood picks up oxygen in the lungs and carries waste carbon dioxide back to the lungs;

it carries excess water and waste to the kidneys for removal; it picks up nutrients absorbed by the digestive tract and distributes energy around the body; and it transports hormones from the endocrine glands to where they are needed.

It was once thought that the lungs were responsible for the circulation of the blood, but a bright spark called William Harvey (1578–1657), court physician to Queen Elizabeth I, discovered that the heart was responsible for pumping blood around a closed circuit.

BLOOD

Human blood is a red fluid tissue made up of cells floating in a liquid called **plasma**. Plasma makes up about 54 per cent of our blood volume and, as well as blood cells, contains nutrients from food, hormones and waste products from the organs. **Corpuscles** are categorised as red blood cells (**erythrocytes**), white blood cells (**leucocytes**) and platelets (**thrombocytes**).

- The red blood cells are the delivery men of the body; they carry the oxygen and carbon dioxide to and from the tissues.
- The white blood cells are the body's army; they protect the body from infection and disease. They are divided into different groups which deal with disease cells in different ways. Some types of white blood cell attack diseases by ingesting the dangerous cells in a marvellously gruesome-sounding process called **phagocytosis**. Another group, called **lymphocytes**, sends out antibodies to destroy hostile cells. **Antibodies** are like Special Ops forces. They are proteins that recognise certain disease cells and kill only those specific cells. Lymphocytes also include the chillingly named **natural killer cells** which mercy-kill the body's own infected or damaged cells.
- **Platelets** are only found in the blood of mammals. They are responsible for causing the blood to **coagulate** (clot) if blood vessels are damaged. Babies have a low number of platelets until they are three months old, which is one good reason to keep them wrapped up safely rather than take them rock climbing.

LYMPH

Unlike its showy scarlet sister, lymph is a pale and colourless fluid. It carries certain types of white blood cells and is a key part of the immune system. Antigens travel from the blood to the lymph nodes (also called the lymph glands) via the lymphatic system, where they are destroyed by defensive white blood cells – this vigorous clean-up activity is the reason why the lymph nodes in your neck, armpits and groin sometimes swell up when you have an infection. Lymph is also responsible for transferring nutrients and fluids from the organs to the blood. Unlike the heart-pumped blood circuit, the network of lymph channels makes up an open circulatory system which allows lymph to flow freely around the organs. Lymph is encouraged round the body by the movement of muscles.

THE SEAT OF WISDOM: THE BRAIN

Ah, our blessed grey matter, the source of all our joy, anxiety and curious habits. The human brain is a marvel, and weighs in at an easily portable average of 1.5kg. The three major parts of the brain are: the **cerebrum**, the **brainstem** and the **cerebellum**.

• The cerebrum is the largest part of the brain and is responsible for the senses, speech, thought, memory and other high-level functions. Imagine how dull we'd be without it. Different parts of the cerebrum are responsible for different jobs, which is why when brain injuries occur they can cause strangely specific effects – for example, there is a rare condition called foreign accent syndrome, which was first identified during World War II, when a Norwegian woman, hit by shrapnel, developed a strong German accent, making her very unpopular.

The cerebrum is divided into left and right hemispheres separated by the **longitudinal fissure**. Each hemisphere controls the movement of the opposite side of the body. Every individual has one

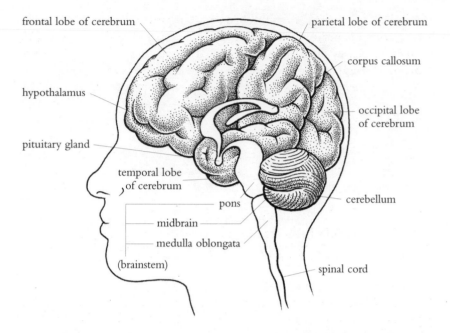

frontal lobe of cerebrum

parietal lobe of cerebrum

corpus callosum

hypothalamus

occipital lobe
of cerebrum

pituitary gland

temporal lobe
of cerebrum

pons

cerebellum

midbrain

medulla oblongata

(brainstem)

spinal cord

hemisphere that is dominant and which dictates whether you are right- or left-handed. Your mathematical, analytical and linguistic abilities are usually based in one hemisphere and your spatial awareness, emotions and how easily you can recognise faces are based in the other.

- The brainstem connects the cerebellum with the spinal cord through which the brain controls the nervous system that runs through the body. It consists of the rather ponderous-sounding **pons**, the **midbrain** and the **medulla oblongata**. The brainstem controls body functions which are automatic and involuntary such as digestion, blood pressure and breathing. When your brainstem stops working you are officially dead – doctors writing out death certificates check for signs of any activity in the brainstem before signing their names.

- The cerebellum is at the back of the skull (cranium) and is responsible for muscular activity.

Another important part of the brain is the **hypothalamus** which controls body temperature, sleep, hunger and thirst. So the next time you're dying for a cup of tea or a refreshing gin and tonic blame it on your hypothalamus.

Below the hypothalamus is the **pituitary gland** which is part of the **endocrine** system. The pituitary gland secretes hormones responsible for growth and water balance and also regulates most of the rest of the endocrine system.

I WANNA HOLD YOUR GLAND: THE ENDOCRINE SYSTEM

The endocrine system is made up of glands that secrete hormones into the bloodstream which contribute to, and stimulate, a huge array of processes such as growth, saliva and sweat production, fertility and digestion. One of the most common hormones vividly experienced by humans is adrenalin, produced by the adrenal glands just above the kidneys. This hormone is always present in the bloodstream but in times of stress or trauma greater quantities are secreted as adrenalin acts to prepare the body for physical exertion: this is also known as the 'fight or flight' response.

A CYTOLOGICAL CELEBRATION

All plants and animals are made up of tiny building blocks called cells. The study of cells is known as **cytology**. Some creatures, such as amoebae, are made of only one cell, but humans are made of trillions of cells. The cells in our bodies come in different shapes and sizes and are designed to carry out different tasks: brain cells do different things to blood cells, for example; liver cells have different jobs to gall bladder cells. Lots of cells of the same type together form tissue, and tissues, grouped together, form organs. Plant and animal cells are different (one difference is that plant cells contain chlorophyll) but they both generally have a cell membrane which is filled with a fluid called **cytoplasm** and which contains the **nucleus** of the cell. The nucleus houses the organism's **DNA**. Some organisms, like bacteria, don't have nuclei: these are called **prokaryotes**. Organisms which have cells containing a nucleus are called **eukaryotes**.

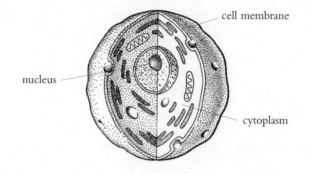

cell membrane

nucleus

cytoplasm

RESPIRATION, RESPIRATION, RESPIRATION

It's slightly exhausting to think of it, but cellular respiration is the constant process that happens in all living organisms where glucose is used to make energy, usually by combining it with oxygen. This energy is stored in a chemical present in all cells called **ATP** (adenosine triphosphate). It is used to fuel all the functions that keep an organism alive and active. So even if you have spent half the day reclining on the sofa staring at the television, you can legitimately claim to have been very busy respiring. Carbon dioxide and water are waste products of respiration. Do not confuse **cellular respiration** with **human respiration**, which is a term that refers to breathing.

SKIN DEEP: HUMAN SKIN

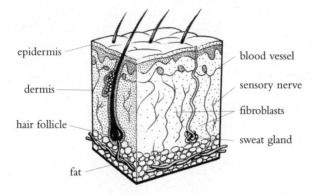

epidermis

dermis

hair follicle

fat

blood vessel

sensory nerve

fibroblasts

sweat gland

Skin is one of the most important organs of the human body – it protects our other organs, regulates our temperature and allows us to touch things and feel them. The average adult has about 2m² of skin (which weighs about 3.2kg).

- Skin is divided into two layers: the outer layer is called the **epidermis**, and is in turn divided into four layers. The outermost layer is called the **stratum corneum** and is made up of dead cells that are continually renewed by the innermost epidermal layer, the **basal cell layer**. These cells are made of **keratin** which is a protein that helps the skin retain moisture. They can also absorb moisture from their surroundings, such as baths and swimming pools, which causes them to swell and expand in relation to the cells below and makes the skin surface wrinkle when immersed in water for long periods. This effect is particularly noticeable on the hands and feet which have a thicker layer of keratin-rich cells because they require more protection than other areas of the body and also don't have the waterproofing provided by the oil-producing sebaceous glands in the hair follicles that cover the rest of our bodies.

- The inner layer is called the **dermis** and this contains the blood vessels, the nerve endings, the hair follicles and the sweat glands that all help the skin do its job.

You should take with a pinch of salt beauty companies' claims that their unguents, elixirs and serums can rebuild the structure of your skin to prevent the effects of ageing. Father Time is a merciless master and no rose-scented lotion will stand in his way. The best you can do for your skin is to keep it clean and hydrated.

SEEING IS BELIEVING: THE HUMAN EYE

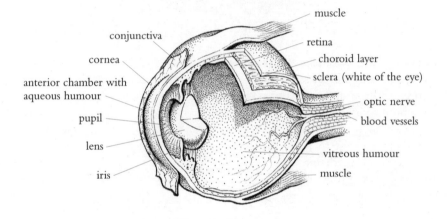

Many people argue that the daedal complexity of the human eye is proof of the existence of God's artistry. Whatever you believe, there's no denying that the eye is a marvel of design.

Cornea: The transparent layer that covers the front of the eye.
Lens: The transparent structure that focuses (through the use of the eye muscles that change its shape) light onto the retina.
Iris: The coloured part of the eye that surrounds the pupil. The iris controls the size of the pupil to let more or less light in depending on the darkness of the surroundings.
Pupil: The hole in the centre of the eye which lets the light through onto the retina.
Retina: The light-sensitive layer of cells on the back of the eyeball

which converts light into electrical impulses that travel to the brain via the optic nerve to create a visual image. The retina is made up of **rod** and **cone cells**. Cone cells are responsible for recognising colour and detail, and rod cells are responsible for vision at low light levels.

Aqueous humour: The fluid in the eye containing the nutrients that nourish the eye.

Vitreous humour: The clear jelly that sits behind the lens.

BIOLOGICAL HERO: ALEXANDER FLEMING AND PENICILLIN

In 1928 the Scottish scientist Alexander Fleming (1881–1955) noticed that some penicillium mould had grown on a culture plate he had prepared containing the staphylococcus bacteria. This bacteria is responsible for diseases including skin and bone infections and some pneumonias. Fleming observed that the intrepid mould had killed the bacteria nearest to it – an observation that led to one of the greatest advances in medicine ever made. Investigation of penicillium's bacteria-killing properties resulted in a usable medicine that was named penicillin: the first antibiotic. It became widely used in the 1940s and saved countless lives during the Second World War. Now there are many different types of antibiotics prescribed to treat a huge array of diseases.

DEFINING DNA

OK, pay attention now – it gets rather complicated here. Francis Crick and James D. Watson are the scientists famous for publishing the first description of the structure of DNA in 1953, for which they won the Nobel Prize.

DNA (deoxyribonucleic acid) is immensely important because it is the body's genetic instruction manual. It is present in the cells of nearly all living things. In humans DNA is held in the 46 chromosomes which are found in the nuclei of cells. The complete DNA sequence of an organism is called its **genome**.

The DNA molecule is shaped like a spiral staircase in what is known as a double-helix formation. If you took all of the DNA in all of your cells and laid it out end to end, it would stretch to the moon and back about 130,000 times. The DNA molecule is made up of smaller molecules called **nucleotides** which form the two sides of the staircase. Nucleotides are made of sugar, phosphate and the four nitrogenous bases: adenine, thymine, guanine and cytosine. These bases connect together in pairs to form the steps of the staircase, but they are very picky: adenine will only connect with thymine and guanine is always paired with cytosine – this system is called **complementary base pairing**. The combinations of steps in the staircase and the arrangements of each person's DNA are unique, which is why DNA fingerprinting can be used in forensic science to identify the culprits of crimes.

DNA is divided into functional sections called **genes**. Humans have between 20,000 and 30,000 genes. Genes are codes for producing particular types of protein, through a process called **protein synthesis**. Much of our bodies is made up of protein, so genes control the arrangement and growth of cells in our bodies – they are responsible for your hair colour, your body shape and many other things. Your DNA is made up of sections from half your father's and half your mother's DNA.

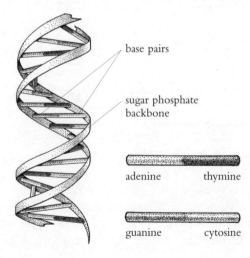

base pairs

sugar phosphate
backbone

adenine   thymine

guanine   cytosine

Amazingly, as well as providing information to produce specific proteins, DNA also replicates itself in order to pass the instructions for protein synthesis on to new cells. Just before a cell divides, catalystic proteins (**enzymes**) break the base pairs (the steps of the staircase) so that the double helix is pulled apart into two separate strands. The bases on the separate strands attract new nucleotides that have been formed by the cell to build new double helices. Complementary base pairing ensures that these new helices are identical to the previous ones. This process enables cells to duplicate their DNA to create new cells.

The only cells we have that don't contain DNA are red blood cells. They find it more useful to carry as much oxygen-storing haemoglobin as possible rather than giving space to a nucleus.

PROACTIVE PROTEINS

Proteins are strings of amino acids made of carbon, oxygen, hydrogen and nitrogen. They link together to take on specific jobs. They make enzymes which control chemical reactions in cells and they also tell cells which bits of DNA to use to decide their specialist function.

CHARISMATIC CHROMOSOMES

To save space, the DNA strands in our cells are wound up together with proteins to form minute structures called chromosomes. Each chromosome stores a different set of genes. Each cell in our bodies has the same set of chromosomes, containing all the genetic orders for all the different functions and facets of our bodies. Humans have 23 pairs of chromosomes – 46 chromosomes in total – in each cell. This 46 is known as the **diploid number** of chromosomes for the human species. African elephants have a diploid number of 56 (they have 28 pairs of chromosomes) and dogs have a diploid number of 78 (they have 39 pairs), but don't get envious – just because the diploid number is higher doesn't mean that they are better than you. Have you ever seen an elephant or a dog get in a fight about the finer details of the offside rule or open five bottles of wine in a single evening? No, we truly are the superior species.

Through the process of sexual reproduction we each inherit 23 chromosomes from our mother and 23 chromosomes from our father. Eggs and
sperm are special cells called **gametes** that have a **haploid number**
of chromosomes – 23 each – that is, half the total number needed to
create a person. When they join together in fertilisation they make up
the full 46. Each of the 23 chromosomes inherited from one parent is
paired with the chromosome that carries the genes that control the same
characteristics from the other parent.

Twenty-two of the pairs of chromosomes are very similar and are called
autosomes. The remaining pair are called **sex chromosomes** and
control the gender of a person. Females have two X chromosomes in
their 23rd pair and males have one X and one Y chromosome. All eggs
carry a female chromosome (known as an X chromosome). Sperm can
carry either the female (X) or male (Y) chromosome from the father's
XY combination. If the egg is fertilised by an X-carrying sperm,
the baby will be a girl. If the egg is fertilised by a Y-carrying sperm, a
bouncing baby boy is on its way.

Problems with the replication of chromosomes during cell division after
fertilisation can lead to genetic disorders. For example, people with
Down's syndrome have one extra chromosome, leading to their diploid
number being 47. This extra chromosome means that the genetic
instructions given by the DNA create different characteristics in people
with Down's syndrome to the majority of people.

SEXUAL EDUCATION:
THE FACTS OF LIFE

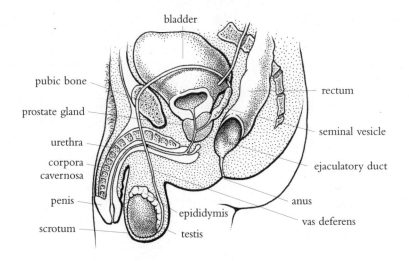

The male reproductive system

No sniggering at the back: there is nothing funny about the miracle of life. Well, perhaps occasionally, but your foibles are your own concern and you don't need to share them with the rest of the class.

After the fireworks, when the male's sperm meets the female's egg in the Fallopian tube, the sperm burrows into the egg until the two nuclei join together and fertilisation occurs. The fertilised egg then travels down the tube to the womb where it makes itself comfortable in the uterine wall and begins to grow.

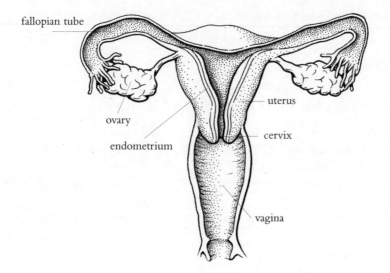

fallopian tube

uterus

ovary

cervix

endometrium

vagina

The female reproductive system

As we have learned, eggs and sperm are special cells known as gametes which carry only half the genetic material necessary to create a human (23 single chromosomes). When they join together in fertilisation, they create a new cell containing 23 pairs of chromosomes. This cell, made up of the two gametes, is known as a **zygote**. When the zygote starts to divide into more cells, through the process of **mitosis**, it is called an **embryo**. Occasionally a zygote will divide in half to make two separate embryos with the same DNA. These will become identical twins (also known as **monozygotic twins**). Fraternal twins (**dizygotic twins**) occur when two separate eggs are fertilised at the same time.

DIVIDE AND RULE: CELL DIVISION

There are two very different ways that cells replicate themselves: mitosis and meiosis.

Mitosis: is cell division which produces daughter cells – cells that have the same number and kind of chromosomes as the parent cell. Mitosis is the process of cell division used in growth and repair. Your hair grows through mitosis.

Meiosis: is cell division that produces egg and sperm cells. These cells have to have half the number of chromosomes of the parent cell as they will join together at fertilisation to produce a zygote with the requisite 46 chromosomes.

OL' BLUE EYES: INHERITING EYE COLOUR

In a zygote, each of the 23 chromosomes inherited from the mother is paired with the chromosome that carries the genes that control the same characteristics from the father. This means that the zygote ends up with two genes that control eye colour – one from the father and one from the mother. Different varieties of the same gene are called **alleles**. **Dominant alleles** prevail over **recessive alleles**.

If your mother has brown eyes and your father has blue eyes you are more likely to have brown than blue eyes because the allele for brown eyes is dominant and the allele for blue eyes is recessive.

Homozygous alleles are two alleles of the same type inherited by the zygote, i.e. blue-eye allele from the father and blue-eye allele from the mother. In this case, even though the blue-eye allele is recessive because both alleles in the zygote are blue-eye the child will have blue eyes.

Heterozygous alleles are two alleles with different information inherited by the zygote i.e. brown-eye allele from the mother and blue-eye allele from the father. In this situation the child will have brown eyes because the brown-eye allele is dominant.

If this heterozygous brown-eyed child grows up and has children then, even though they show brown eyes, they could pass on their blue-eyed allele to their children. If their reproductive partner also passes on a blue-eye allele, even if they are also heterozygous and have brown eyes, then their child will have blue eyes, and there's no need to go pointing the finger at the milkman.

∽ SCIENCE ∽
TEST PAPER

1. **Which of these diagrams correctly represents the organisation of an atom?**

a)

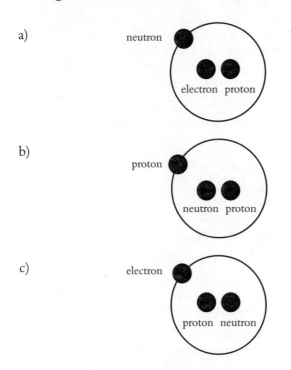

b)

c)

2. **If you are given a bar of gold with a mass of 50g and a volume of 2.59cm³, what do you calculate the density of gold to be?**

3. **Which of the following is a state of matter?**

a) fire   c) gas   e) pineapple
b) untidy   d) brisk   f) water

4. A substance that is made up entirely of the same kind of atoms is called what?

a) a solution
b) a molecule
c) a solid
d) an element

5. Which of the following people has not significantly advanced the cause of physics?

a) William Thompson
b) John Bartram
c) Albert Einstein
d) Isaac Newton

6. Which of the following is the smallest?

a) atom
b) quark
c) proton

7. If Coach Calhoun has a mass of 65kg and he is running at an acceleration of 1.25m/s², what is his driving force?

8. Which of the following are elements?

a) water
b) air
c) gold
d) helium
e) wind
f) bicycle

9. Who is the happiest pair?

a) proton and proton
b) proton and neutron

c) north-seeking pole and north-seeking pole
d) electron and neutron
e) electron and electron
f) proton and electron

10. How can you tell what an atom's element is?

11. Identify which types of energy are being used and transferred in the following scenarios:

a) Mr Dadier eats a bowl of spaghetti and goes for a run.
b) A pendulum inside a grandfather clock swings back and forth.
c) A football is kicked towards goal, hits the crossbar and bounces back off.

12. What is terminal velocity?

13. What is entropy?

a) the total thermodynamic heat content of a system
b) the measure of the unavailability of a system's thermal energy for conversion into mechanical work
c) a warehouse for the temporary storage of goods in transit
d) the process of making silage

14. Identify the problem with the following sentence:

'The cold is seeping into my bones because the temperature has dropped to absolute zero.'

15. Why is radiation a different process from convection and conduction?

16. What colour is lymph?

17. **Which of the following is the definition of this chemical hazard sign?**

a) Corrosive: a substance that can destroy living tissues on contact.
b) Explosive: a substance that may explode when heated or which is more sensitive to shocks than dinitrobenzene.
c) Oxidising: a substance that produces a reaction giving off great heat when in contact with other substances.
d) Terrifying: a substance that may cause the chemist's hair to stand on end.

18. **An exothermic reaction is:**

a) a reaction in which compounds are broken down with the use of electricity
b) a reaction that takes place outside the skeleton
c) a reaction that gives out heat

19. **What colour would your red litmus paper go if you put it into a glass of sea water?**

a) blue
b) green
c) red
d) yellow

20. Draw an arrow from each of the body parts below to where they should go in the human skeleton diagram.

tibia   patella
humerus   scapula
pelvis   clavicle
femur   mandible

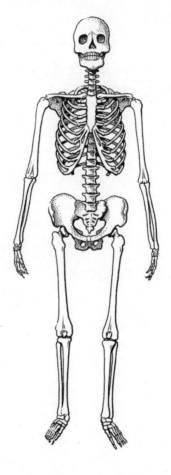

21. What phylum does the octopus belong to?

22. What is 'survival of the fittest'?

a)   a self-help manual for ambitious City workers
b)   a popular name for Darwin's theory of natural selection
c)   a term referring to the process by which organisms that have traits

that help them flourish in their particular environments tend to
survive longer than their rivals and therefore produce more
offspring endowed with these favourable traits
d) the state of the body after strenuous exertion

23. An apple is:

a) an ovary
b) a stamen
c) a pony
d) an anther

24. If Sandy has blue eyes and Danny has brown eyes, they are more likely to have:

a) a brown-eyed baby
b) a blue-eyed baby

25. Where would you find an epididymis?

26. What is air made of?

27. What are bones mainly made of?

28. Where would you find the islets of Langerhans?

∽ BREAK TIME ∽

You may now take a short, well-deserved break. Perhaps have a glass of orange squash and a couple of custard creams to revitalise you for the next lesson, or why not play one of the games below and let off a bit of steam? We expect you back promptly at the bell: pink-cheeked, fired-up and ready to concentrate hard.

GRANDMOTHER'S FOOTSTEPS
Players: 3+

One player stands facing a wall (you can choose who this should be using the tried-and-tested eeny-meany-miney-mo method). According to custom, this player is referred to respectfully as 'It'. Her fellow players form a line four or five metres behind her. At a given signal, they creep up on the player against the wall, freezing whenever she turns round. If the person who is 'It' spots one of the players moving, she can send them back to the start line to begin their creeping progress again. The first player to reach the wall without being spotted has won, and takes their place at the wall for their own go at being 'It'.

CENTURION CAPERS: HOPSCOTCH
Players: 2+

According to some sources, hopscotch was originally a training exercise for Roman soldiers in ancient Britain, so you can muse on the perils of trying to carry out this traditional pastime fully attired in armour.

The first task of the game is to draw the hopscotch grid on the ground. Usually you will be able to find a piece of stone around somewhere that will leave a mark on concrete, otherwise you can scratch a grid in mud with a stick or even arrange individual sticks to create the requisite pattern. Whatever you use, you will need a stone or some other object to use as a marker.

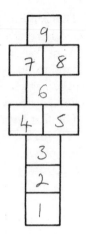

The first player throws the marker into the first square. If he misses the first square, or the stone lands on a line, he misses a turn. If the marker lands successfully in the first square he can hop through the board and back again. It is important that he lands on squares 4/5 and 7/8 with both feet, and that the others are hopped. If he lands on a line or hops the squares in the wrong order, his turn ends in dismal failure. After one successful turn, the marker may then be thrown into the second square and the process repeated. The winner is the first person to successfully complete the course.

PAPER, SCISSORS, STONE
Players: 2

Paper, Scissors, Stone is a very useful and frighteningly addictive game. You can employ it to decide who has to go and pick the kids up from school, who has to do the washing-up, who gets the last chocolate in the box and myriad other tough life decisions. It can even be used just to decide who is the better person.

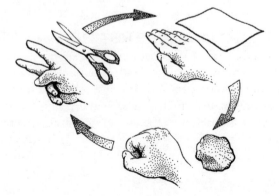

The game is played between two competitors who stand facing one another with their hands behind their backs. To the beat of three they chant 'Paper! Scissors! Stone!' and on the third beat they display their hand to the opposition in the shape of either a pair of scissors, a piece of paper, or a stone. Paper beats stone (as it can wrap it up), stone beats scissors (as it can blunt them), and scissors beat paper (as they can cut it). The first hand gladiator to win three games is the victor.

BRITISH BULLDOG

Players: as many as possible (you may coerce all junior members of staff in the office to join in if you find you're running low on volunteers).

British bulldog is part of the British Commonwealth's glorious heritage. Despite being banned in many schools – it's a slightly violent game to be sure – it remains a source of excitement impossible to capture by almost any other known legal activity. It should be played in a large hall or, even better, in a field or empty car park. To begin you need to mark out two safety havens –

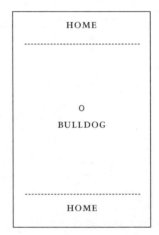

called 'home' – on either side of the playing area near the ends. You can use cardigans or other items of clothing to make these areas clear.

One player is picked to be the first bulldog – it is most satisfying if an aggressive and socially dysfunctional member of the group is elected to this position. All the other players stand in one of the home areas. The game begins with players attempting to run from one home to the other without being caught. It is important to note that once you have left a home you cannot go back to the same one but must try your chances in no-man's-land. The bulldog must try to catch the players and hang on to them long enough to shout, 'British bulldog 1 2 3!'. If the bulldog is successful then the player who has been caught becomes a bulldog too. The other players continue to run back and forth between the two home sides until all but one of them have been caught. The last free player is the winner.

You can also play this game in swimming pools, but it should be referred to as 'sharks' rather than British bulldog in this context and a trained life-guard must be present.

A PERFECTLY SIMPLE PAPER PLANE

1. Take a piece of plain A4 paper and fold it in half lengthways firmly.
2. Unfold the paper and fold the two top corners in to meet the centre fold. Now fold the two edges of that fold in again to the centre fold.

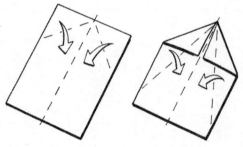

3. Turn the plane over and fold each edge back on itself in what is known in the origami community as a 'mountain fold', again bringing the edge to the centre fold.

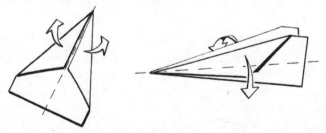

4. Turn the plane over and secure the tip with a paper clip. You may want to experiment with the positioning of this paper clip, as the flight path of your cloud-buster will vary depending on how far down the nose you place it.

5. Launch your plane with a swift decisive throw, aiming the nose in the direction you want it to fly – be that towards the back of an unsuspecting co-worker's head or simply up, up, and away into the big blue sky.

DOUBLE DUTCH
Players: 3+

Double Dutch is a tricky but very impressive skipping game involving two ropes which are spun by two people simultaneously, a bit like an egg beater. A third person then jumps deftly in between the ropes and, avoiding getting tangled, does tricks or gymnastics along to chanted songs such as the exhilarating verse below:

> Jack be nimble, Jack be quick
> Jack jump over the candlestick.
> Mumble, kick,
> Sizzler, split,
> Pop-ups 10 to 1 – Hit it. 10, 9, 8, 7, 6, 5, 4, 3, 2, 1!

At the point where the players chant 'Jack jump over', the jumper jumps up as high as they can and both feet leave the ground.

At 'Mumble', the jumper keeps both feet together and executes little low hops.

At 'Kick', the jumper kicks his or her foot in and out.

At 'Sizzler', they cross and uncross their feet – a move known in double Dutch circles as 'sizzling'.

At 'Split', they jump with their legs as wide apart as possible.

And at 'Pop' the jumper jumps as high as possible with both feet leaving the ground.

KISS CHASE
Players: 3+

Ah, kiss chase. Kiss chase is a form of tag, in which one player is chosen as 'It' and must chase the other players to try to tag them. The player they touch becomes 'It' and the former 'It' joins her fellow classmates in running away from the new 'It'. In kiss chase this very simple concept is complicated by the fact that 'It' must kiss the player they want to tag.

Kiss chase is a complicated game that can reveal social and emotional truths, some people never get tagged, and others may get tagged a little too often. The game ends when the bell is rung to indicate the end of break time.

⚬ 6 ⚬

RELIGIOUS EDUCATION

'**Religion** *n*. the belief in a superhuman controlling power, esp. in a
personal God or gods entitled to obedience and worship'
Oxford Concise English Dictionary

'My country is the world, and my religion is to do good'
THOMAS PAINE (1737–1809), *The Rights of Man*

From the Crusades to the conquistadors, from the French Wars of
Religion to Northern Ireland and the terrorist attacks taking place with
horrific regularity in the Middle East today, we are constantly reminded
that throughout history religion has played a part in the majority of
the world's conflicts, so it is sometimes hard to appreciate just how
much the world's major religions have in common. In addition, much
mumbo-jumbo is spouted about religion; from what the immaculate
conception really is, to the true meaning of 'jihad', and it can be
difficult to work out what to think about what other people are said to
believe.

Over the last century Britain has become a predominantly secular
country, and many of its citizens would consider themselves atheists
(people who don't believe in God), agnostics (people who believe that
no one can ever know whether God exists or not) or Jedis (a fictional
warrior group from the *Star Wars* films that a surprising number of
people state as their religion on census forms). However, there are also
many people who are seriously committed to a particular faith, to a
greater or lesser degree, and this can influence their attitudes, actions
and aspirations in daily life in a variety of ways. In our cosmopolitan
community, it is not merely useful and respectful to have a grasp of the
basic beliefs and rituals of our neighbours, but it is also crucial in these
days of polarised cultures and simultaneous globalisation to have an
understanding of different faiths in order to comprehend international
politics, history, philosophy, art and literature.

Religion is a subject that can ignite strong passions – along with politics it is one of the topics that etiquette guides recommend guests avoid at formal dinner parties. Throughout history people's faiths have been the cause of both amazing achievements and great oppression – from the awe-inspiring splendour of religious architecture and art, to the horror of religious wars and persecution. Today, in its multifarious forms, it can be a cause of both unity and division both in local communities and internationally. Whether you believe in something or nothing, the study of religion investigates the most fundamental questions of human existence: how our world was created, how we should live, what our values and morals should be, whether we have eternal souls, where we have come from and where we should be going.

This chapter will help clarify the central principles of the major world faiths and also refresh your memory about their histories, significant religious leaders, their holy books and their festivals. Approach it with an open mind.

HINDUISM

Hinduism is a very ancient religion; in fact, it is considered to be the oldest major belief system in the world that is still in existence. It is thought to have originated around 1,800 BCE in India and it is practised by 80 per cent of the population there today. Hinduism has changed form over time and many different beliefs and approaches to reaching union with God are held by different Hindus. The central principles include the ideas of **samsara**, **karma** and **Brahman**.

Samsara means 'wandering' and refers to the Hindu belief in reincarnation. Hindus believe that after death an individual's soul (**atman**) is repeatedly reborn in different bodies – working its way up from lower life forms like animals to humans – until it becomes one with God (Brahman), a process called **moksha**. A person can reach moksha through various means, such as meditation, prayer and good deeds. Living a good life and performing charitable actions can lead to a better subsequent life through reincarnation. This is because Hindus believe that every action (**karma**) a person takes causes a result that they are responsible for and will experience in their current life or one of their future lives.

It may surprise you to learn that Hindus believe in one God who exists as the external and internal universe, known as Brahman. Everything in existence is part of Brahman. A person's soul is also part of Brahman. Brahman is worshipped by Hindus in many forms, illustrating different aspects of God. The three primary personifications of God are known collectively as the **Trimurti**, which includes Brahma, Vishnu and Shiva.

*   **Brahma** is the personification of God as creator. He is represented with four heads looking in four different directions.

*   **Shiva** is the personification of God as destroyer. He has four arms and is often depicted meditating or dancing with fire. Shiva's son with his wife **Parvati**, is the elephant-headed god **Ganesh**.

*   **Vishnu** is the personification of God as preserver. He is often represented with blue skin and with four arms each holding a different object. Whenever evil threatens to overcome the world Vishnu becomes incarnate as an avatar. **Rama**, the hero of the great

Hindu epic the Ramayana, is an avatar of Vishnu, as is **Krishna** who appears in the other major Sanskrit epic, the Mahabharata.

RITES OF PASSAGE: HINDU SAMSKARAS

During the different stages of life, a Hindu undergoes various ceremonies known as **samskaras**. These sacraments help to counteract the negative effects of karma. There are sixteen samskaras that encompass prayers and rituals carried out at certain points in a person's life: pre-conception, during pregnancy, after seven months of pregnancy, at birth, at naming, at the first look at the sun, during the eating of the first solid food, at the first haircut, at ear piercing, at first learning of the alphabet at the age of about five, at the beginning of studies, at the first study of the scriptures, at the first shaving of the beard, on returning home after studying, at marriage and at death.

An illustration of Vishnu

The most important of these rituals are the naming ceremony (Namakarana), the ceremony at the beginning of studies (Upanayana), the marriage ceremony (Vivaha) and the funeral rites (Antyeshti).

BUDDHISM

Buddhism is often thought of in the West as something to do with Hollywood actors meditating in tropical retreats and not stepping on insects, but it is actually an intellectually rigorous philosophy developed by an extraordinary man in the sixth century BCE.

Prince Siddhartha Gautama was born near the India-Nepal border around 563 BCE. When he was twenty-nine years old Gautama left his father's palace because he found court life unfulfilling. On his travels one day, he saw an old man, a sick man and a funeral, which brought home to him the suffering in the world. He then saw a serene monk, which made him realise his destiny and renounce his previous life. These events are known as the **Four Sights** and the **Great Renunciation**. After studying and living as a Hindu monk without achieving inner peace, in about 528 BCE Gautama experienced the **Great Enlightenment** while meditating under a bodhi tree. This experience revealed to him the path to ultimate truth which he began to preach throughout the Ganges region of India. Gautama is known by his followers as **Buddha** which means 'the enlightened one'.

The **Four Noble Truths** of Buddhism are: that life is filled with suffering; that suffering is the result of desires; that the removal of desires results in a state of no suffering called **nirvana**; and that the **Noble Eightfold Path** leads to nirvana.

The Noble Eightfold Path involves:

1. right views
2. right intentions
3. right speech
4. right action
5. right livelihood
6. right effort
7. right-mindedness
8. right contemplation

These central teachings were supplemented with the **Five Precepts**: to avoid harming any living thing; to avoid stealing; to avoid sexual misconduct; to avoid unworthy speech; and to avoid substances which cloud the reason such as drugs and alcohol.

Buddha also taught that human beings are constantly changing creatures and do not have a permanent soul – this doctrine is known as **anatman**. In Hindu belief, the permanent soul is reborn into different bodies through reincarnation. Buddhists also believe in rebirth – but of the consciousness rather than the unchanging soul. Living a life full of good actions (good karma) and following Buddha's advice leads to a release from the cycle of rebirth and the achievement of nirvana.

JUDAISM

Judaism is a **monotheistic** religion (a faith where believers worship one God) which began over 3,500 years ago in the Middle East. Its history is told in the holy book, the **Torah** (Genesis, Exodus, Leviticus, Numbers and Deuteronomy). According to the Torah, the father of the Jews is Abraham. In the early history of Judaism, God promised Abraham that if he worshipped and obeyed Him as the one single omnipotent deity, Abraham would be the father of God's chosen people who would set an example of goodness to all people in the world. God also promised that Abraham and his descendants would own the territory known then as Canaan (which is in the same area as modern Israel). God's agreement with Abraham is known as the **First Covenant**. Circumcision is practised on Jewish boys as a symbol of this covenant.

Abraham originally came from what is now Iraq and, after God's promise, he and his people (known as the Hebrews) moved to Canaan (also called the Promised Land) until famine drove his descendants into Egypt. By the thirteenth century BCE the Hebrews were being persecuted and enslaved by the Egyptian Pharaoh. Moses, a Hebrew raised by an Egyptian princess, led the Hebrews out of Egypt back to Canaan – a journey called the Exodus. He also received the central laws of Judaism from God, including the **Ten Commandments.**

Moses died just before he reached their final destination and Joshua took over the leadership of the Hebrews, establishing them in Canaan.

In 586 BCE King Nebuchadnezzar of Babylonia conquered the Jewish territory, the kingdom of Judah, destroyed the Temple of Solomon and deported many Jews to Babylonia. This period is known as the **Babylonian Exile** and the beginning of the Jewish **Diaspora**. Diaspora means 'scattering' in ancient Greek and the term refers to the dispersal of Jews among different countries away from their homeland. Many Jews returned to Judah after the Persians defeated the Babylonians in 539 BCE and rebuilt their capital city of Jerusalem and the Temple.

In 333 BCE Alexander the Great took control of the territory of Israel from the Persians and it was later ruled by the Egyptians and Syrians but was taken back by the Jews after the revolt of the Maccabees (168–164 BCE). This period ended in 63 BCE with the Roman conquest, which led to a long period of rule and rebellion during which the Temple was destroyed once more in 70 CE and the Jews were expelled from Judea in 135 CE. After the Romans, this territory went on to be successively governed by Byzantine and Arab powers up until the time of the Crusades. ·

THE ABRAHAMIC FAITHS

As well as Judaism, Christianity and Islam are also known as Abrahamic religions because they also recognise Abraham as an important figure in their histories. In Christianity Abraham is revered as an example of great faith in God, and in Islam he is known as an important prophet (called Ibrahim) and ancestor of the Arab people.

THE TEN COMMANDMENTS

The Ten Commandments were given directly by God to Moses while he was praying on Mount Sinai during his journey from Egypt to Canaan. They were then engraved on two stone tablets. These rules are followed by both Jews and Christians: Jewish tradition divides the commandments up as follows, but Christian tradition conflates the first two here and separates the probation on coveting your neighbour's wife into a separate commandment from coveting his property.

1. Thou shalt have no other gods before me.
2. Thou shalt not make unto thee any graven image, or any likeness of any thing that is in heaven above, or that is in the earth beneath, or that is in the water under the earth. Thou shalt not bow down thyself to them, nor serve them: for I the Lord thy God am a jealous God, visiting the iniquity of the fathers upon the children unto the third and fourth generation of them that hate me. And showing mercy unto thousands of them that love me, and keep my commandments.
3. Thou shalt not take the name of the Lord thy God in vain; for the Lord will not hold him guiltless that taketh His name in vain.
4. Remember the sabbath day, to keep it holy. Six days shalt thou labour, and do all thy work. But the seventh day is the sabbath of the Lord thy God: in it thou shalt not do any work, thou, nor thy son,

nor thy daughter, thy manservant, nor thy maidservant, nor thy cattle, nor thy stranger that is within thy gates. For in six days the Lord made heaven and earth, the sea, and all that in them is, and rested the seventh day: wherefore the Lord blessed the sabbath day, and hallowed it.

5. Honour thy father and thy mother: that thy days may be long upon the land which the Lord thy God giveth thee.
6. Thou shalt not kill.
7. Thou shalt not commit adultery.
8. Thou shalt not steal.
9. Thou shalt not bear false witness against thy neighbour.
10. Thou shalt not covet thy neighbour's house, thou shalt not covet thy neighbour's wife, nor his manservant, nor his maidservant, nor his ox, nor his ass, nor any thing that is thy neighbour's.

King James Bible*, Exodus 20:2–17

JEWISH DIETARY LAWS

The system of dietary laws followed by Orthodox Jews is called **kashrut**. These laws were laid down by God in the Torah. They were given to Moses on Mount Sinai at the same time as the Ten Commandments. The dietary laws help the Jewish community, wherever it may be in the world, retain a sense of identity and obedience to God's will. Foods which are permitted are known as **kosher** (meaning 'proper') foods.

*   Fish that have both fins and scales are kosher. Shellfish are not.
*   Birds that are not birds of prey or scavengers are kosher. (There are lists of forbidden birds in Leviticus and Deuteronomy.)
*   Mammals that chew the cud and have cloven hooves are kosher. For example, pigs do not chew the cud and so pork is not kosher.
*   Meat and dairy foods must not be eaten together. Different utensils must be used for preparing these two types of food.

*The King James Bible is the beautifully written translation of the Bible that was commissioned by King James I of England in 1604. It is also known as the Authorised Version.

- Jews are not permitted to eat blood, therefore there is a special kosher way of slaughtering animals (*shechitah*) that must be observed in order for their meat to be deemed kosher.
- Forbidden foods are known as *terefah*. Rodents, reptiles, amphibians and insects are all *terefah*.

CHRISTIANITY

There are almost two billion Christians in the world and Christianity's influence has spread widely across the globe. Most of us know something of the story of Jesus, even if it's just that he was laid in a manger after his birth while around him the 'cattle were lowing'. This is because Christianity has been the major religion in Britain since the eighth century CE. However, people often become confused about what happened in Jesus's life between the manger and the cross and this short summary will help you to understand why he is such a significant figure.

Jesus was a Jewish carpenter who was born in Bethlehem and raised in Nazareth during the time of Roman rule. According to Christian belief, Jesus was the son of God and the **Messiah**, or spiritual saviour, promised by the Jewish holy books who would save mankind. He is known as Jesus Christ because '*christos*' is the ancient Greek word for 'messiah'. Jesus's life and the moral directions and stories (**parables**) he told were collected after his death by the four Gospel writers, Matthew, Mark, Luke and John, and these books form the key basis of the New Testament which is the central part of the Christian Bible.

Jesus was a religious teacher who gathered together a band of disciples to spread the word of his new approach to religion, which emphasised love for one's fellow man and God's forgiveness of sins. He is also celebrated in the Gospels for performing miracles and particularly healing the sick. Jesus was very critical of the official clergy of the time and they reported him to the Roman ruler, Pontius Pilate, who condemned him to death for sedition.

On the last night before his arrest Jesus ate a meal (known as the **Last Supper**) with his disciples where he indicated that he knew one of them would betray him to the authorities. Judas would later hand Jesus over to Roman soldiers while he was praying in the Garden of Gethsemane. Judas indicated to the soldiers who Jesus was by kissing him. After his trial, Jesus was flogged and forced to carry his cross up to a hill called Golgotha near Jerusalem where he was crucified. However, three days later he proved his divinity by resurrecting from the dead and, forty days later, ascending into heaven.

Most Christians believe that God is one being (made up of the **Trinity** of God the Father, Jesus and the Holy Spirit), is omnipotent, omniscient and is good. They believe that humans became distanced from God through sin and that Jesus and his teachings help redeem them from sin so that after death they can be reunited with God in heaven.

DIFFERENCES BETWEEN CHRISTIANS

If asked, many in Britain would define their religion casually as Christianity, because they know how to sing a few hymns from the school assemblies of their youth, or they occasionally tip up to their parish church on Christmas Day. However, as with all things to do with religion, it's not just a simple case of being 'a Christian'. Depending on what kind of parish church you go to, you will find many differences between the main strands of Christianity practised in the world today.

There are broadly three major Christian Churches – **Roman Catholic**, **Orthodox** and **Protestant**. The early Christian Church developed directly from the teachings of followers of Jesus who travelled widely spreading the new religion and passing on the Gospels. By the end of the fourth century CE Christianity was the official religion of the far-reaching Roman Empire. The Christian Church was one unified body until the **East-West Schism** in 1054 when the Eastern Orthodox Church, under the authority of the Patriarch of Constantinople, split off from the Western Church that had become centred around Rome under the authority of the Pope. The Pope and the Patriarch both angrily excommunicated each other (**excommunication** is the worst punishment you can inflict on a member of a religious community as it means they are expelled from the Church). The cultural traditions of these two groups of Christians had been developing in different ways for many years, but things came to a head over specific questions of doctrine, such as the use of unleavened bread in Mass and the concept of the Trinity. The Orthodox Church and the Roman Catholic Church have been separate organisations since this point.

The sixteenth century saw another break in the Western Church when religious reformers such as Martin Luther and John Calvin challenged the authority of the established Church and set up a third branch of Christianity known as Protestantism. Protestantism developed in part because of disillusionment with the moral corruption rife among the leaders of the Catholic Church at the time and was also a concerted effort to go back to the original beliefs of the early Christian Church and reject the layers of doctrine that had been established over the years by tradition. Protestantism is a broad term that now covers many different, but related, Christian Churches.

Roman Catholics believe in the authority of the established Church and its representatives, and at the head of their community sits the Pope, who holds the position of Church leader established by one of Jesus's disciples, St Peter. Protestants, on the other hand, believe in the **priesthood of all believers**, which states that all people have equally direct contact with God and do not need the clergy to mediate for them. They also believe in the primacy of the scriptures in deciding Christian belief and practice where Catholics also depend on the traditions of the Church. Protestants believe in **justification by grace alone** through faith (**grace** is God's favour, which He can grant to individuals and which 'justifies' them or redeems them from their sins) where Catholics believe that partaking of the sacraments (religious ceremonies) and doing penance and good works all help to invite God's grace. Many other differences between Roman Catholic and Protestant practice and doctrine have developed over time, including different views concerning the books of the Bible, the celibacy of clergy, homosexuality, abortion, contraception and the gender of clergy.

THE IMMACULATE CONCEPTION

All Christians believe that the mother of Jesus, Mary, was a virgin when she conceived Jesus through the Holy Spirit. People often make the mistake of thinking that this is what is known as the Immaculate Conception. However, only Roman Catholics believe in the doctrine of the Immaculate Conception, which states that Mary herself was conceived without original sin (the essential sinfulness of mankind passed on to each human being through procreation right back to Adam and Eve).

RELIGIOUS SYMBOLS IN CHRISTIAN ART

- The Chi-Rho symbol (above) incorporates the first two letters of the Greek word for Christ, χ (chi) and ρ (rho).
- The Four Evangelists (often depicted together): a man – St Matthew; a lion – St Mark; an ox – St Luke; an eagle – St John.
- The lily represents purity and the Virgin Mary; a lily among thorns represents the Immaculate Conception.
- The Greek letters *alpha* and *omega* represent the eternity of God.
- Three circles intersecting represent the Holy Trinity.
- The dove represents the Holy Ghost.
- The fish represents Jesus. This was a secret symbol used by Christians during their persecution under the Roman Empire. The letters of the Greek word for fish, *ichthus*, stand for Jesus Christ Son of God the Saviour in Greek.
- The olive tree represents peace.
- The flaming sword represents judgement.
- The keys represent the Church or St Peter.

PATRON SAINTS

Saint's Day	Name	Patron Saint of:
1 March	St David	doves, Wales
17 March	St Patrick	engineers, Ireland
23 April	St George	England, horses, lepers, saddle-makers, shepherds, skin diseases, soldiers
20 May	Bernadine of Siena	advertising, gambling addicts, lungs, public relations personnel
2 June	St Erasmus	stomach ache, childbirth, explosives workers, sailors, seasickness
13 June	St Anthony of Padua	amputees, domestic animals, elderly people, lost objects, pregnant women, swineherds
29 June	St Peter	bakers, butchers, fishermen, locksmiths, shipbuilders, shoemakers, stonemasons, watchmakers
25 July	St Christopher	bachelors, bookbinders, bus drivers, epileptics, gardeners, travellers
18 August	St Helena	archaeologists, difficult marriages, divorced people, empresses
27 August	St Monica	alcoholics, disappointing children, housewives, victims of adultery, widows
4 October	St Francis of Assisi	animals, birds, lacemakers, tapestry workers, zoos
28 October	St Jude	lost causes, hospital workers
22 November	St Cecilia	martyrs, musicians, poets
30 November	St Andrew	fishmongers, Scotland, singers, sore throats, spinsters
6 December	St Nicholas of Myra	brewers, judges, murderers, newly-weds, pawnbrokers, pharmacists, prisoners, schoolchildren, shoe shiners, thieves

ISLAM

Islam is the second largest religion in the world after Christianity and people who belong to the Islamic faith are called Muslims. Islam is an Arabic word meaning 'submission' and all Muslims seek to 'submit' to the will of God. Muslims believe that Islam has always existed but was revealed over time through prophets such as Abraham, Moses and Jesus, and most importantly through the last great prophet Muhammad (peace be upon him) (570-632 CE). (Because Muhammad is so important in the Islamic religion, whenever Muslims say or write his name they follow it with the words 'peace be upon him', or the abbreviation 'pbuh', as a mark of respect.)

Muhammad was born in Mecca (in present-day Saudi Arabia) and after he began preaching he travelled to Medina on a journey know as the **Hegira** (migration) where he found many new followers; both these cities are sacred to Muslims (as is Jerusalem, since it was from here that Muhammad made a miraculous journey to heaven). Muhammad was an intensely spiritual man and in 610 CE, while praying in a cave on Mount Hira he had a vision and the Angel Jibreel (known as Gabriel in Judaism and Christianity) inspired him to recite the words of the one, true, eternal, benevolent, omniscient and omnipotent God, **Allah**. God's revelation through the mouth of Muhammad was recorded and became the Muslim holy scripture, the **Qu'ran**. The Qu'ran is regarded as the direct word of God and gives guidance on how Muslims should live in accordance with Allah's will. Muslims also follow the example set by Muhammad's life, called the **Sunna**. After the Prophet's death, scholars travelled around carefully collecting his sayings, called **Hadith**, from people so that Muslims could live by his words.

THE SIX ARTICLES OF FAITH

These are the basic components of the Islamic faith and are taken from the Qu'ran.

* Belief in Allah as the only God.
* Belief in the angels.
* Belief in the holy books; these include the Torah of Judaism and the Christian Gospels, which also preach belief in the one God.

However, only the Qu'ran is the pure word of God, unadulterated by human interests and error.

- Belief in the prophets; these include figures revered in other religions including Adam and Ibrahim, Musa, Dawud and Isa (known as Abraham, Moses, David and Jesus in Judaism and Christianity). The most important and final prophet is Muhammad.
- Belief in the Day of Judgement; Muslims believe in eternal life after death and that the Day of Judgement is the day that will come at the end of time when everyone will be judged by Allah and sent to paradise or hell depending on their actions in life.
- Belief in Allah's control of man's destiny; Muslims believe in fate but also in free will.

THE FIVE PILLARS OF ISLAM

The five pillars are the religious duties of all Muslims.

- *Shahadah*: Declaration of faith. In order to be a Muslim a person must sincerely recite the profession of faith: 'There is no God but Allah and Muhammad is the prophet of Allah.' The concept of one, omniscient and omnipotent God is called *tawhid* and is of central importance to Islam.
- *Salah*: Prayer. Muslims should pray five times a day: *fajr* in the early morning; *zuhr* in the early afternoon; *asr* in the late afternoon, *maghrib* at sunset and *isha* last thing at night. In Islamic countries you will hear the muezzins (callers) reciting the call to prayer from the minarets of the mosques. Muslims pray after carrying out specific ablutions, and they always pray facing in the direction of Mecca. This is why, if you fly on Muslim airlines, you will notice that the GPS image of the aeroplane on the TV screens also shows the direction of Mecca.
- *Zakat*: Giving alms. Muslims believe that it is every person's duty to give money to the less fortunate. *Zakat* is normally paid annually during the festival of Ramadan.
- *Sawm*: Fasting. During Ramadan, Muslims are required to abstain from food, drink and sex between sunrise and sunset.
- *Hajj*: Pilgrimage. If they possibly can, once in each Muslim's life they should perform the journey to Mecca called the *hajj*. This takes place

at a specific time in the Islamic calendar and pilgrims wear special white clothes and visit key holy sites on their journey.

SUNNI AND SHIA MUSLIMS

When Muhammad died in 632 he left behind a large Muslim community in need of political and religious guidance. He was succeeded by Abu Bakr as caliph (leader) who was elected by the majority. However, a smaller group believed that Muhammad's successor should have been a member of his family. They wanted Muhammad's son-in-law and cousin, Ali, to become the first caliph. This smaller group became known as the Shia and the larger group became known as the Sunnis. Today 90 per cent of the world's Muslims are Sunnis but the Shia form the majority of the population in Iran and Iraq. The two groups both believe that Muhammad wanted their chosen leader to succeed him and they have different collections of Hadith which support their claims.

After Abu Bakr, Umar ibn al-Khattab and Uthman ibn'Affan were the next caliphs, and were also supported by the Sunni community. However, the Shia choice, Ali, became the fourth caliph and the first Imam of the Shia. In 661, Ali was murdered and Mu'awiya, a cousin of the third caliph, Uthman, founded the Umayyad dynasty that provided the next thirteen caliphs. Mu'awiya's son Yazid, killed Ali's son, who was challenging him for the caliphate, at the Battle of Karbala (in present-day Iraq) in 680. Karbala still holds great significance for Shia Muslims and is a site of pilgrimage for them. Sunnis supported the Umayyad dynasty, but Shia regarded the Imams as their sole, infallible religious leaders.

The term Imam is used by Shia Muslims to designate specific hereditary spiritual leaders, descended from Muhammad. Different groups of Shia believe that there have been different numbers of Imams, though the largest group believe that there have been twelve and that the twelfth, Imam Mahdi, disappeared as a child in 878, but will return again at the end of the world. In the absence of the Imam, religious scholars called ayatollahs have the authority to spiritually guide Shia Muslims.

Sunnis use the term imam differently, to refer to various theologians and chiefs or the leaders of prayers in a mosque. Sunnis believe that the caliphs before Ali were legitimate and that the leader of their community is not divinely ordained but should be elected. Instead of looking to a living leader for religious guidance, Sunnis solve religious issues through consensus (*ijma*) and the works of past theologians. Sunni and Shia practices differ in various respects because of their different inter-pretations of Muhammad's wishes, but both groups believe in the same fundamental basics of Islam.

SIKHISM

Sikhism is the newest major religion in the world – it is over three thousand years younger than Hinduism. It is centred in the Punjab province of India and the second largest Sikh population in the world is in the United Kingdom. The most holy place in the Sikh religion is the Golden Temple in Amritsar which was built in 1604 CE by Guru Arjan. Sikhism was founded in the fifteenth century by Guru Nanak (1469–1539), who travelled and studied both Hinduism and Islam for many years. Like Hindus, Sikhs believe in karma and reincarnation and the aim of life being to free oneself from this cycle, but they believe that this liberation can only be reached with God's grace rather than through a person's actions. Sikhs believe that all men and women are equal and reject the Hindu caste system, which states that people of different social and occupational groups have different levels of religious purity. Sikhs also believe in one God, who is present inside all people, and that God should be worshipped through good deeds rather than rituals. It is very important to Sikhs to have an honest job and to be charitable to others.

THE TEN GURUS

Shortly before his death, Guru Nanak named one of his followers as his successor as religious adviser and guide to the Sikhs. There have been ten gurus in total, each of whom has contributed to the religious principles and practices of Sikhism: Guru Nanak, Guru Angad (guru from 1539 to 1552), Guru Amar Das (1552–74), Guru Ram Das (1574–81), Guru Arjan (1581–1606), Guru Hargobind (1606–44), Guru Har Rai (1644–61), Guru Har Krishan (1661–4), Guru Tegh Bahadur (1664–75),

Guru Gobind Singh (1666–1708). Guru Gobind Singh decreed that the Sikh holy scriptures, called Guru Granth Sahib, should act as guru for the Sikhs from his death onwards.

THE KHALSA

During the seventeenth century Sikhs were oppressed and discriminated against by the ruling powers in India, so in 1699 Guru Gobind Singh set up the Khalsa as a trained armed force of Sikhs prepared to defend their faith. Guru Gobind Singh's father, Guru Tegh Bahadur, had been executed in 1675 by the Mughal Emperor Aurangzeb for not accepting Islam, and for helping some Hindus who Aurangzeb also wanted to convert. The Khalsa today binds the community of Sikhs together with a strict code of conduct which involves prayers, avoiding intoxicants, moral behaviour, obedience to God and charity towards the less fortunate. All Sikhs can be initiated into the Khalsa and after initiation all Sikh men take the surname 'Singh', meaning 'lion', and all Sikh women take the surname 'Kaur', meaning 'princess'. Members of the Khalsa wear five signs of their membership, called the Five Ks: *kesh* (uncut hair), *kirpan* (the sword), *kangha* (a comb), *kara* (a steel bracelet) and *kachera* (underwear shorts). These symbols all remind the wearer of his or her responsibilities and beliefs as a Sikh.

DAYS OF CELEBRATION: MAJOR FESTIVALS

DIWALI

The most popular festival in Hinduism is Diwali, which is celebrated over five days in the Hindu month of Kartika (October/November) and marks the end of the Hindu year. Diwali means 'row of lights' and the festival is celebrated with special prayers, displays of lights in people's homes, fireworks and the exchanging of gifts.

The festival celebrates the triumph of light over darkness and commemorates an episode in the Ramayana featuring the hero Rama, with his wife Sita and his brother Lakshmana. In this story Rama is denied his right to the throne of the kingdom of Ayodhya and is sent into exile with his wife and brother for fourteen years. While they are away the demon king of Sri Lanka, Ravana, kidnaps Sita. With the help of the monkey god Hanuman, Rama rescues Sita and kills Ravana. On the last day of the year, he then returns with his wife and brother to take the throne of Ayodhya. As the trio return at night, the inhabitants of the city greet them and guide their way by setting out rows of lights.

Sita is regarded as an incarnation of Vishnu's wife, the goddess Lakshmi, who is particularly celebrated at Diwali. Lakshmi is the goddess of prosperity, and Diwali also marks the beginning of the new business year. Many households leave their doors open during this festival so that Lakshmi can visit them and bring them good fortune.

Sikhs also celebrate Diwali. For them the festival commemorates an event in the life of their sixth guru, Guru Hargobind. The Muslim Mughal Emperor Jahangir, who controlled most of India in the early seventeenth century, felt threatened by the growing community of Sikhs and executed the fifth guru, Guru Arjan, Guru Hargobind's father. Guru Hargobind built up a defensive force of Sikhs and because of this was arrested and imprisoned in Gwalior Fort by Jahangir in 1619. Eventually the emperor decided to release Guru Hargobind, but the guru refused to leave without the fifty-two other prisoners in the fort. The emperor told him he could only leave with the number of prisoners who could walk out of the prison holding onto his coat, so Hargobind had a special cloak made with lots of long tassels and saved all the prisoners with it. The Sikh community welcomed Hargobind back to Amritsar by lighting lamps and this is why the lights are set out for them at Diwali. The lights also remind Sikhs of the inner light that leads them towards God.

HANUKKAH

The Jewish festival of lights is called Hanukkah, which means 'dedication'. It is celebrated for eight days in the Jewish month of Kislev (November/December) and commemorates the victory of the Maccabees over the Syrians, who ruled much of the Middle East, in 165 BCE. In 168 BCE King Antiochus IV of Syria banned Judaism and forced everyone to worship the Greek god Zeus. The Jewish priest Mattathias killed a worshipper who profaned the Temple with a sacrifice to Zeus and then he and his family, known as the Hasmonaeans or Maccabees, fled into the mountains and began a guerrilla war against the Syrians. Mattathias's son Judas Maccabeus conquered Jerusalem in 165 BCE.

When Judas Maccabeus returned to Jerusalem he could only find a tiny amount of holy oil to light the sacred lamp needed to resanctify the Temple. Miraculously, the lamp burned for eight days and Hanukkah celebrates this sacred event. Special candlesticks called Hanukkah menorahs are used during the festival and one candle is lit each day. Jews also say special prayers, play games and exchange gifts over Hannukah.

CHRISTMAS

On 25 December Christians celebrate the anniversary of the birth of Jesus Christ. According to the story of the Nativity, the Angel Gabriel announced to the Virgin Mary that she would conceive miraculously through the Holy Spirit and give birth to the son of God. While heavily pregnant, Mary had to travel with her husband Joseph, by donkey, to Bethlehem, because of a census called by the Romans. On their arrival they could not find a place to stay and so they bedded down in a stable. That night, Jesus was born and the family received visits from shepherds and wise men who had been guided to them by a star appearing in the night sky. Christians celebrate Christmas by going to church, singing carols (hymns about the Nativity), displaying cribs (models of the stable with the holy family), enacting Nativity plays and exchanging gifts. This final part of the traditional Christmas rituals has become the most important in our modern age, a fact that is oft lamented by people who want us to be reminded of the true spirit of Christmas. However, receiving colossal consumerist crates of Action Men, Bratz, games consoles and other wholeheartedly plastic entertainment does seem to give the children a great deal of joy and at least remind them that Christmas is a time of celebration, even if it provides an experience that is worlds away from that humble manger. In fact, Christmas is often now celebrated as a gift-giving festival all over the world, even in non-Christian countries.

Is Christmas really Jesus's birthday?

Christian tradition holds that Jesus was born on 25 December 1 AD (standing for Anno Domini meaning 'in the year of the Lord' in Latin). BC stands for 'Before Christ' but it is now thought that Jesus was born between 8 and 4 BC. The Gregorian calendar is used widely throughout the world and many non-Christians refer to BC years as BCE years (standing for Before the Common Era) and AD years as CE years (standing for Common Era). Many scholars consider it unlikely that Jesus's birthday actually fell on 25 December but rather that early Christians chose to replace the established pagan celebrations of the winter solstice with this Christian festival. Many of the traditions around Christmas, such as the use of mistletoe and holly for decorations and the giving of gifts, stretch back to solstice rituals.

EID UL-FITR

Eid ul-Fitr is a three-day festival celebrated by Muslims at the end of Ramadan, the ninth month of the Islamic calendar. The Islamic calendar is lunar and so doesn't match up with the Gregorian calendar – this means that Eid is celebrated on a different date in the Gregorian calendar each year. Each month of the calendar begins and ends with the new moon. Some Muslims begin and end the month according to when the new moon is first sighted in their own country and some base their celebrations around sightings of the moon in Saudi Arabia. During Ramadan Muslims fast to commemorate the revelation of the Qu'ran to Muhammad. Eid ul-Fitr means 'festival to break the fast' and Muslims celebrate by taking part in communal prayers, wearing their best clothes, eating a special meal and decorating their homes.

RELIGIOUS EDUCATION TEST PAPER

1. The Hindu god Ganesh is which other god's son?

2. What are the Five Ks of the Sikh Khalsa?

3. What do the following terms relating to the Hindu faith mean?
a) *samsara*
b) *karma*

4. What is a samskara?

5. Name the twelve apostles of Jesus.

6. Who is the patron saint of Wales?

7. Who is the patron saint of stomach ache?

8. What are the eight precepts of the Noble Eightfold Path of Buddhism which lead to nirvana?

9. What is the golden rule?

10. What kind of tree was Buddha sitting under when he gained enlightenment?

11. What does nirvana mean?

12. What is meditation?

13. Why is it often difficult to buy condoms in Catholic countries?

14. Who is the father of the Jews?

15. Name the Twelve Tribes of Israel.

16. When was the Jewish Temple in Jerusalem destroyed?

17. Who built the first Jewish Temple in Jerusalem?

18. What is the significance of the menorah used by Jews during the festival of Hanukkah?

19. Why would it be inappropriate to serve king prawn spring rolls or pork belly at a Jewish wedding reception?

20. List the seven deadly sins.

21. Name all of the Ten Commandments.

22. What is the Torah?

23. What is the Immaculate Conception?

24. What does the word 'islam' mean?

25. What does the word 'jihad' mean?

26. **Name three differences between Protestants and Catholics.**

27. **Who was Ephraim?**

28. **If, last Sunday, you built a shrine to George Clooney and wrote 'George is God' on a sign on top of it, how many of the Ten Commandments would you have broken?**

29. **What are the Five Pillars of Islam?**

30. **When does Ramadan take place?**

31. **What should all good Muslims abstain from between sunrise and sunset during Ramadan?**

32. **Are the majority of Muslims in the world Sunni or Shia?**

33. **Who was the first Sikh guru?**

34. **What happens in a gurdwara?**

35. **Which is the most holy city in the world for Muslims?**

36. **Where was Jesus born?**

37. **What is original sin?**

38. **In the Book of Genesis, what was Eve's special punishment for eating the forbidden fruit in the Garden of Eden?**

❦ 7 ❦

GEOGRAPHY

'**Geography** *n*. the study of the earth's physical features, resources, natural and political divisions, climate, population, products, etc'
Oxford Concise English Dictionary

'So geographers in Afric-maps
With savage-pictures fill their gaps;
And o'er unhabitable downs
Place elephants for want of towns'
JONATHAN SWIFT (1667–1745)

Hello, sky! Hello, birds! Hello, trees! Geography isn't just learning about sheep farming and different types of rock, it is a way of understanding the most spectacular natural phenomena we see around us: voluptuous volcanoes spewing incandescent crimson lava into the sky; glimmering stars burning the candle at both ends far away in the cosmos; purple-headed mountains disappearing up into the lowering clouds; gorgeous glaciers; impressive eclipses; rapids and rivers and the good old British rain. It is also the study of human life in different places – a country's, society's, or person's geography influences them just as much as their history.

Our sense of the planet's geography has changed over generations – we no longer worry about sailing off the edge of the world, or believe ourselves to be the centre of the universe; we know that America and India are different places and that pitiable Pluto is not actually a planet after all. But do you *really* know where Brunei is? Or the Federal States of Micronesia? Do you know how to differentiate a Strombolian from a Plinian volcanic eruption? Or what causes tsunamis? Or how fast the wind has to be blowing to qualify as a hurricane? Or how an oxbow lake forms? Or when the vernal equinox falls? We all have our geographical black holes, but this chapter should help fill them in.

BANG!: THE BIG BANG THEORY

Most thinkers now accept that the universe was formed as described in the Big Bang theory. Only the extremely dim, or religiously motivated, still believe that the world was literally created in six days (with a well-deserved tea break on the seventh). Scientists have worked out, using complicated mathematical formulae the layman probably wouldn't be able to grasp even after reading the Mathematics and Physics chapters of this book, that the universe is continually expanding outwards and, at the same time, cooling.

The theory goes that the universe began its life as a dense fireball which contained all the matter and energy that currently makes up our universe as it exists today. This fireball exploded hundreds of millions of years ago, in what must have been a pretty impressive show, and, as it cooled, galaxies, solar systems, stars and planets were formed. The force of this explosion is still continuing today, which is why the galaxies in the universe are measurably moving away from each other over time.

Thinking about how big the universe is can sometimes bring people out in goosebumps, so we'll break it down into slightly more manageable gargantuan pieces. **Galaxies** are swirling systems of millions of stars bound together by gravitational force and there are thought to be over 100 billion of them in the universe. Our galaxy is often referred to as the Milky Way. **Solar systems** are the arrangement of planets and other bodies around a single star. The solar system we call home, arrayed around our sun, is approximately 4,600 million years old.

MY VICIOUS EARTHWORM:
THE ORDER OF THE PLANETS

It is difficult for our minuscule minds to think about much outside our own experience: in general we are a combination of a bit baffled and a bit lazy in our efforts to contemplate the magnitude of space. But for an easy way to digest a sense of our planet's place in the great void, you can imagine the solar system in this human-friendly way. If the sun were reduced to roughly the size of a beach ball, following on the same scale the eight planets could be represented relatively thus:

Mercury – a grain of mustard 15.2 metres away from the beach ball
Venus – a pea 23.7 metres away
Earth – a pea 33.2 metres away
Mars – a currant 49.9 metres away
Jupiter – an orange 170.6 metres away
Saturn – a tangerine 312.1 metres away
Uranus – a plum 627.8 metres away
Neptune – a plum 984.5 metres away

(Pluto *was* a pinhead up to 1.6 kilometres away, but in 2006 its status was demoted to a minor planet so it shouldn't really be included in this list. Poor Pluto.)

The best way to remember the order of the planets is by repeating this sentence: '**My Vicious Earthworm Might Just Swallow Us Now**.'

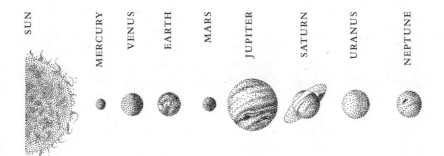

SUN   MERCURY   VENUS   EARTH   MARS   JUPITER   SATURN   URANUS   NEPTUNE

EARTHLY POSSESSIONS: OUR PLANET

Scientists divide the Earth into four areas:

- The **atmosphere** is a band of useful gases that surrounds the Earth, like a blanket cushioning us from the frigid, airless void of space. It is divided into six layers: the **troposphere** (nearest the Earth's surface), the **stratosphere**, the **mesosphere**, the **thermosphere**, the **ionosphere** and the **exosphere**. The atmosphere is one of the special attributes of our planet, making it capable of supporting life as it incorporates gases like oxygen and nitrogen which plants and animals need in order to live and breathe. It also protects the Earth from harmful ultraviolet rays in sunlight and keeps the temperature of the Earth habitable.

- The **biosphere** is the part of the Earth in which living things exist. It includes all animals and plants both on land and in the sea.

- The **hydrosphere** refers to all the forms of water that exist on, under and over the surface of the Earth: clouds, snow, ice, fresh water and the seas and oceans.

- The **internal structure** of the Earth includes the crust, the mantle and the core.

Our planet is made of a mixture of what some clever clogs call volatile-depleted primitive material and the rest of us call rock and metal. Its core is about the same size as the moon. The **inner core** is mainly made of solid nickel and iron, the **outer core** is liquid nickel and iron, and the **mantle** and the **crust** are made of rock. The crust is the small sliver of the planet that we actually can call our own. Its circumference measures 40,076km and it is covered on the surface with the oceans, mountains, forests, plains and deserts that are our stamping grounds. However, deep down below the crust, Gaia is less hospitable. The earth's core is hotter than a chestnut roasting on an open fire, hotter than a snake's bum in a wagon-rut, hotter than a sauna in the Sahara and possibly hotter than hell. With temperatures estimated to be capable of reaching 7,000°C, it is even hotter than the surface of the sun.

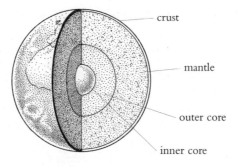

crust

mantle

A cross-section
of the Earth

outer core

inner core

DID YOU FEEL THE EARTH MOVE?:
WHAT CAUSES EARTHQUAKES

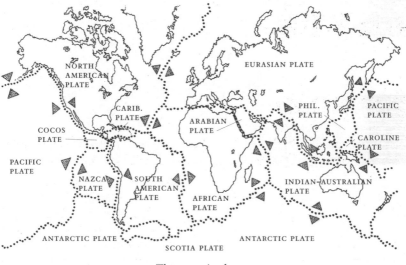

The tectonic plates

The ground beneath our feet is a captivating place. The Earth's rock crust is not quite as solid as you think. It is divided into huge slabs called **tectonic plates** which float on the **magma** (liquid rock) below. The word 'tectonic' comes from the ancient Greek word '*tekton*' meaning 'carpenter' and the plates fit together just like the different parts of an elaborate piece of furniture. However, as they move about on the magma they can pull apart, rub up and crash against each other, causing earthquakes and volcanic eruptions.

The source point of an earthquake within the crust is called the **hypocentre** and the point on the Earth's surface directly above the hypocentre is called the **epicentre** (and is not a great place to be for a relaxing time). If the earthquake begins at a hypocentre that is deep within the crust, then you're lucky as the earthquake will be less severe. Shallow hypocentres cause much stronger earthquakes.

The friction between the plates at the hypocentre causes different types of scismic waves to flow through the crust (the word 'seismic' means 'related to earthquakes'). The three types of seismic waves are categorised according to the way they move: **P-waves**, **S-waves** and **L-waves**. P-waves and S-waves move through the Earth under the surface, but L-waves are the most dangerous as they affect the surface of the Earth, causing the ground to move, knocking down buildings, opening up fissures and creating tsunamis. An easy way to remember the different wave types is that P-waves **p**ush and **p**ull, S-waves **s**hake and **s**hear, and L-waves travel the **l**ongest route over the surface of the Earth.

If you are caught in an earthquake, the best place to position yourself is under a door frame, away from windows, or under a sturdy piece of furniture. If you're outside, move away from buildings, trees or power lines that could collapse on you, and lie flat on the ground with your hands over your head.

Many people believe that dogs and other animals can sense when an earthquake is coming as they are more sensitively attuned to vibrations than people. So if Rover suddenly starts acting strangely and the air goes quiet of birdsong, make a beeline for the nearest door frame.

THE RICHTER SCALE

The severity of earthquakes can be measured on a number of different scales but the most famous is the Richter magnitude scale, drawn up by the American seismologist Charles F. Richter in 1934. Earthquakes are designated a Richter scale number according to the amplitude of the largest seismic wave recorded for that particular earthquake. These waves are recorded by scientific instruments called **seismometers**. Earthquakes measuring less than 2 Richter magnitudes are not felt on the surface at all, an earthquake measuring 4 will cause the objects in your house to rattle and shake, and earthquakes measuring 9 devastate areas for thousands of miles from the epicentre. The biggest earthquake ever recorded measured 9.5 on the Richter scale – it occurred in Chile in 1960, killing nearly two thousand people and causing 25-metre-high tsunami waves. To give you a sense of perspective, the most recent significant earthquake in the United Kingdom occurred on 27 February 2008 in Lincolnshire, causing damage to buildings in the immediate area and tremors which were felt as far afield as Dumfries and Kent. It measured 5.2 on the Richter scale.

DRIFTING CONTINENTS

Today we commonly recognise six continents:

Africa	Antarctica	Australia
America	Asia	Europe

In some parts of the world pupils are taught that there are seven continents with North and South America separated; or that there are a slightly different six: Africa, Antarctica, Australia, Eurasia, North America and South America.

In 1915 a sharp-minded scientist called Albert Wegener published a theory that hundreds of millions of years ago all today's continents were part of one huge supercontinent – which he called **Pangaea** – which later split into the current arrangement of land masses. He came up with this idea of **continental drift** after noticing the similarities of fossil animals that he found in continents separated by thousands of miles. Wegener's only problem was that he couldn't explain convincingly why the continents had moved apart in this way. The development of the theory of tectonic plates in the 1960s filled this gap in our understanding of how the continents came to be.

Pangaea

THE REALM OF THE DIVINE
BLACKSMITH: VOLCANOES

The amazing pyrotechnical displays; the ungodly, sulphuric stink; the ominous, creeping lava; the fatal clouds of poisonous gas – what's not to like about volcanoes? In ancient Greece volcanoes were thought to lead down through the Earth to the forge of the blacksmith god of fire, Hephaestus. Hephaestus was called Vulcan in ancient Rome and it is from his name that we get the word 'volcano'. In fact, a volcano is a rupture in the Earth's crust caused by tectonic-plate activity, through which lava, steam and ash are expelled. It is estimated that there are about 1,500 active volcanoes in the world. Vulcanologists classify volcanoes as **extinct**, **dormant** or **active**, depending on how frisky they are (the volcanoes rather than the vulcanologists.) Kilauea on Hawaii is the world's most active volcano, followed by Etna in Italy and Piton de la Fournaise on Réunion island.

TYPES OF VOLCANO

Volcanoes are mountains of a sort. They are formed of a build-up of their own **lava** (molten rock), **ash flows** and **tephra** (ejected ash and rock). Usually they are conically shaped and built around a vent that connects with reservoirs of searing magma below the Earth's surface. From the beautiful daily flare-ups of the Aeolian island of Stromboli to the menacing blasts of Popocatépetl in Mexico, volcanoes, and their eruptions, come in all different shapes and sizes.

Volcano type	Volcano shape	Eruption type
Scoria or cinder cone	straight sides with steep slopes; large summit crater	Strombolian
Shield volcano	very gentle slopes	Hawaiian
Stratovolcano or composite volcano	gentle lower slopes, but steep upper slopes; small summit crater	Plinian

- **Strombolian eruption**: a low-level volcanic eruption named after the Italian island of Stromboli.
- **Hawaiian eruption**: an eruption where lava flows from the vent in

a relatively gentle course, characteristic of Hawaiian volcanoes. Very little volcanic ash is produced by these eruptions.

- **Plinian eruption:** an eruption similar to the eruption of Mount Vesuvius in AD 79 that killed Pliny the Elder after he ventured out in a boat to have a closer look at it. In an evocative letter Pliny the Elder's nephew, imaginatively called Pliny the Younger, described the eruption:

> A cloud, from which mountain was uncertain, at this distance (but it was found afterwards to come from Mount Vesuvius), was ascending, the appearance of which I cannot give you a more exact description of than by likening it to that of a pine tree, for it shot up to a great height in the form of a very tall trunk, which spread itself out at the top into a sort of branches; occasioned, I imagine, either by a sudden gust of air that impelled it, the force of which decreased as it advanced upwards, or the cloud itself being pressed back again by its own weight, expanded in the manner I have mentioned; it appeared sometimes bright and sometimes dark and spotted, according as it was either more or less impregnated with earth and cinders.

Pliny the Younger, *Letters*, Book VI, Letter 16

ON TOP OF THE WORLD: MARVELLOUS MOUNTAINS

From the mighty Mount Everest in Nepal to the more modest Sutter Buttes of California and our own dear Ben Nevis, mountains are formed by volcanic activity, glaciation and tectonic plates pushing up against each other and crumpling the Earth's crust into ridges. If these mounds rise for less than 600 metres they only qualify as hills, but anything over 600 metres makes a mountain. Mountains exist on every continent and even at the bottom of our great oceans. As the peaks of land mountains rise so high they trap the clouds, forcing them to cool and turn into rain or snow. All the world's major rivers take their water from mountain sources.

Mount Everest (Nepal) is the world's highest mountain, measuring, from sea level, 8,850 metres.

K2 (Pakistan) is 8,611 metres.
Kanchenjunga (Nepal) is 8,586 metres.
Lhotse (Nepal) is 8,516 metres.
Makalu (Nepal) is 8,462 metres.

Ben Nevis reaches 1,343 metres, and South Butte, the largest of the
Sutter Butte range, at 645 metres, only just makes the mountain league
and is lucky not to be languishing with the humiliating title of 'large
hill'.

The highest mountain on Earth from the seabed is Mauna Kea in Hawaii.
It is only 4,206 metres above sea level but 10,200 metres from its base to
its summit.

THE BIG BLUE: OCEANS AND SEAS

Let's switch our attention to the watery depths. You may not realise it
but all the oceans and seas on our planet are actually part of the same
body of water. However, officially there are four oceans – the **Pacific**,
the **Atlantic**, the **Indian** and the **Arctic** – although, as with all 'facts',
there are differing viewpoints on this subject and some people add in the
Southern Ocean, or claim that the Arctic Ocean is part of the Atlantic.

If your knee-jerk reaction when asked how many seas there are is seven,
then you really aren't thinking clearly about the world you're familiar
with. Most people can manage to name at least eight and in fact there
are many more. There isn't any broad consensus on an exact number but
the major ones include:

South China Sea	Caribbean Sea	Mediterranean Sea
Bering Sea	Gulf of Mexico	Sea of Okhotsk
East China Sea	Hudson Bay	Sea of Japan
Andaman Sea	North Sea	Black Sea
Red Sea	Baltic Sea	Persian Gulf
Gulf of St Lawrence	English Channel	Irish Sea

Please don't make the mistake of including the Dead Sea in this list as
this will immediately mark you out as an amateur. It is not a sea but a
hypersaline lake.

NAILING NAVIGATION:
LONGITUDE AND LATITUDE

To find out exactly where you are in the world you should use the time-honoured system of longitude and latitude. To understand the old L & L, think of the Earth as a chocolate orange, divided into many little segments running from the top to the bottom. Bands of **longitude** (sometimes represented by the Greek letter λ) are the segment lines of the orange. They measure distance east or west of an imaginary line running from the North Pole through Greenwich, in England, to the South Pole. This imaginary line defines 0° longitude and is called the **prime meridian**. Other longitude lines are also called meridians. All longitude lines meet at the North and South Poles. If you go to Greenwich, just off the A206, you can stand with one foot in the eastern hemisphere and one foot in the western hemisphere.

Latitude, sometimes represented by the Greek letter Φ, gives the location of a place on the chocolate orange north or south of the **equator** (the band of ° latitude that runs east and west around the middle of the Earth). Places that are located north of the equator are in the northern hemisphere. Places located south of the equator are in the southern hemisphere.

Each latitude line forms an imaginary circle around the Earth. Because these circles are parallel to the equator, they are sometimes called **parallels**. The further the circles are from the equator, the smaller they are, until they become points at the **North** or **South Poles**. The latitude of the North Pole is 90° north, and the South Pole is 90° south.

The five celebrity circles of latitude are: the equator, the **Arctic Circle** and the **Antarctic Circle**, and the **tropics of Cancer and Capricorn**. The tropic of Cancer lies 23°26′ to the north of the equator and the tropic of Capricorn lies 23°26′ to the south. The Arctic Circle lies 66°33′ north, and the Antarctic Circle lies 66°33′ south.

One way to remember which 'L' runs north to south and which runs east to west, is to recall that 'longitude' contains an 'n' for 'north' and thus lines of longitude run north to south.

THE ARRANT THIEF: OUR MOON

The moon is the Earth's satellite and our nearest celestial neighbour, being only 384,400km – couple of days' travel in a shuttle – away from us. It takes 27 days, 7 hours and 43 minutes for the moon to orbit the Earth. It takes the same amount of time to spin on its own axis, so from the Earth we always see the same side of the moon, which gives us plenty of opportunity for us to get familiar with the craggy good looks of the man in the moon. Contrary to a million love songs describing moonlight, this serene satellite gives off no light of her own, but only reflects light from the sun.

MOON FACTS

Lunar phases: The changing positions of the Earth and moon in relation to the sun mean that different proportions of the moon's face are visible as the moon moves around the Earth. A **waxing** moon changes from **new moon** to **full moon**, a **waning** moon changes from full moon to new moon.

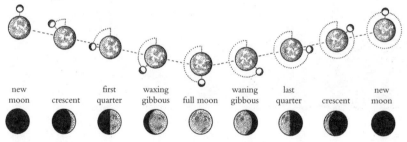

new moon	crescent	first quarter	waxing gibbous	full moon	waning gibbous	last quarter	crescent	new moon

Eclipses: An eclipse of the sun occurs when the shadow of the moon comes between the Earth and the sun. An eclipse of the moon occurs when the shadow of the Earth covers the moon.

Tides: Tides are periodic rises and falls of the oceans and seas that, amazingly, are caused by the gravitational pull of the moon and the sun as the Earth rotates. Because the moon is closer to the Earth, its effect on the tides is twice that of the sun. When the sun, moon and earth align – this occasion has the extremely sexy name of **syzygy** (remember this for Scrabble) and occurs every 14.5 days – the sun's gravitational pull reinforces the moon's, causing a **spring tide**, where the range between high and low tide is greatest. During **neap tides** the difference between high and low tide is smallest. Neap tides occur when the sun and moon form a right angle with the Earth so that the overall gravitational pull is dissipated.

BLUE SKY THINKING: CATEGORISING CLOUDS

As with psychiatrists' ink blots, the wondrous things people see in the sky probably have interesting things to say about the mental state of the person gazing skywards. Where one fellow might see a monkey in a nun's habit skiing downhill, another might see a murderous fish with a ravening maw trawling for victims at the bottom of the ocean. Whatever we see, the cold, icy fact remains that clouds are made of frozen droplets of water. These droplets are suspended in the sky because of changes in temperature that take place in the Earth's atmosphere.

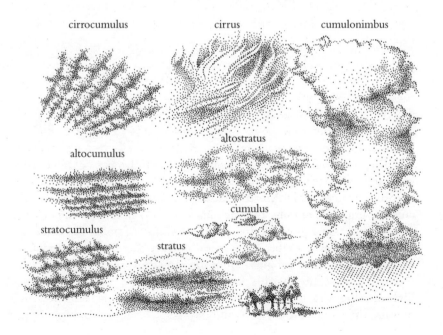

Outside the imaginations of cloud-spotters, it is true that, whether skiing monkeys or feeding fish, different cloud formations indicate different types of weather. On a fair day, you're likely to see puffy, sheep-like clouds called **cumulus**, friend of picnics. In a clear blue sky, you may see high feathery clouds called **cirrus**. **Stratus** clouds will appear on a rainy, overcast day, and big, bad **cumulonimbus** clouds signify stormy weather ahead.

NB Be sure to remember that **nephology** is the study of clouds but **nephrology** is quite a different matter, being the branch of medicine dealing with the kidneys.

WHY DOES THE WIND BLOW?

Wind is air that moves because of differences in **atmospheric pressure**. Atmospheric pressure can also be called **air pressure** or **barometric pressure** and it can be measured, and the weather predicted, using elegant devices called barometers, which also make good presents for people you don't know particularly well but who seem to have every-thing.

Put simply, atmospheric pressure is the pressure of the air above the Earth pressing down on it. Logically, it's higher near sea level, where there is lots of air piled up, and lower the higher up you go – which is why when you are in an aeroplane that is gaining height your ears 'pop' as the pressure between the air inside and outside your ears equalises.

In areas of high pressure the air is sinking and becoming warmer which is why high pressure is associated with barbecues, rounders and general good weather; whereas in low pressure areas the air is rising and becoming cooler, which creates clouds. On weather maps, areas of high and low pressure are indicated with lines called **isobars**, which connect areas of the same pressure together – like the contour lines on an Ordnance Survey map that show you how steep the hill you're about to climb is. If one area has high atmospheric pressure and next door is a region of low atmospheric pressure, then the air will move from the high-pressure area to the low as wind. The greater the difference in pressure the harder those gusts will blow.

The intensity of winds and storms is measured using a table called the Beaufort scale, invented by the Irish naval admiral Sir Francis Beaufort in 1805.

THE MAGNIFICENT SEVEN:
THE SEVEN WONDERS OF THE WORLD

- the Pyramids of Giza
- the Hanging Gardens of Babylon
- the temple of Artemis at Ephesus
- the statue of Zeus at Olympia
- the Colossus of Rhodes
- the Pharos of Alexandria
- the Mausoleum at Halicarnassus

The Seven Wonders of the World are a selection of the top tourist sites visited by the ancient Greeks. In ancient Greece the word for the wonders was '*theamata*' which translates as 'must-sees' and your diligent ancient tour operator would surely have loved to load you onto an oxen-drawn bus to visit every one of them. Just take a moment to reflect on how extraordinary that holiday would have been. Alas, the only wonderful wonder surviving today is the Great Pyramid of Giza in Egypt.

THE BIG SMOKES: CAPITAL CITIES

Afghanistan – Kabul
Albania – Tirana
Algeria – Algiers
Andorra – Andorra la Vella
Angola – Luanda
Antigua and Barbuda – St John's
Argentina – Buenos Aires
Armenia – Yerevan
Australia – Canberra
Austria – Vienna
Azerbaijan – Baku
The Bahamas – Nassau
Bahrain – Manama
Bangladesh – Dhaka
Barbados – Bridgetown
Belarus – Minsk
Belgium – Brussels
Belize – Belmopan
Benin – Porto-Novo
Bhutan – Thimphu
Bolivia – La Paz
Bosnia-Herzegovina – Sarajevo
Botswana – Gaborone
Brazil – Brasilia
Brunei – Bandar Seri Begawan
Bulgaria – Sofia
Burkina Faso – Ouagadougou
Burundi – Bujumbura
Cambodia – Phnom Penh
Cameroon – Yaoundé
Canada – Ottawa
Cape Verde – Praia
Central African Republic –
  Bangui
Chad – N'Djamena
Chile – Santiago

China – Beijing
Colombia – Bogotá
Comoros – Moroni
Congo – Brazzaville
Congo, Democratic Republic of
  – Kinshasa
Costa Rica – San José
Côte d'Ivoire – Yamoussoukro
Croatia – Zagreb
Cuba – Havana
Cyprus – Nicosia
Czech Republic – Prague
Denmark – Copenhagen
Djibouti – Djibouti
Dominica – Roseau
Dominican Republic – Santo
  Domingo
East Timor (Timor Leste) – Dili
Ecuador – Quito
Egypt – Cairo
El Salvador – San Salvador
Equatorial Guinea – Malabo
Eritrea – Asmara
Estonia – Tallinn
Ethiopia – Addis Ababa
Fiji – Suva
Finland – Helsinki
France – Paris
Gabon – Libreville
The Gambia – Banjul
Georgia – Tbilisi
Germany – Berlin
Ghana – Accra
Greece – Athens
Grenada – St George's
Guatemala – Guatemala City

Guinea – Conakry
Guinea-Bissau – Bissau
Guyana – Georgetown
Haiti – Port-au-Prince
Honduras – Tegucigalpa
Hungary – Budapest
Iceland – Reykjavik
India – New Delhi
Indonesia – Jakarta
Iran – Tehran
Iraq – Baghdad
Ireland – Dublin
Israel – Jerusalem
Italy – Rome
Jamaica – Kingston
Japan – Tokyo
Jordan – Amman
Kazakhstan – Astana
Kenya – Nairobi
Kiribati – Tarawa Atoll
Korea, North – Pyongyang
Korea, South – Seoul
Kosovo – Priština
Kuwait – Kuwait City
Kyrgyzstan – Bishkek
Laos – Vientiane
Latvia – Riga
Lebanon – Beirut
Lesotho – Maseru
Liberia – Monrovia
Libya – Tripoli
Liechtenstein – Vaduz
Lithuania – Vilnius
Luxembourg – Luxembourg
Macedonia – Skopje
Madagascar – Antananarivo
Malawi – Lilongwe
Malaysia – Kuala Lumpur

Maldives – Male
Mali – Bamako
Malta – Valletta
Marshall Islands – Majuro
Mauritania – Nouakchott
Mauritius – Port Louis
Mexico – Mexico City
Micronesia, Federated States of –
    Palikir
Moldova – Chişinău
Monaco – Monaco-ville
Mongolia – Ulan Bator
Montenegro – Podgorica
Morocco – Rabat
Mozambique – Maputo
Myanmar (Burma) – Nay Pyi Taw
Namibia – Windhoek
Nauru – no official capital;
    government offices in Yaren
Nepal – Kathmandu
Netherlands – Amsterdam
New Zealand – Wellington
Nicaragua – Managua
Niger – Niamey
Nigeria – Abuja
Norway – Oslo
Oman – Muscat
Pakistan – Islamabad
Palau – Melekeok
Panama – Panama City
Papua New Guinea – Port
    Moresby
Paraguay – Asunción
Peru – Lima
Philippines – Manila
Poland – Warsaw
Portugal – Lisbon
Qatar – Doha

Romania – Bucharest
Russia – Moscow
Rwanda – Kigali
St Kitts and Nevis – Basseterre
St Lucia – Castries
St Vincent and the Grenadines
 – Kingstown
Samoa – Apia
San Marino – San Marino
São Tomé and Príncipe –
 São Tomé
Saudi Arabia – Riyadh
Senegal – Dakar
Serbia – Belgrade
Seychelles – Victoria
Sierra Leone – Freetown
Singapore – Singapore
Slovakia – Bratislava
Slovenia – Ljubljana
Solomon Islands – Honiara
Somalia – Mogadishu
South Africa – Pretoria
Spain – Madrid
Sri Lanka – Colombo
Sudan – Khartoum
Suriname – Paramaribo
Swaziland – Mbabane
Sweden – Stockholm
Switzerland – Bern

Syria – Damascus
Taiwan – Taipei
Tajikistan – Dushanbe
Tanzania – Dar es Salaam
Thailand – Bangkok
Togo – Lomé
Tonga – Nuku'alofa
Trinidad and Tobago –
 Port-of-Spain
Tunisia – Tunis
Turkey – Ankara
Turkmenistan – Ashgabat
Tuvalu – Vaiaku
Uganda – Kampala
Ukraine – Kiev
United Arab Emirates – Abu Dhabi
United Kingdom – London
United States of America –
 Washington D.C.
Uruguay – Montevideo
Uzbekistan – Tashkent
Vanuatu – Port-Vila
Vatican City (Holy See) – Vatican
 City
Venezuela – Caracas
Vietnam – Hanoi
Yemen – Sana'a
Zambia – Lusaka
Zimbabwe – Harare

FUELLING THE FIRE:
FOSSIL FUELS

There are three types of fossil fuel - **coal**, **gas** and **oil** - which are all made of the fossilised carbon remains of animals and plants that have been covered and squashed by layers of sedimentary rock over millions of years. Fossil fuels spell bad news for the poor old Earth as they can only be mined out of the crust and, unlike library books, are non-renewable, so will one day run out. Unfortunately, there isn't any good news to counteract that blow, as they are also bad for the environment. When they are burned to release the energy in them – for example, to drive a car or heat a bowl of parsnip soup on a stove – they release more carbon dioxide into the atmosphere than can be absorbed by the Earth's natural processes and this contributes to the negative effects of **greenhouse gases**.

IT'S GETTING HOT IN HERE:
THE GREENHOUSE EFFECT

Despite the bad press they receive, the processes behind the greenhouse effect are not all bad. They are, in fact, responsible for keeping the Earth's perfectly calibrated temperature in balance. Without it, the temperature of the Earth's surface would be a chilly -23°C, which, to put it bluntly, means we wouldn't exist. Luckily, our diligent atmosphere traps some of the heat received from the sun, rather than letting it reflect back into space, thereby maintaining a habitable temperature on our planet.

Greenhouse gases make the atmosphere more insulating. Carbon dioxide and methane are both greenhouse gases that have increased in the atmosphere over time due to human activity. Burning fossil fuels increases carbon dioxide, and livestock and rice farming and drilling for oil produce increasing levels of methane. The rise in these gases is called the **greenhouse effect**, which is contributing to the rise in the Earth's temperature, or **global warming**, and may prove disastrous not just for the polar bears who run out of puff swimming between their melting ice caps, but also, eventually, for us.

HOLEY O₃: THE OZONE LAYER

The ozone layer is a crucial layer of ozone gas high in the stratosphere, 10km above our heads. Ozone molecules (O_3) are made of three oxygen atoms, and they occur naturally in the stratosphere. The ozone layer works like a protective pair of sunglasses, as it is responsible for filtering out a large proportion of the destructive ultraviolet rays from the sun that are harmful to humans. In the recent past scientists discovered the shocking fact that the ozone layer has been damaged by atmospheric pollutants, particularly CFCs (chlorofluorocarbons), chemicals that were widely used in fridges and aerosol sprays.

WATER WORKS:
THE HYDROLOGICAL CYCLE

The hydrological cycle is the endless system whereby water moves from the ocean (evaporation) and from plants (transpiration) through the atmosphere, falls to Earth as **precipitation** (rain, snow, sleet and hail) and then travels back to the ocean in a continuous loop.

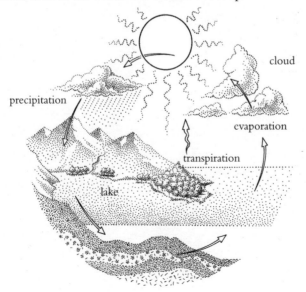

RIVERS

Rivers are part of the hydrological cycle, and also a crucial part of human existence – settlements have always sprung up around them because they provide food, drink, transport and irrigation, as well as water sports and handy places to dump dead bodies and sewage. Rivers beribbon our lands and flow from higher ground down into lakes, seas and oceans. They can run for huge distances: the longest river in the world is the Nile, which runs for 6,695km from Lake Victoria through Uganda, Sudan and Egypt to the Mediterranean. The starting point of a river is called the **source** and the place where the water pours out into the sea is called the **river mouth**. The source can be fed in different ways, such as through rain or snowfall collecting in a **drainage basin** (an area of land from which water seeps into the river course). Separate drainage basins are divided by hills, ridges, or mountains known as **watersheds**. Other ways for sources to fill themselves up include water flowing from glaciers, springs, lakes or marshes.

Confluence: the point where two rivers join.
Tributary: a smaller river that joins the main channel.
Meanders: the large horseshoe-shaped bends rivers make as they flow.
Oxbow lake: due to erosion, meanders become tighter and eventually
    break. The remaining horseshoe separated from the river is called an
    oxbow lake.

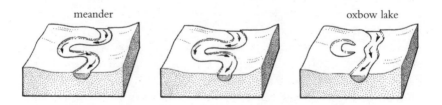

meander   oxbow lake

Deltas: occur at the mouth of rivers where the river deposits mud and
    rock carried with it. There are three types of delta: **arcuate**, or
    fan-shaped, deltas occur when the river splits into lots of small rivers
    as it reaches the sea; **cuspate** deltas occur when the river deposits
    sediment either side of itself as it flows into the sea, creating a
    pointed promontory; a **bird's foot** delta occurs when the river splits

into smaller rivers and also deposits sediment around each river, creating a shape like a bird's foot stretching out into the sea.

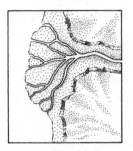 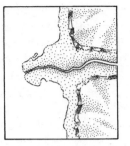 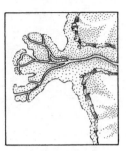

arcuate delta   cuspate delta   bird's foot delta

SLIP, SLIDING AWAY: COASTAL EROSION

Next time you're licking a lolly on the beach, being soothed by the sound of the waves lapping against the shore, remember that a process fascinating to geographers is taking place right in front of you. **Erosion** is the means by which coastal land constantly changes shape. There are various different methods that the weather and the waves use to have their wicked way with the shore. They can create features such as rugged cliffs, bays, crags, caves, beaches, spits and tombolos by breaking up the rock or earth of the coastline, carrying it away and dropping it in other places (this is called **deposition**). Waves also erode the coastline through the hydraulic action of their repeated battering against the shore and by throwing sand against cliff faces day in and day out (this is called **abrasion**). Bigger waves can even carry rocks along with them and if these bash into other rocks they break down in a process called **attrition**. On a more subtle level, the chemicals in seawater also act to break down certain types of rock (this is called **corrosion** or **solution**).

HANG ON TIGHT:
STALACTITES AND STALAGMITES

Stalactites and stalagmites are naturally formed stone pillars that are made when water containing calcium carbonate drips from the roofs of caves.

The way to remember the difference between them is that stalac**tites** hold **tight** to the roof, and that if they achieve their slow-dripping, patient dreams, young stalag**mites might** one day reach the roof.

❧ GEOGRAPHY ❧
TEST PAPER

1. Which is the correct order of the planets from the sun?

a) Mercury, Venus, Mars, Earth, Uranus, Jupiter, Neptune, Saturn
b) Mercury, Venus, Earth, Mars, Jupiter, Saturn, Uranus, Neptune
c) Neptune, Earth, Jupiter, Uranus, Mars, Venus, Saturn, Mercury

2. Why does the wind blow?

a) hot air rises from the Earth and creates a vacuum.
b) precipitation causes changes in humidity.
c) differences in air pressure lead to airflow.
d) cumulus clouds release their droplets of water.

3. What is a meander?

a) a high feathery cloud
b) the discharge of a river into the sea
c) the barrier between two watersheds
d) the bends a river forms as it flows

4. Which of the following is not one of the Seven Wonders of the World?

a) the temple of the Vestal Virgins in Rome
b) the Temple of Artemis at Ephesus
c) the Mausoleum at Halicarnassus
d) the statue of Zeus at Olympia

5. What is the name of the huge continent described in Albert Wegener's theory of continental drift?

6. Name all four oceans.

7. Name the six continents.

8. Which mountain is the highest in the world?

9. When does spring start?

10. What are clouds made of?

11. What is the difference between nephology and nephrology?

12. Where is Timbuktu?

13. Which seismic waves are the most dangerous?
a) P-waves
b) S-waves
c) L-waves

14. What should you do in an earthquake?

15. What inspired Albert Wegener to come up with the theory of continental drift?

16. If you see these clouds in the sky, what sort of weather should you expect?

17. What is the capital of Tanzania?

18. Which country is Ouagadougou the capital of?

19. Where would you find the exosphere?

20. What is O_3?

21. Name three types of precipitation.

22. Which river is the longest in the world?

23. What is a watershed?

24. What is the name for the source point of an earthquake within the Earth's crust?

CLASSICS

The chapter number "8" appears above the title with decorative flourishes.

'**Classics** *n.pl.* Ancient Greek and Latin literature, art, or culture'
Oxford Concise English Dictionary

'*Mediocribus esse poetis*
Non homines, non di, non concessere columnae'
(Not gods, nor men, nor even booksellers have put up
with poets being second-rate)
HORACE (65–8 BCE), *Ars Poetica*

There's more to ancient Greece and Rome than eccentric emperors, ponderous philosophers, togas and tragedies. The study of the Classics transports us to the cradle of our own civilisation – politics, philosophy, literature, law, architecture, drama, science, art, mathematics, medicine and the A5 would not be what they are today without the influences of ancient Greece and Rome.

We have no time for those who protest that Latin is a dead language or that Socrates has nothing to do with them. All around us we can see evidence of the important place that these cultures have in our everyday lives. When you look out of your window, you will see the columns and architraves of classical architecture all around you. When you talk about how your television is malfunctioning, you are using ancient Greek and Latin words ('*tele*' means 'far away' in ancient Greek and 'vision' comes from the Latin verb '*videre*' meaning 'to see', '*mal*' comes from the Latin '*malus*' meaning 'bad' and 'function' from the verb '*fungi*' meaning 'to perform'). When you admire a beautiful Renaissance sculpture, you are looking at the aesthetic principles of ancient Greece refracted through the prism of a joyous period in the fifteenth century when artists and writers fell in love with their classical forebears.

Cast aside those memories of mindless recitations of *amo, amas, amat* and struggles with the ablative absolute: in this chapter we unveil these grammatical mysteries but you will also discover the beauty of Homeric poetry, the drama of Greek myths, the inimitable indulgence of Roman banquets, the secrets of philosophy and the correct names for the various parts of a legionary's armour.

Versa folium! Prepare for a classic adventure!

ALEXANDER TO AUGUSTUS: A SHORT HISTORY OF THE GREAT CLASSICAL EMPIRES

Archaeologists believe that European civilisation pushed up its first green shoots in the Mediterranean, with the bull-leaping Minoan society that flourished on the island of Crete in the second millennium BCE. Simultaneously, an organised community, called **Mycenae**, grew up in the south of mainland Greece on the pulchritudinous Peloponnesian peninsula.

By the fifth century BCE, mainland Greece was divided into many independent *poleis* (city states), the most powerful of which were energetic **Athens** and sober **Sparta**. These *poleis* were the first roots of the era we refer to as **classical civilisation**. From 499 to 479 BCE the Greek states were constantly threatened by the powerful **Persian Empire** with whom they battled repeatedly, in famous conflicts at Marathon, Thermopylae, Salamis and Plataea among others. Not content with fighting external enemies, the two main city states took each other on in the **Peloponnesian War** (431–404 BCE) which ended with Sparta victorious (with a little help from their old enemy Persia).

However, Sparta's reign as top *polis* came under threat in 359 BCE, with an ambitious young man called Philip and his usurpation of the throne of the state of **Macedon**. By the time pugnacious Philip popped his clogs, Macedon held sway over almost all of Greece. However, even this achievement would be bettered by his son, the amazing **Alexander the Great** (356–323 BCE). Alexander created a huge empire that stretched as far as India and Egypt, spreading Hellenic values and language across the world. And all by the age of thirty-two, when he carelessly caught a fever and died. After Alexander, the Greek Empire fragmented as his generals took control of different areas.

This left the way clear for a power-hungry city in Italy called **Rome** to fully assert itself on a global scale. Rome had been a simple Etruscan kingdom, but around 510 BCE its citizens declared their home town a **republic** and began to conquer the surrounding territories. Thanks to its exceptional army, Rome had great success and the eventual defeat of its arch-enemy, **Carthage**, in the **Punic Wars** (264–241 BCE, 218–201 BCE and 149–146 BCE) took Roman expansionism to a new level, bringing Spain, Sicily and North Africa under its control, and in 197 BCE Rome invaded Greece. By the end of the first century BCE, Rome controlled the shores of the entire Mediterranean, including Palestine, Egypt and Libya.

In 27 BCE the Roman Republic ended when **Augustus** became **Emperor**. Under the aegis of successive emperors, Rome continued its relentless march: over the course of its illustrious history the empire's territories stretched from the borders of Scotland in the north to Egypt in the south, Spain in the west and Iraq in the east.

However, as everyone knows, all good things come to an end. After the Emperor Diocletian (245–313 CE) divided the Roman territories into **Eastern** and **Western Empires**, Rome's power diminished until the final Western Emperor, Romulus Augustulus, was deposed by the **Goths** in 476 CE. The Eastern or **Byzantine Empire**, which had flourished under the Christian Emperor Constantine (c.274–337 CE), continued until 1453 when the capital city he had established, **Constantinople** (a contracted form of 'Constantinopolis' meaning '*polis* of Constantine'), was finally overrun by the Turks.

WHAT'S SO SPECIAL ABOUT THE SPARTANS?

When we use the adjective 'spartan' to describe a hotel room or a selection of canapés, we are using it as a synonym for 'frugal' or 'austere'. This is because the Spartans had a reputation for leading disciplined, harsh existences without comfort or luxury. Spartan boys were subject to extremely rigorous military training from the age of seven in order to make them outstanding soldiers. In fact, babies who were born weak or disabled were left outside to die because they would never contribute to Sparta's great army of *hoplites* (foot soldiers).

The Olympian Family Tree

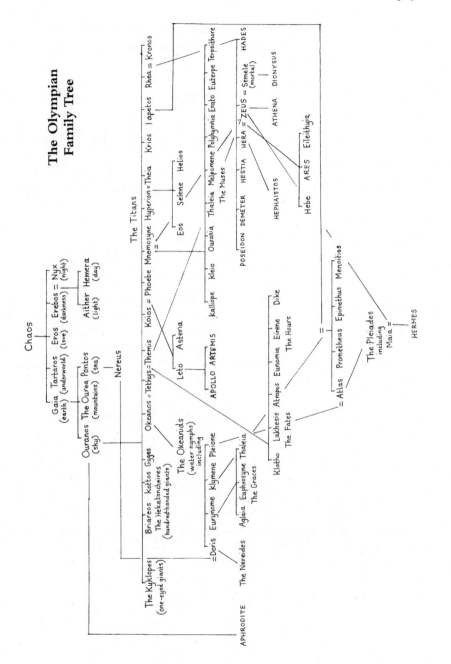

ALPHA TO OMEGA: THE ANCIENT GREEK ALPHABET

Greek capital letter	Greek lower-case letter	Name of Greek letter	English pronunciation
A	α	alpha	fat or father
B	β	beta	boy
Γ	γ	gamma	girl
Δ	δ	delta	dog
E	ε	epsilon	pet
Z	ζ	zeta	wisdom
H	η	eta	hair
Θ	θ	theta	theatre
I	ι	iota	pit or meet
K	κ	kappa	pickle
Λ	λ	lambda	long
M	μ	mu	mother
N	ν	nu	nice
Ξ	ξ	xi	axe
O	o	omicron	boat
Π	π	pi	cap
P	ρ	rho	radish (but rolled)
Σ	σ (or ς at end of words)	sigma	sigh or zoo
T	τ	tau	stop
Y	υ	upsilon	fool
Φ	φ	phi	philosophy
X	χ	chi	kite
Ψ	ψ	psi	slips
Ω	ω	omega	boat

ANCIENT GREEK PHILOSOPHY

The word 'philosophy' comes from the ancient Greek 'φιλοσοφια' ('*philosophia*') meaning 'love of wisdom'. Once you know that the stem 'phil' means love you'll see that it pops up in lots of English words such as 'philanthropic' (meaning 'loving people'), 'philharmonic' (meaning 'loving music'),'bibliophile' (meaning 'book lover') and 'Phillip' (meaning 'horse lover'). From '*sophos*' meaning wisdom we get the word 'sophisticated' and the name 'Sophie'. Philosophy is the practice of attempting to understand and organise the true facts of our existence, our universe and our behaviour. It is concerned with using rational argument to get to the bottom of formidable concepts such as truth, justice, morality, beauty and knowledge. The ancient Greeks are famous throughout history for their contribution to this field of study.

The Presocratics (*c.* sixth century BCE)
The Presocratics were chiefly concerned with the investigation of the nature of the world around them. They rejected mythological explanations for phenomena and sought instead to understand their surroundings in terms of mathematics, astronomy and biology. They were fascinated by the idea of the gap between how things appear to human beings and how they really are. Pythagoras, Empedocles, Thales and Heraclitus can be counted among them, and while many of the theories they proposed were eventually rejected (Heraclitus' belief that everything around us is born from fire and Thales' theory that everything is really made of water, for example), their manner of questioning has informed the basis of what we think of as Western philosophy and has also influenced the field of science. The group of teachers known as the **sophists** emerged from this tradition – they believed that morality did not exist in any objective form; rather that it was a structure forced upon humans by kings or states. They also emphasised the power of rhetoric and argument in politics.

Socrates (469–399 BCE)
It is tricky to identify exactly what our favourite ugly genius Socrates believed as none of his own writings survive and we only have the works of his followers like Plato to rely on. We do know that he rejected the sophist idea that morality did not exist and focused his philosophical

enquiry on the subject of ethics. He encouraged self-knowledge and attempted to define wisdom, knowledge and beliefs. Two of the most famous quotes attributed to him are: 'I know nothing except the fact of my own ignorance' and 'The unexamined life is not worth living'. His major contribution to philosophy lies in his invention of the **Socratic method**, in which a series of questions are posed to a person or group and through rigorous questioning the underlying principles of the person or group emerge in a distilled form. Socrates was condemned to death in 399 BCE for corrupting the youth of Athens. Despite his friends' best efforts, he refused to attempt an escape because he was committed to living by the laws of Athens and therefore felt he had to accept his sentence. He died by drinking poison made with hemlock.

Plato (429–347 BCE)
Plato was a pupil of Socrates who, after his mentor's death, devoted his life to continuing his teachings. In 387 BCE he founded the **Academy** in Athens where pupils were taught subjects such as metaphysics, natural science, mathematics, ethics and politics. The Academy existed in some form for nearly a thousand years. Plato believed that the world was divided into two realms; the visible, which we understand with our senses; and the intelligible, which we understand with our minds. He also proposed the idea of **Forms**, which stated that properties such as goodness, beauty and truth, exist as timeless unchanging entities in parallel to the visible world and that what we are capable of perceiving in our world are imitations of these Forms. In his work *The Republic*, Plato explains this theory with an allegory narrated by Socrates, where he likens most of unenlightened humanity to people sitting in a cave with a fire behind them watching shadows on the cave wall. Philosophers are the people who venture out of the cave and see things as they really are, rather than simply the shadows.

Aristotle (384–322 BCE)
Aristotle was educated at Plato's Academy and later, after acting as tutor to Alexander the Great, set up his own school called the **Lyceum** in Athens. He wrote and taught on many subjects, including logic, mathematics and psychology. The aim of Aristotle's writings on logic (known as the *Organon*) was to develop a method of reasoning that could be used to learn everything one could want to learn about reality.

Aristotle's method uses **syllogisms**. A syllogism is a way of coming to a conclusion by linking two separate propositions: e.g. All men are mortal: Socrates is a man: therefore, Socrates is mortal. Aristotle rejected Plato's theory of Forms and developed his own theories of reality and on the structure of the universe, biology, drama, ethics and the soul.

Stoicism (*c.* fourth century BCE to second century CE)
Stoicism was founded by Zeno of Citium (344–262 BCE) in the third century BCE and was named after the *Stoa Poikile* or 'Painted Porch' of the marketplace in Athens where its followers were taught. It was a school of thought that held as its central tenet that the world is created by a divine being and man must accept his fate and not be governed by negative emotions, but instead try to live according to virtue, which Zeno believed to be the highest good and source of happiness.

Epicureanism (*c.* fourth century BCE to fourth century CE)
This very influential school of Greek thought was founded by Epicurus of Samos (341–271 BCE) who believed that pleasure was the essence of a happy life. By pleasure, Epicurus did not mean sensual enjoyment, but rather the absence of pain. He taught moderation because excess would ultimately cause pain. The Epicureans also believed that the world was made up solely of atoms and void. They included the soul in this theory and therefore believed that there could be no life after death, as the soul must deteriorate into its component atoms after death just as the body does.

Scepticism (*c.* fifth century BCE to third century CE)
This was a school of thought formalised by Pyrrho of Elis (*c.*360–272 BCE), and also followed by some later members of Plato's Academy, which states that man can only ever know things through the veil of his own perception, rather than knowing the nature of things as they actually are. This being accepted, a wise person will never believe in absolute or final truths.

**WOODEN HORSES AND WARRIOR HEROES:
THE TROJAN WAR (twelfth or thirteenth century BCE)**

When Paris, the son of King Priam of Troy, eloped with Helen, the extraordinarily beautiful wife of King Menelaus of Sparta, Agamemnon, Menelaus' brother and King of Mycenae, led a Greek army, including famous heroes such as Odysseus and Nestor, to attack Troy and retrieve Helen (hence Marlowe's reference to Helen's 'face that launched a thousand ships'). The war lasted ten years, at the end of which the Greeks launched a false retreat, leaving behind a gift of a huge wooden horse. Concealed inside the horse was a band of men who attacked and brought down the city from within. It is not known how much of the story is legend, but it has remained embedded in the world's imagination, and the phrase 'beware Greeks bearing gifts' derives from this tale.

THE WRATH OF ACHILLES: THE *ILIAD*

Homer's *Iliad* is an ancient Greek epic poem in twenty-four books which was probably composed in the eighth century BCE but describes events that took place four centuries earlier: the last gasps of the **Trojan War**. The war provides a background for the main story of the poem: the anger of the Greek hero and warrior **Achilles**.

Achilles was the son of the water nymph Thetis, who, when the Fates predicted Achilles would be killed in the Trojan War, dipped her son into the River Styx to make him immortal – however, she missed a spot on the ankle which she held him by (hence the phrase 'Achilles heel' referring to a person's weak spot). Achilles is the greatest and most magnificent hero of the war, but he gets in a huff and refuses to fight when he's insulted by Agamemnon, who insists he must give up his slave woman, Briseis. After Achilles' withdrawal the Greeks begin to suffer heavy losses, and try to persuade him to return. Achilles still refuses, but agrees to a plan formulated by the oldest and wisest of the Greek commanders, Nestor, to allow his dearest friend **Patroclus** to fight in his place wearing his armour. When Troy's top fighter, **Hector**, kills Patroclus (thinking he is Achilles), Achilles is overcome with anger towards the Trojans and after he kills Hector, he desecrates his body by dragging it behind his chariot for many days. In ancient times, it was held that a hero who dies on the battlefield should be burned on a funeral pyre and his bones and remaining ashes buried separately, so this is a terrible sacrilege. The poem closes with **Priam**, King of Troy and Hector's father, coming to Achilles to ask for the body of his son to be returned so he can be given the proper burial. Achilles is deeply moved by the old king, and with uncharacteristic grace and pity he finally returns Hector's body. Both sides temporarily agree to a truce and Hector is given a hero's burial.

The *Iliad* forms part of the ancient Greek oral tradition, where laws, stories, poetry and events were committed to memory and recited rather than written down. It's a poem full of beautiful and unforgettable epithets that serve to bring both colour and life to the words, but also to help the audience to identify their favourite characters. There is, for example, much mention of 'rosy-fingered Dawn', 'swift-footed Achilles' and, loveliest of all, 'cow-eyed Hera'.

EPIC WANDERINGS: HOMER'S *ODYSSEY*

Unlike the *Iliad*, which has a fairly simple structure and only one setting, Homer's *Odyssey* is much more sophisticated in scope and style. It also uses techniques of flashback, multiple narratives, characters and scenes. It is generally thought to be one of the greatest poems ever written and has had a huge influence on world literature.

Like the *Iliad* the *Odyssey* begins by plunging *in medias res* (into the middle of things). Ten years after the end of the Trojan War, the wily Greek hero **Odysseus** is held captive on a remote island by the goddess Calypso, who has taken a shine to him. All the other Greeks have been allowed to return home, but Odysseus, stalled by **Calypso** and the wrath of **Poseidon** (whose son, Polyphemus, Odysseus had blinded), has yet to return home to Ithaca where his wife **Penelope** and son **Telemachus** wait for him. **Athena**, Odysseus' great champion among the gods, persuades Zeus to let him escape.

The story then cuts to Ithaca, where the lovely Penelope is pursued by 108 suitors desperate for her hand. Telemachus is visited by Athena in disguise who tells him that Odysseus is still alive and that Telemachus should travel to Pylos, the kingdom of Nestor, and Sparta, the kingdom of Menelaus, to discover where his father is. In fact, neither have news of him, but in Sparta Telemachus is told of Odysseus' bravery and cunning while hiding inside the wooden horse which eventually led to the overthrow of Troy and the safe return of Helen.

Meanwhile, the gods reconvene to discuss Odysseus' fate, and Zeus sends Hermes to order Calypso to release him. Odysseus heads for home in a small boat but Poseidon, still furious, sends a storm to shipwreck him, until finally, with Athena's help, he reaches the shore. He wakes to find himself in the land of the **Phaeacians**, where he is received hospitably and at a banquet the next night is asked to recount the story of his journey from Troy to Calypso's island.

He then tells of his extraordinary adventures – the escape from the **Lotus Eaters**, whose flowers make memories fade, and from the Cyclops **Polyphemus**, who kills two of his men to make his supper; of **Aeolus**, King of the Winds, who gives him a bag of winds which his shipmates open and waste, forcing him to row to the island of the king of the **Laestrygonians**, who eats his scouts and destroys the ships by throwing huge rocks. Only Odysseus' ship survives and he sails to the house of the goddess **Circe**, who drugs his men and turns them into pigs. After Odysseus defeats her he stays with her as her lover for a year. Finally she tells him he must travel to the underworld to speak to **Tiresias**, the blind prophet who will guide him home. He also tells of the **Sirens**' song, which lures sailors into the sea, and which he manages to resist by tying himself to the mast of his ship and filling his crew's ears with wax; of the terrifying passage between the sea monsters **Scylla** and **Charybdis**; and the slaughter of the **cattle of the sun** on the island of Thrinacia which resulted in the death of his entire crew.

These terrifying adventures amuse the Phaeacians and they send him home on a ship the next morning. Finally, after twenty years' absence, Odysseus returns to Ithaca. Athena meets him on the path home and warns him that his wife's suitors may kill him. While she goes to collect Telemachus, Odysseus disguises himself as a beggar and seeks refuge at the house of **Eumaeus**, who fails to see through his disguise but receives him warmly. Odysseus' old dog, however, recognises his master's voice. Telemachus and Odysseus are reunited and go to Penelope, who does not realise that the stranger at her door is her husband. She announces she will hold a contest: she will marry whichever of the suitors can string and shoot with Odysseus' mighty bow. All fail, except Odysseus, who is embraced by his wife before he turns his arrows on the suitors, killing each one of them. He is pursued by their angry relatives but again Athena intervenes and the poem ends with Zeus promising peace to Ithaca.

ARISTOTLE'S *POETICS*

Many of the concepts and terms that we still use to discuss literature come from an influential work by the ancient Greek philosopher Aristotle (384–322 BC). His *Poetics* only partially survives but it has exerted its influence for centuries. In the *Poetics* Aristotle discusses ancient Greek poetry and, in particular, tragedy. He divides tragedy into six separate elements: plot, character, thought, language, melody and spectacle. Aristotle saw plot as the most important and believed that good tragedies have:

- unity of action – the action of the play follows one main plot
- unity of time – the action should take place in the course of one day
- unity of place – the action of the play should take place in one setting only

According to Aristotle, plays should include
only action that is probable and necessary for
the plot of the story. Famous terms that come
from the *Poetics* are:

Catharsis – meaning 'purgation' – the experience of strong emotion while watching
a play that benefits the audience by
purging them of extreme feelings and
leaving them in a calmer state.

Hamartia – meaning 'error' – the crucial
mistake that a hero in a drama makes,
causing the climax of the action. In later centuries *hamartia* was
interpreted to mean 'tragic flaw', referring to a moral weakness
inherent in the hero rather than just a mistake he makes.

Anagnorisis – meaning 'recognition' – the moment in a play where the
hero realises some crucial truth that had been previously hidden
from him.

Peripeteia – meaning 'reversal' – the climax of a play where the
fortunes or character of the hero change.

CLASSICAL GENRES

In classical times, different types of verse literature were divided into
three genres: **epic**, **lyric** and **drama**. Since that time various other
genres have been identified in ancient Greek and Roman literature.
Some of the major genres and their prime identifying characteristics are
listed below.

Epic: Common characteristics of epic poems are that they are long, deal
with elevated subjects, are set in the heroic past and are written in
epic metre. The most famous ancient Greek epics are the *Odyssey*
and the *Iliad* by Homer and the most famous Roman epic is the
Aeneid by Virgil.

Lyric poetry: This is poetry that expresses the personal feelings of the
poet in certain recognised metres. Originally lyric poems were sung
to the accompaniment of a lyre. Pindar and Sappho are considered

the top ancient Greek lyricists and Catullus is probably the most
famous Roman lyric poet. One of his most powerful poems is only
two lines long:

Odi et amo: quare id faciam, fortasse requiris.
Nescio, sed fieri sentio et excrucior.

(A rough translation would read: 'I hate and I love: you might ask
why I do this. I don't know, but I feel it and am crucified.' It's much
more brutally hard-hitting in the Latin.)

Elegiac poetry: This is poetry written in a specific metre and is considered a shorter form of epic poetry. The most famous ancient
Greek elegiac poet is Callimachus and the most famous Roman
elegiac poets are Catullus and Ovid.

Drama – Tragedy: Tragedy is a form of serious drama which usually
focuses on a hero who makes some kind of mistake that leads to a
change in his or her fortunes. Classical tragedy does not involve
many characters, the actors wear masks, and much of the action
occurs offstage and is reported. The three great ancient Greek
tragedians whose work survives today are Aeschylus, Sophocles and
Euripides. Not much Roman tragedy survives apart from a few
works by Seneca.

Drama – Comedy: Classical comedy tends to focus around one
central idea or conflict and involves humorous situations designed to
make the audience laugh. The most famous ancient Greek comedy
writer is Aristophanes and the most famous Roman comedy
writers are Terence and Plautus. We do have to admit that what
made the ancients giggle doesn't seem to have the same effect today.

Satire: This is writing that attacks something or someone using biting
humour. The term was invented in Roman times and the two
most famous Roman satirists are Horace and Juvenal. Juvenal was a
cutting wit – one of his most famous phrases, *'panem et circenses'*
('bread and circuses'), comes from a passage where he states that
rulers can keep the masses docile so long as they ply them with
entertainment and keep them well fed as this is all they care about.
Think about that next time you're enjoying a pizza in front of *Strictly
Come Dancing*.

History: History was generally written in prose in classical times. The
most prominent ancient Greek historians are Herodotus, Plutarch

and Thucydides. The most famous Roman historians are Livy and
Tacitus.

LA BELLA ROMA:
THE FOUNDING MYTH OF ROME

In ancient Rome of the eighth century BCE, the only female figures in
the state religious system were the Vestal Virgins – the priestesses whose
duty it was to maintain the sacred fire of Vesta, the goddess of the hearth,
home and the family. After their initiation, they were bound to thirty
years of service as virgins. Unlike the nuns in *The Sound of Music*, the
Romans weren't terribly sympathetic to Vestals who found it hard to
deny the pleasures of the flesh: a Vestal who broke her vow of chastity
was buried alive.

According to Virgil's *Aeneid*, Ilia (also known as Rhea Sylvia) was the
daughter of Numitor, King of Alba Longa, and a descendant of Aeneas.
When Numitor's brother Amulius seized the throne, he killed Numitor's
son and forced Ilia to become a Vestal Virgin, thereby ensuring Numitor
would have no male heirs to his throne. But Mars, the god of war, raped
Ilia in the forest – as the ancient Greek and Roman gods were wont to
do on a casual basis – and she conceived twin boys, Romulus and
Remus. When Amulius discovered Ilia was pregnant, he ordered that she
be buried alive, and the boys killed. However, the boys were saved by a
kind servant and set adrift on the River Tiber, where the river god
Tiberius rescued them and gave them to a she-wolf to be looked after.
Tiberius later rescued and married Ilia, and Romulus and Remus over-
threw Amulius to restore Numitor to the throne. They then founded a
city on the banks of the river
that had saved their lives, Rome.
This fraternal teamwork wasn't
to last, however, as Romulus
killed Remus after a dispute over
which brother had the support
of the gods to rule the city.

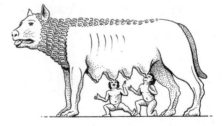

THE ROMAN GODS

From the ninth century BCE the ancient Roman civilisation began to grow in prominence in the Italian peninsular. The Romans absorbed many elements of Greek culture, including their religion, and they essentially worshipped the same gods but with different names. These gods were the official religion of Rome – although other cults such as that of Mithras and Isis were also introduced as the empire expanded its territories – until the Emperor Constantine brought Christianity to the empire in 313 CE.

Ancient Greek Name	Roman Name	Speciality
Zeus	Jupiter or Jove	king of the gods, god of the sky
Hera	Juno	Zeus/Jupiter's wife, goddess of marriage
Poseidon	Neptune	god of the sea
Hermes	Mercury	messenger of the gods
Ares	Mars	god of war
Aphrodite	Venus	goddess of love
Athena	Minerva	goddess of wisdom
Artemis	Diana	goddess of hunting
Apollo	Apollo	god of music, poetry and healing
Hephaestus	Vulcan	crippled god of fire
Dionysus	Bacchus	god of wine
Ceres	Demeter	goddess of crops
Hades or Pluto	Dis Pater	god of the underworld

COMMENTARII DE BELLO GALLICO
BY JULIUS CAESAR

Between 58 and 51 BCE, Julius Caesar, while he was still predominantly a military leader and long before his absolute rule of Rome and his 'Et tu Brute' moment, carried out a series of wars against various tribes in Gaul (a territory which roughly corresponds with modern-day France). He recorded his experience of these wars in the *Commentarii de Bello Gallico*, which used to be much studied for its simple, clean Latin prose (rather than for its thrilling storyline). It gives great insight into the practical considerations of running a military campaign and is also an expert example of political propaganda. The comic series *Asterix* by René Goscinny and Albert Uderzo is set in the period just after the Gallic wars when Gaul was under Roman rule.

> *Gallia est omnis divisa in partes tres, quarum unam incolunt Belgae, aliam Aquitani, tertiam qui ipsorum lingua Celtae, nostra Galli appellantur. Hi omnes lingua, institutis, legibus inter se differunt. Gallos ab Aquitanis Garumna flumen, a Belgis Matrona et Sequana dividit. Horum omnium fortissimi sunt Belgae, propterea quod a cultu atque humanitate provinciae longissime absunt, minimeque ad eos mercatores saepe commeant atque ea quae ad effeminandos animos pertinent important . . .*

All Gaul is divided into three parts, one of which the Belgae inhabit, the Aquitani another, those who in their own language are called Celts, in ours Gauls, the third. All these differ from each other in language, customs and laws. The river Garonne separates the Gauls from the Aquitani; the Marne and the Seine separate them from the Belgae. Of all these, the Belgae are the bravest, because they are farthest from the civilization and refinement of [our] Province, and merchants least frequently resort to them and import those things which tend to effeminate the mind . . .

Translated by W. A. MacDevitt (1851)

LEARNING TO LOVE LATIN

Latin was the most important language in Europe for almost 2,000 years and was still in use as the international language of diplomacy up until the eighteenth century. It is the basis for the French, Italian and Spanish languages spoken today, as well as being a source for thousands of words in English. Its prominence in Europe spread with the conquests of the Roman Empire. After the end of the empire its power continued as it remained the official language of the Roman Catholic Church.

The language of classical Latin literature is known as classical Latin, which is more formal than the Latin that was actually spoken by the Romans in their day-to-day lives. Once you know the rules of Latin grammar it becomes clear that Latin is a very logical language and you will gradually realise that it is an enormous lark to puzzle out Latin prose or poetry, looking for clues in the endings of words and the arrangements of sentences.

BASIC LATIN GRAMMAR

Latin is a marvellous, muscular, satisfying language and the poetry and prose it has given us in its literature, carefully copied out by all those diligent scribes over the years, is a treasure trove. Being able to translate it probably isn't most pupils' priority, but it is surprising how much you can work out when reading inscriptions in churches and ancient ruins if you can just grasp a few of the basics.

NOUNS

In Latin nouns are always masculine, feminine or neuter.

Nearly all nouns ending in '-*us*' are masculine, such as '*lupus*' meaning 'wolf', '*amicus*' meaning '(male) friend' and '*equus*' meaning 'horse'.

Nearly all nouns ending in '-*a*' are feminine, such as '*puella*' meaning 'girl', '*amica*' meaning '(female) friend' and '*taberna*' meaning 'shop' or 'inn'.

Nearly all nouns ending in '-*um*' are neuter, such as '*templum*' meaning 'temple' and '*alimentum*' meaning 'food'.

The plurals of masculine '-*us*' nouns end in '-*i*'; '*lupi*' means 'wolves'. The plurals of feminine '-*a*' nouns end in '-*ae*'; '*puellae*' means 'girls'. The plural of neuter '–*um*' nouns end in '-*a*'; '*templa*' means 'temples'.

Nouns in Latin also change their endings depending on their role in the sentence. This is known as changing case. The complete list of cases for one type of noun is called a **declension**. The cases of nouns are important for working out the sense of a Latin phrase, as word order is different in Latin to in English; in particular, the verb usually comes at the end of a sentence. There are also no articles ('the' or 'a') in Latin so you have to decide which is most appropriate when translating.

The subject of a sentence is in the **nominative** case: '**The girl** called the dog.'

If someone or something is being called or addressed, they are in the **vocative** case: '**Dog**! Come here!'

The object of a sentence is in the **accusative** case: 'The girl called **the dog**.'

The **genitive** case is used to show possession: 'The **girl's** dog'.

The indirect object of a sentence is in the **dative** case: 'The girl gave the food **to the dog**.'

The **ablative** case is used with certain prepositions and for nouns describing when or where something happened, or how it happened. It is usually translated into English with the addition of either 'by', 'with' or 'from' before the noun: 'The girl gave the food to the dog **with love**.'

Latin nouns can belong to any of five declensions. All nouns of the same declension change their endings in the same way.

When you look up a Latin noun in a dictionary, as you no doubt often find yourself doing of a winter's evening, it gives the nominative singular case, the ending of the genitive singular case and the gender. This is all the information you need to let you know how to decline the noun as the genitive case is different in each of the five declensions, so you can identify which declension a noun belongs to simply by looking at the genitive ending.

You also only need to know these two cases in order to identify the **stem** of a noun – the stem is the basic form of a noun to which the various case endings are added. Sometimes stems change from how they appear in the nominative case, and the genitive given in the dictionary will show this stem change. For example, the word for tooth, '*dens*', appears in the dictionary as '*dens, dentis* m'. From this you can work out that '*dens*' is from the third declension and that the stem you should add the different endings to is '*dent-*'. English words that derive from Latin tend to be based on the stem – for example 'dentist'.

First declension: *puella*, *-ae* f – girl (NB the stem of *puella* is *puell-*)
Second declension: *amicus*, *-i* m – friend
Third declension: *canis*, *-is* f – dog
Fourth declension: *gradus*, *-us* m – step
Fifth declension: *dies*, *-ei*, m or f – day

The first declension

First declension nouns end in '*-a*' and are usually feminine.

Nominative: *puella*
Vocative: *puella*
Accusative: *puellam*
Genitive: *puellae*
Dative: *puellae*
Ablative: *puella*

Nominative plural: *puellae*
Vocative plural: *puellae*
Accusative plural: *puellas*
Genitive plural: *puellarum*
Dative plural: *puellis*
Ablative plural: *puellis*

Absolutely ablative

Ablative absolutes are groups of nouns (or nouns and a participle) in the ablative case which are participial phrases that are separate from the rest of a sentence. Participial phrases are one of the trickier concepts one comes across when learning Latin, but there's really nothing to be afraid of, although many pupils regard them with the same horror Odysseus (Ulysses in Latin) regarded the Cyclops as he chowed down on his friends. They are best translated into English by adding the words, 'with', 'when', 'since' or 'because' at the start of the phrase.

Nocte appropinqante, puella dormit
Literal translation: Night approaching, the girl sleeps.
This can be more elegantly phrased as: As night approaches, the girl sleeps.

Alimento dato, canis laeta erat.
Literal: The food having been given, the dog happy he was.
Again, more smoothly translated as: When he had been given his food, the dog was happy.

Endings for the five declensions

SINGULAR	First (m or f)	Second (m, f or n)	Third (m, f or n)	Fourth (m or n)	Fifth (m or f)
nominative	-a	-us/-ius/ -er (neuter -um)	various	-us (neuter -u)	-es
vocative	-a	-us changes to -e/-ius changes to -i/-er stays as -er (neuter -um)	same as nominative	-us (neuter -u)	-es
accusative	-am	-um	-em (neuter – same as nominative)	-um (neuter -u)	-em
genitive	-ae	-i	-is	-us	-ei
dative	-ae	-o	-i	-ui or -u	-ei
ablative	-a	-o	-e (neuter -e or -i)	-u	-e

PLURAL					
nominative	-ae	-i (neuter -a)	-es (neuter -a or ia)	-us (neuter -ua)	-es -es
vocative	-ae	-i (neuter -a)	-es (neuter -a or -ia)	-us (neuter -ua)	-es
accusative	-as	-os (neuter -a)	-es (neuter -a or -ia)	-us (neuter -ua)	-es
genitive	-arum	-orum	-um or -ium	-uum	-erum
dative	-is	-is	-ibus	-ibus	-ebus
ablative	-is	-is	-ibus	-ibus	-ebus

ADJECTIVES

Adjectives in Latin, infuriatingly or fantastically depending on how Roman you're feeling, must match the noun they describe in number, gender and case, but not in declension. Sadly, the endings of adjectives don't simply match the ending of the noun they are describing. Each adjective belongs to one of two of its own groups: the first group being made up of first- and second-declension adjectives and the second group being made up of third-declension adjectives. So a first-declension noun can be described by a third-declension adjective and thus the noun and adjective will have different endings even though both will be of the same number, gender and case. (There are a few irregular adjectives that don't abide by the following rules but most of them fit into these patterns.)

The endings of the first group of adjectives match the endings of first-declension nouns in the feminine form (i.e. when the adjective is describing a feminine noun) and of second-declension nouns in the masculine and neuter form.

In the dictionary first- and second-declension adjectives appear like this:

novus, -a, -um – new
magnus, -a, -um – big
laetus, -a, -um – happy

Nouns are displayed in the dictionary with their nominative and genitive singular cases and gender in order to let you know their declension, stem and gender. You don't need these different forms for adjectives as you get this information from the three nominative-case endings for the different genders that are shown instead. All first- and second-declension nouns are shown in the dictionary with '*-us, -a, -um*' endings.

The second group of adjectives' endings match the endings of third-declension nouns apart from the following differences: the ablative singular form for all genders ends in '*-i*', the genitive plural form for all genders ends in '*-ium*', and the nominative, vocative and accusative neuter plural ends in '*-ia*'. Is your head swimming? Don't worry, it is unlikely that a centurion is going to stride up to you and embarrass you in the supermarket by testing you on this.

In the dictionary third-declension adjectives appear like this:

omnis, -e – all
ferox, -ocis – ferocious
celer, celeris, celere – fast

As you can see these three adjectives all appear differently in the dictionary even though they are all third-declension adjectives. This is because there are three types of third-declension adjective, but do not despair as they only look different in their nominative singular cases.

The first type, of which '*omnis*' is one, has the same form for the masculine and feminine nominative singular ('*omnis*') and a different form for neuter nominative singular ('*omne*').

The second type, of which '*ferox*' is one, has the same form in the masculine, feminine and neuter nominative singular ('*ferox*'). For this reason, so that you can work out the stem, the genitive singular form ('*ferocis*') is given as well – just like with nouns. As you can see, this lets you know that the stem changes to '*feroc-*' in the cases that aren't nominative.

The third type, of which '*celer*' is one, has different forms for the masculine ('*celer*'), feminine ('*celeris*') and neuter ('*celere*') nominative singulars.

VERBS

The form of the verb in a Latin sentence changes according to the subject of the verb, the tense of the verb and sometimes the gender of the subject as well. There are four different types of regular verbs, called conjugations. Any verb that is part of each conjugation will change the endings that are added to its stem in the same way.

The first conjugation is for all verbs which end in '*-are*' in the infinitive, such as '*amare*' meaning 'to love'. The second is for '*-ere*' verbs, such as '*habere*' meaning 'to have'. The third is for a different set of '*-ere*' verbs (where the '*e*' of '*-ere*' is a short rather than long sound), such as '*mittere*' meaning 'to send'. The fourth is for '*-ire*' verbs, such as '*audire*' meaning 'to hear'.

In Latin dictionaries the first-person singular form of a verb is given first and then the infinitive. So the verb '*amare*' appears as '*amo, amare*'. You can find the present stem of a verb by removing the '*-are*', '*-ere*', or '*-ire*' from the infinitive, although you should be aware that stems can change in certain tenses.

First conjugation

TO LOVE: *Amare*

PRESENT	PAST	FUTURE
I love: *amo*	I loved: *amavi*	I will love: *amabo*
you love: *amas*	you loved: *amavisti*	you will love: *amabis*
he/she loves: *amat*	he/she loved: *amavit*	he/she will love: *amabit*
we love: *amamus*	we loved: *amavimus*	we will love: *amabimus*
you (plural) love: *amatis*	you (plural) loved: *amavistis*	you (plural) will love: *amabitis*
they love: *amant*	they loved: *amaverunt*	they will love: *amabunt*

Second conjugation

TO HAVE: *Habere*

PRESENT	PAST	FUTURE
I have: *habeo*	I had: *habui*	I will have: *habebo*
you have: *habes*	you had: *habuisti*	you will have: *habebis*
he/she has: *habet*	he/she had: *habuit*	he/she will have: *habebit*
we have: *habemus*	we had: *habuimus*	we will have: *habebimus*
you (plural) have: *habetis*	you (plural) had: *habuistis*	you (plural) will have: *habebitis*
they have: *habent*	they had: *habuerunt*	they will have: *habebunt*

Third conjugation

TO SEND: *Mittere*

PRESENT	PAST	FUTURE
I send: *mitto*	I sent: *misi*	I will send: *mittam*
you send: *mittis*	you sent: *misisti*	you will send: *mittes*
he/she sends: *mittit*	he/she sent: *misit*	he/she will send: *mittet*
we send: *mittimus*	we sent: *misimus*	we will send: *mittemus*
you (plural) send: *mittitis*	you (plural) sent: *misisti*	you (plural) will send: *mittetis*
they send: *mittunt*	they sent: *miserunt*	they will send: *mittent*

Some third-conjugation verbs are called *-io* verbs as they conjugate slightly differently – with an 'i' before the endings of the 'I' and 'they' forms.

TO MAKE: *Facere*

PRESENT	PAST	FUTURE
I make: *facio*	I made: *feci*	I will make: *faciam*
you make: *facis*	you made: *fecisti*	you will make: *facies*
he/she makes: *facit*	he/she made: *fecit*	he/she will make: *faciet*
we make: *facimus*	we made: *fecimus*	we will make: *faciemus*
you (plural) make: *facitis*	you (plural) made: *fecisti*	you (plural) will make: *facietis*
they make: *faciunt*	they made: *fecerunt*	they will make: *facient*

Fourth conjugation

TO HEAR: *Audire*

PRESENT	PAST	FUTURE
I hear: *audio*	I heard: *audivi*	I will hear: *audiam*
you hear: *audis*	you heard: *audivisti*	you will hear: *audies*
he/she hears: *audit*	he/she heard: *audivit*	he/she will hear: *audiet*
we hear: *audimus*	we heard: *audivimus*	we will hear: *audiemus*
you (plural) hear: *auditis*	you (plural) heard: *audivistis*	you (plural) will hear: *audietis*
they hear: *audiunt*	they heard: *audiverunt*	they will hear: *audient*

A LIVING LANGUAGE:
SOME INDISPENSABLE LATIN PHRASES

There are many phrases in Latin that are used in the English language today. You should try to sprinkle your conversation with as many of them as possible – for example, in Tesco when you are offered two for the price of one on chicken nuggets, feel free to shout '*Cui bono?*' at the unsuspecting cashier.

ad hoc (to this) – for a particular purpose

quid pro quo (something for something) – something given as compensation

et cetera (and the other) – and the rest

e.g. (*exempli gratia* – for the sake of example) – for example

QED *(quod erat demonstrandum* – which was to be shown) – which was the thing to be proved or shown.

ad nauseam (to sickness) – to an excessive or disgusting degree

a priori (from what is before) – proceeding from causes to effects

cum grano salis (with a grain of salt) – with a pinch of salt

cui bono? (a benefit to whom?) – who stands to gain?

in flagrante delicto (in blazing crime) – in the act of committing an offence

modus operandi (way of operating) – the particular way something or someone operates

non compos mentis (not having control of one's mind) – not in one's right mind

magnum opus (great work) – a great work of art, or the most important work of an artist

ibid (ibidem – in the same place) – in the same book or passage

de facto (in fact) – in fact, whether by right or not

mea culpa (by my fault) – my fault or mistake

in vitro (in glass) – taking place in a test tube or elsewhere outside a living organism

non sequitur (it does not follow) – a conclusion that does not logically follow from the premises

per se (by itself) – by or in itself

persona non grata (a not pleasing person) – an unwelcome person

rigor mortis (stiffness of death) – stiffening of the body after death

sine qua non (without which not) – an indispensable condition

terra incognita (unknown land) – an unknown or unexplored region

ROMAN NUMERALS

1	I	14	XIV	27	XXVII	150	CL
2	II	15	XV	28	XXVIII	200	CC
3	III	16	XVI	29	XXIX	300	CCC
4	IV	17	XVII	30	XXX	400	CD
5	V	18	XVIII	31	XXXI	500	D
6	VI	19	XIX	40	XL	600	DC
7	VII	20	XX	50	L	700	DCC
8	VIII	21	XXI	60	LX	800	DCCC
9	IX	22	XXII	70	LXX	900	CM
10	X	23	XXIII	80	LXXX	1000	M
11	XI	24	XXIV	90	XC	1600	MDC
12	XII	25	XXV	100	C	1700	MDCC
13	XIII	26	XXVI	101	CI	1900	MCM

CULINARY CLASSICS: ROMAN FOOD

The Romans are famous for having eaten elaborate food at their banquets, such as stuffed dormice, larks' tongues and peacocks. They drank diluted wine with everything and used a lot of honey to sweeten their food. They also used spices such as cinnamon, pepper, nutmeg and cloves, brought from outposts of their vast empire. Less wealthy Romans ate bread and porridge made of wheat or barley, beans and vegetables with olive oil, and fruit. Interestingly, the common people also used garlic in their food, but this was not favoured by the patrician classes in their cooking. The only Roman cookbook that has survived is *De re coquinaria* by a writer known as Apicius; dating from the first century CE, it gives recipes for upper-class meals.

APICIUS' RECIPE FOR LENTILS WITH CHESTNUTS

Lenticulam de castaneis: accipies caccabum novum, et castaneas purgatas diligenter mittis. Adicies aquam et nitrum modice, facies ut coquatur. Cum coquitur, mittis in mortario piper, cuminum, semen coriandri, mentam, rutam, laseris radicem, puleium, fricabis. Suffundis acetum, mel, liquamen, aceto temperabis, et super castaneas coctas refundis. Adicies oleum, facies ut ferveat. Cum bene ferbuerit, tudiclabis [ut in mortario teres]. Gustas, si quid deest, addes. Cum in boletar miseris, addes oleum viridem.

Here is a modern interpretation of this recipe:

Serves 6 as a side dish

375g puy lentils
200g chestnuts (or peeled cooked chestnuts in a packet)
½ tsp black peppercorns
1 tsp cumin
½ tsp coriander seeds
a few chopped leaves of mint
one stalk of very finely chopped rosemary leaves
1 tbsp vinegar
1 tsp honey
1 tsp of fermented fish sauce (optional)
2 tbsp olive oil

Boil the lentils in water for 20 minutes. Meanwhile, grind up the spices and then mix in with the vinegar, honey, fish sauce and olive oil. In another pan, boil the chestnuts for a few minutes in salted water until they are tender. Drain and carefully remove the chestnuts from their skins. (If you are using pre-cooked and peeled chestnuts just gently heat them through in a frying pan for a few minutes instead.) Stir the spicy oil into the chestnuts. Check the lentils are tender, then drain and mix with the chestnuts. Serve, remembering that the Romans' concept of a delicious meal was somewhat different to our own.

ANCIENT ATTIRE: ROMAN CLOTHING

Roman attire was stuffed full of sartorial signifiers: one could tell a person's class, status, sex and even profession by the type of clothes they wore. Roman commoners, shepherds and slaves wore tunics made of rough material, while patricians' and magistrates' tunics were made of softer white wool or linen. Free Roman men wore a toga draped over their tunic and consuls' and senators' tunics were often edged in purple.

Roman women were not so defined by their clothes as men, but they did wear a *stola*, which showed that they were married. In addition, respectable women wore a *palla*, or large shawl, when outside.

Military tunics were not as long as those worn by civilians. An ordinary legionary soldier, *miles legionarius*, wore a fairly standard uniform of armour held together with strips of leather, a metal helmet, boots and a belt to which was attached a short dagger and a sword. He also carried a large shield and a javelin, which was cleverly designed to bend on impact – thereby ensuring the enemy could not reuse a thrown weapon.

SUETONIUS
AND THE TWELVE CAESARS

Gaius Suetonius Tranquillus (*c*.70–*c*.130 CE) was a Roman man of letters during the rule of the Emperor Hadrian. His biography of the first twelve emperors of Rome was hugely influential and contains much fascinating historical information as well as a great deal of scurrilous gossip. His analysis of these absolute rulers includes descriptions not only of their military campaigns but also of their matrimonial disputes, not just their history-changing laws but also their hairstyles. Below, you will find an easy-reference table summing up Suetonius' more vivid anecdotes about his subjects.

Emperor	*Highlights of Reign*
Julius Caesar (100–44 BCE)	Had a comb-over. Was an example of moderation and clemency – allowed some pirates to have their throats cut before crucifying them. Had a prophetic dream about flying through the clouds before his murder.
Augustus (63–14 BCE)	Handsome and popular emperor who considered executing his difficult and promiscuous daughter. Bashed his head against the wall in disappointment after his general Varus lost three legions in an ambush in Germany. Was born with birthmarks on his body in the shape of the constellation of the Bear.
Tiberius (42 BCE–37 CE)	Was overly fond of wine and small boys. Broke the legs of children after abusing them. Had spots and could see in the dark. Jubilation in Rome upon news of his death.

Emperor	Highlights of Reign
Caligula (12–41 CE)	Slept with all of his sisters. Tried to make his horse Incitatus a consul. Ominously spattered with blood from a sacrificial flamingo before being assassinated on his way to dinner.
Claudius (10 BCE–54 CE)	Had a stutter. Enjoyed his food and a drink. Loved gambling so much he had his chariot adapted so he could play while on the move. Was probably assassinated by poisoned mushrooms given to him by his wife.
Nero (37–68 CE)	Loved horses, baths and poetry – sang a poem about Troy while watching the great fire of Rome. Married a eunuch and raped a Vestal Virgin. Kicked his pregnant wife Poppaea to death for complaining about him being late. Committed suicide after the senate turned against him.
Galba (3 BCE–69 CE)	Bald with blue eyes. Had a penchant for old catamites. Emperor for only seven months. Killed by soldiers loyal to Otho.
Otho (32–69 CE)	Bandy-legged, somewhat bald first husband of Nero's doomed wife Poppaea. Emperor for only three months. Stabbed himself in the chest after losing a decisive battle to Vitellius.
Vitellius (15–69 CE)	Extremely tall and greedy general who managed to hold onto the title of emperor for eight months. After much of the army decided to support Vespasian as emperor instead, Vitellius was dragged half-naked out of hiding and assassinated, before his body was thrown into the Tiber.

Emperor	Highlights of Reign
Vespasian (9–79 CE)	Relatively decent ruler. Keen on imposing taxes. Died of diarrhoea.
Titus (39–81 CE)	Surrounded himself with catamites. Put on a show at the amphitheatre involving 5,000 wild beasts.
Domitian (51–96 CE)	Titus' younger brother who gained the throne after allowing Titus to die of an unattended fever. Liked impaling flies on pins. Sensitive about his baldness. Personally depilated his concubines. Murdered by his friends with the collusion of his wife.

THE *AENEID*

The *Aeneid* is a Latin epic poem about the origins of Rome written by the poet Virgil (70–19 BCE). It describes the adventures of the Trojan Aeneas after he flees his city as it is being destroyed by the Greeks at the end of the Trojan War. After his escape he spends years travelling before settling in Italy, defeating hostile native tribes and marrying a local princess, starting the history of the city that would become Rome. The *Aeneid* is based on Homer's *Odyssey* and *Iliad*, legends about Aeneas, and contemporary political events – the poem was written in praise of the Emperor Augustus (emperor from 27 BCE to 14 CE) who ruled during Virgil's lifetime.

∾ CLASSICS ∾
TEST PAPER

1. Name two bald Roman emperors.

2. Write 'He loves the dog' in Latin.

3. Name two amours of Aeneas.

4. What does '*arma virumque cano*' mean?

5. According to Caesar's account of the Gallic Wars, which of the Gaulish tribes was the bravest?

6. When and how did the Emperor Claudius meet his maker?

7. What is a *polis*?
   a) a Scottish term for the law-enforcement community
   b) a three-piece 1980s rock band
   c) an Ancient Greek city-state
   d) a headdress worn by Roman women in the second century CE

8. How old was Alexander the Great when he died?

9. What was Alexander the Great's horse called? If you can also name two other famous classical horses you can gain extra bonus points!

10. Who was Rome's greatest enemy during the establishment of the Roman Empire?

339

11. **How did doomed Dido die?**

12. **Which Roman ruler is Asterix resisting in the cartoon stories of his adventures?**

13. **What was the Emperor Diocletian's most significant act during his reign?**

14. **What does Constantinople literally mean?**

15. **Who were the fathers of Cleopatra's children?**

16. **Write 'The ferocious dog of the good girl' in Latin.**

17. **Give the following Greek gods their Roman names:**
a) Zeus
b) Hera
c) Hermes
d) Apollo
e) Dionysus

18. **Who is the ancient Greek god of medicine?**

19. **Who is the ancient Greek goddess of war?**

20. **What does φιλοσοφια mean?**

21. **What do sceptics believe?**

22. **If someone tells you to take your wife's criticism of your new outfit 'cum grano salis', what do they mean?**

23. How long did the Trojan War last?

24. Where was Odysseus' home?

25. What was Achilles so cross about in the *Iliad*?

26. If Gaius Cornelius '*sub arborem sedet*' what is he doing?

27. If Aurelia gets her *stola* covered in lark-tongue juice, what does she need to do?

28. What does *in medias res* mean?

29. What does catharsis mean?

30. What was lyric poetry originally accompanied by?

a) a lyre   c) a flute
b) a piano   d) an elaborate dance

31. Who invented the phrase '*panem et circenses*'?

32. Who would you rather fight out of the Greek gods Ares and Hephaestus?

33. Who said 'The unexamined life is not worth living'?

34. Which of the following are not characters in the *Iliad*?

a) Orestes   c) Sophocles
b) Nestor   d) Hector

9

PHYSICAL EDUCATION

'**P.E.** *n*. instruction in physical exercise and games'
Oxford Concise English Dictionary

'*Mens sana in corpore sano*'
(A healthy mind in a healthy body)
JUVENAL (*c*.60–130), *Satires*

Who among us can forget afternoons spent freezing on the sports field, knees knocking in large navy blue pants or shorts, as rugby balls sail overhead and out of reach, or your tennis partner shouts at you once again for missing the return? Or the dreaded group showers after on-field exertion? Or the horror of your terrifying sports mistress checking that your name is sewn onto your Aertex shirt and every sweat-soaked sock? Or sports day, where competitive parents cheer little Belinda into first place as you come limping in last, hobbled by your own sack? For many of us, school sports don't provide the fondest of memories, and indeed, some may be plagued by nightmares swirling with the scent of linseed oil, verruca socks and the bitter tears of defeat.

Even if you never set foot on the athletics track again, a knowledge of the rules and ethics of the various games we learned at school, from cricket to football, and from rugby to lacrosse, will enrich your conversation and enjoyment of those great sporting events that feature on every pub television across the land. Sport can also be a powerful metaphor for the interactions of society – cast your mind back to the excruciating torment of watching the most aggressive and powerful members of your class pick-ing the best to be in their teams, while leaving the weak and lame till last. But equally, sport has the power to unite and it can also provide a positive and instructive guide to living: the value of preparation and self-discipline, fair play, teamwork, grace in defeat and humility in triumph – all of these qualities can be transferred from the muddy pitch to real life.

Grab your hockey boots, remove any watches and jewellery, snap on that swimming hat, slam in that mouth-guard and rub that cricket ball to a brilliant shine against your whites . . . It's time to play!

ORGANISED LOAFING:
THE ART OF CRICKET

Traditionally, cricket is the game of gentlemen. Unlike its rougher cousin football, in cricket there is no applause for cheating or attempting to win by underhand means: cricket tests your moral fibre as well as your physical prowess. It's impossible to establish exactly when cricket was invented, but we know the English game started life in the rural south-east of England. Hambledon Club in Hampshire claims to be the 'Birthplace of Cricket', but the most influential club is the Marylebone Cricket Club (MCC) at Lord's in London. The laws of cricket were formally set in stone by the MCC in 1835.

A cricket strip or wicket

Cricket is played by two teams of eleven players. One team **bats** by sending two players onto the pitch to score runs. The other team **bowls** and fields. Each team has players who specialise in either batting or bowling. The game is played in **overs** in which a bowler bowls the ball at the batsman standing in front of the edifice of sticks shown below from one end six times. At the end of an over a second bowler will bowl six balls from the other end, and so on.

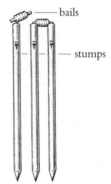

The bowler attempts to get the batsmen out by hitting the **wicket** and dislodging the **bails** that the batsman protects. The word 'wicket' can refer to both the strip the game is played on and the stump and bails. The batsmen also try to score **runs**. A run is scored when the two running batsmen cross in the centre of the wicket, but they must also ground their bat in the **opposite popping crease**. If they have time, they may then return for more runs straight away. Runs can also be scored without the batsmen running if the ball is hit out of the field of play: aerially for **six** runs or along the ground for **four**. The score is kept as a ratio between runs to batsmen who have gone out: e.g. 382 for 8 means 382 runs have been scored and 8 batsmen have gone out.

Fielders are positioned around the field of play to catch or intercept the ball when the batsman hits it, thereby restricting the number of runs scored. There are various ways in which the fielding team can get a batsman 'out'. For example, if the ball is caught by a fielder off the batsman's bat without it touching the ground (**full toss**) then the batsman is out. If the batsman hits the ball along the ground, the fielders attempt to stop it and throw it to the **wicketkeeper** (the fellow standing behind the stumps), who uses it to dislodge the bails on the wicket. If the batsman is outside the **popping crease** when the bails are dislodged, then he is out. When one batsman is out, the team sends another batsman on to replace him and so on until all eleven players have batted and ten are out. When the batting team are all out their **innings** has ended. They then become the fielding team and the fielding team now comes in to bat.

The game is refereed by two **umpires** who are on the field at all times and whose word is final. The umpires make all the decisions regarding whether a batsman is in or out, how many runs have been scored (e.g. four or six) and other issues surrounding the legitimacy of each ball. If the fielding side thinks that a batsman is out then they appeal to the umpire by bellowing '**Howzat?**' or '**Howzee?**'. If the umpire agrees with the fielding side he raises his finger and the batsman walks off the field.

There are two main types of cricket match: **Test match** cricket, which involves two innings per team and takes place over five days, and **limited overs** cricket whereby each team has one innings of a specified and equal number of overs.

A GLOSSARY OF CRICKETING TERMS

Leg side: The side of the cricketing field to the left of the facing batsman.

Off side: The side of the cricketing field to the right of the facing batsman. (If the batsman is left-handed then these terms are reversed.)

A duck: A batsman is out for zero runs.

A golden duck: A batsman is out first ball.

Leg before wicket (lbw): If the batsman fails to hit the ball with his bat but intercepts it with part of his body, he is deemed out lbw if that ball would have gone on to hit the stumps. There are a number of conditions that need to be met, however, before an lbw decision is given. If a shot is played, then a batsman may not be given out if the ball hits him outside of the line of off stump. A batsman also may not be given out if the ball has pitched outside of the line of leg. The batsman can reduce the likelihood of being out lbw by taking a large stride down the wicket as he goes for the ball.

Wide: A delivery is deemed to be out of reasonable reach of the batsman.

No-ball: A bowler oversteps the crease when bowling, giving him an unfair advantage.

Bye: If the ball misses the batsman and his bat, then the batsmen are allowed to attempt a run. This will normally happen if the wicket-keeper fails to catch the ball.

Leg bye: A run that is scored after the ball hits the body of the batsman rather than the bat. The batsman must be playing a shot for a leg bye to be valid.

Extra: A run that is scored other than by the ball being hit by the batsman, for example leg byes. Australians refer to these as 'sundries'.

Maiden: An over that is bowled during which no runs are scored off the bat.

Swing bowling: The ability of a bowler to arc the ball during its flight either towards the leg side (**in-swing**) or towards the off side (**away-swing**).

Spin bowling: The ability of a slow bowler to impart spin on a ball so that when it pitches on the wicket it moves either from leg to off (**leg spin** or **leg break bowling**) or from off to leg (**off spin** or **off break bowling**).

Fast bowling: Bowling which is very fast and very straight, sometimes moving towards leg or off stump when the ball's raised stitching hits the wicket.

All-rounder: A player who excels in two of the three core cricketing skills aside from fielding (i.e. batting, bowling and wicketkeeping).

Bouncer: When a fast bowler aims to bounce the ball directly at the head or chest of the batsman.

Beamer: A high full toss bowled at the batsman. This is dangerous and unacceptable behaviour, especially if bowled by a quick- or medium-pace bowler.

Googly: A ball delivered with the apparent bowling action of a leg break (see spin bowling) but actually spinning in the opposite direction so that when it lands it becomes an off break.

Doosra: A ball delivered with the apparent bowling action of an off break (see spin bowling) but actually spinning in the opposite direction so that when it lands it becomes a leg break.

Sledging: Controversial heckling of the batsman by the close fielders. Sledging never takes place as the ball is bowled but is used to unsettle batsmen between deliveries. Aggressive sledging is viewed in a dim light.

THE BEAUTIFUL GAME: FOOTBALL

As Bill Shankly so memorably put it, 'Some people think football is a matter of life and death . . . I can assure them it is much more serious than that.' Football is played in virtually every country in the world by more than one and a half million teams and 300,000 clubs – not including school and youth clubs. Part of football's universal appeal lies in its simplicity; schoolchildren everywhere play with just a ball, a flat area and, of course, jumpers for goalposts.

The game is played by two teams of eleven players, each trying to score goals by passing, dribbling and shooting the ball into the opposition's goal. Players can use any part of their body other than their hands and arms to achieve this, apart from the **goalkeeper**, who can defend his goal using any part of his body. Broadly speaking, teams are split into **defenders**, **midfielders**, **wingers** and **attackers**; however formations vary considerably. The role of the coach, aside from training, is to organise the team into formations: for example, the classic 4–4–2 means 4 defenders, 4 midfielders and 2 attackers or strikers.

Since the first thirteen rules were laid out at a pub in Lincoln's Inn Fields in London in 1863, the rules of the game have been many and varied, but the trickiest rule, and the one that referees, linesmen and spectators get wrong all the time is the **offside rule**. Here is the latest definition:

> A player is in an offside position if he is nearer to his opponents' goal line than both the ball and the second-last opponent when the ball is played to him. A player cannot be offside if he is in his own half and nor can he be if the referee deems him to be 'inactive' to the play.

RUCKING AND MAULING: RUGBY

In 1823, at Rugby School in Warwickshire, William Webb Ellis picked up the ball during a game of football, and ran at the goal. Instead of being dismissed from the field, as the schoolboy no doubt should have been, the game of rugby was born. And instead of having black marks against his name in perpetuity, Webb Ellis has the World Cup trophy named in his honour. The game quickly caught on at other schools and universities, and the English Rugby Union was formed in 1871 to establish and set down the rules. In the 1890s a schism formed between the working men's rugby clubs of the north, and the upper-class clubs of the south over whether players should be paid for any wages lost while playing. The **Rugby Union** clubs of the south voted against professionalism, and the northern clubs broke away to form the **Northern Union** in 1895 which would become the **Rugby Football League**.

Rugby Union
Rugby union is played by two teams of fifteen players. Each team consists of eight **forwards** (numbers 1–8) and seven **backs** (numbers 9–15).

The game is played in two halves each lasting forty minutes and each started by a kick from the halfway line.

During the match the teams attempt to score **tries** by running the ball over the opposition try line and touching it down. They do this by passing the ball to one another in an effort to evade the opposition's defence. A pass may only be made sideways or backwards – never forwards. A team may also opt to kick the ball forward in an attempt to gain ground. The defending team can stop the attacking team by tackling the player with the ball as long as the contact is below shoulder height. If a player is brought to the ground with the ball he must immediately release the ball. A **ruck** is then formed, whereby both teams (usually the forwards) will attempt to retrieve the ball while remaining on their feet by driving over it. The ball is then passed to the backs who will attempt to run it over the try line. Occasionally a **maul** will form whereby a player has the ball and remains upstanding while being grappled by one or more of the opposition.

The referee reserves the right to decide when a maul becomes a ruck and, if the ball is not forthcoming, awards a **scrum** to the team driving forward. A scrum is also awarded against the offending team if the ball is passed forward or knocked on (other than when kicked). A scrum involves the forwards of each team 'scrumming' or 'packing' down in formation in a seething mass of limbs. The ball is then rolled in to the middle of the scrum by the **scrum half** and is controlled by the **hooker** who hooks the ball with his foot back towards his own team while the rest of the forwards push against their opponents. The scrum half then retrieves the ball from the back of the scrum and passes it to the back line who pick it up and attempt to run the ball over the try line.

If a ball is kicked or passed out of play then a **line-out** ensues, whereby the forwards of each team line up against one another and the hooker throws the ball in. The forwards will then jump like graceful hares, usually assisted by a friendly hand on their haunches from their teammates, to catch the ball so that they can pass it out to the fleet-of-foot back line.

During the run of play, penalties are awarded for various infringements, such as being **offside**. A player is considered offside if he is in front of the player carrying the ball, though he will only be penalised if he then takes part in the play. Other penalty infringements include high or dangerous tackles, tripping, purposefully bringing down a maul and violent conduct. A penalty provides an opportunity for a team to score points by **place-kicking** the ball through the posts or to gain ground by kicking it out of play further up the field and being awarded the subsequent line-out. Alternatively they can opt to have a scrum or just continue to run the ball from the point at which the penalty was awarded.

Points are awarded as follows: for scoring a try, when a player touches a ball down behind the opposition's goal line, 5 points; a **conversion**, when after a try has been scored the team is given the opportunity to convert it into more points by kicking the ball between the opposition's goalposts, a further 2 points; a **drop goal**, which occurs during open play when a player opts to drop-kick the ball between the opposition's goalposts, 3 points, or a penalty kick, when the ball is place-kicked between the opposition's posts as a result of a penalty being awarded, 3 points.

Rugby League
The principles of rugby league are exactly the same as those of union in that points are scored in the same way. Their value, however, differs, as does the run of play. Each team is made up of thirteen players, again split into backs and forwards. From the kick-off, the receiving team has six chances or **tackles** to break the opposition defence and score a try. If they fail to do so the ball is given to the other team who themselves have six tackles to score. Each time a player is tackled and they keep hold of the ball, the defence retreats ten yards, and play continues from the point of tackle. If, during the course of a team's possession, they opt to kick the ball, then the tackle count goes back to zero. Scrums do exist in rugby league, but are not as aggressively contested as in union. Line-outs do not occur, and if a team allows the ball to go out it is simply given to the opposition. A try is worth 4 points, a conversion a further 2, and a drop-goal or penalty is worth 1 point.

LUCKY LAX: LACROSSE

Lacrosse was invented in its earliest form by Native Americans and was known as 'baggataway'. It was initially employed as a form of martial training and bore no resemblance to the modern game as it could be played between teams of well over a hundred and matches could last for days. The game was adopted by French-Canadians and remains the official summer sport in Canada. The word 'lacrosse' derives from the name given to the handled stick used by players, which was called '*la crosse*' in French as it resembled a bishop's crosier.

The rules of men's and women's lacrosse differ slightly in the number of players and the length of a match but the fundamentals of the sport are the same (although physical contact is only permitted in the men's version of the game). The object of the game is to send the ball, using the crosse, into the opponent's goal. Each goal is worth 1 point and the team scoring the most points at the end of play is the winner. Each team comprises a **goalkeeper, defenders, midfielders** and **attackers**. Players catch, carry and throw the ball using the crosse, never with the hands – only the goalkeeper is allowed to use his or her hands and other parts of the body to block shots on goal.

JOLLY HOCKEY STICKS! FIELD HOCKEY

Field hockey is one of the oldest stick-and-ball games and is known to have been played in some form or other by the ancient Egyptians, Romans, Persians and Arabs. The game takes its name from the old French word '*hoquet*' ('shepherd's crook') due to the curved shape of the hockey stick.

The game is comprised of two teams of eleven players, each battling to score goals by hitting, pushing, passing or dribbling the ball into the opponents' goal. One of the eleven players acts as **goalkeeper** and the other ten **field players** are made up of **defenders**, **midfielders** and **attackers**. The stick has a rounded, curved face and a flat face and the ball is manoeuvred between players using only the flat face. Players, except for the goalkeeper, are not allowed to use their feet to kick the ball. During open play, goals may only be scored from within the **shooting circle**. Goals can also be scored from a **penalty corner** or a **penalty stroke**, which are awarded for infringements.

A SHORT GLOSSARY OF RACKET SPORTS

Lawn tennis: Tennis played between two individuals (**singles**) or two pairs of individuals (**doubles**). Players use a strung racket to hit a tennis ball back and forth over a net in order to score points.

Real tennis: Famously played by Henry VIII, real tennis follows a similar format to lawn tennis, but it has much more complicated rules and a detailed scoring system. Real tennis is played on a special, and slightly bizarre, indoor court, and no two courts are identical. Players may also play the ball off the walls and buttresses.

Badminton: Badminton developed from a game played in the fifth century BCE in China called *ti jian zi* or 'kicking the shuttle'. By the 1860s this game had developed into *poona* in India, where a shuttlecock was hit with paddles over a net. British soldiers brought the game back to our shores.

Squash: A game called rackets began life in London's King's Bench and Fleet debtors' prisons as a pastime played by inmates and the rules were later formalised at Harrow School. Squash was invented when some schoolboys realised that a punctured rackets ball would squash when it hit the wall, leading to different styles of shot. It's played in a similar fashion to rackets, but on a smaller court, and is much slower.

Table tennis (also called **ping-pong**): This sport was developed by well-heeled Victorians, who, after an evening's merriment, would divert themselves by recreating a tennis court on a table. The game is played in singles or doubles, and involves hitting a small, light-weight ball back and forth across a net.

PIVOT AND PASS: NETBALL

Ah, the blooming young ladies of the netball team – they set an example to all with their elegance and energy, unlike the muddy terrier-like hockey players with their socks round their ankles and their bruised shins. Netball is played by two teams of seven players. At each end of a netball court is a goal consisting of a post topped with a hoop and net. The object of the game is to pass an inflated ball through the opposing team's goal. The ball is thrown from player to player; there should be no physical contact between players and players are not permitted to run with the ball.

Each of the positions is confined to specific areas or zones on the court and each position has a set role:

GS (**goal shooter**) – scores goals and works in and around the goal circle with GA.

GA (**goal attack**) – works with GS to score goals.

WA (**wing attack**) – feeds the circle players to give them a chance to shoot.

C (**centre**) – links defence and attack and takes the **centre pass** (from the middle of the court) after a goal has been scored.

WD (**wing defence**) – a defensive player who attempts to intercept passes from WA to the circle players.

GD (**goal defence**) – reduces goal-scoring opportunities of the GA and tries to win the ball from the attackers.

GK (**goalkeeper**) – works with the GD to protect the goal and reduces scoring opportunities of the GS.

HOW TO CLIMB A ROPE

For some, the exhortation of the teacher to climb a rope in gym class can be slightly daunting. Follow these simple instructions and you will be shimmying through the air like a proper Tarzan.

1. Hold the rope over your head using both hands, ensuring that your stronger hand (your left if you are left-handed, your right if you are right-handed) is above the other.

2. Pull down, and, at the same time, jump up and use your legs to encircle the rope. This sounds trickier than it is: your body will instinctively do this to avoid falling.

3. Create an anchor using pinched rope at your feet. You should be able to untense your grip in your hands and still feel secure. Test this out when you are at the bottom of the rope rather than at the top.

4. When the anchor is secure, move your hands a little higher, and as you pull up, simultaneously release your feet and bring up your knees to pinch another anchor further up.

5. Repeat steadily until you have reached the top.

6. Slide slowly down – fast sliding will result in burns – nasty!

TIPS: Tying knots in the rope will provide anchors, and it's always a good idea to place a mat at the bottom of the rope, too.

PHYSICAL EDUCATION
TEST PAPER

1. In cricket, what is a 'beamer'?

a) a flash car
b) a smiling friend
c) an over bowled during which no runs are scored off the bat
d) a dangerous high full toss

2. How many rules did football originally have?

3. Explain the offside rule.

4. Where was rugby invented?

a) Harrow School
b) Rugby School
c) its origins are unknown but it is thought to have developed on the streets of Birmingham

5. How do men's and women's lacrosse differ?

6. When would you see a man dressed entirely in white jumping up and down and shouting, 'Howzat?'

7. If you have got a golden duck, it means that you are:

a) a champion cricketer b) a terrible cricketer

8. In which of the following sports might you find a hooker?

a) football c) swimming
b) equestrian dressage d) rugby

9. Who invented lacrosse?

10. How many players are there in a hockey team?

ART

'**Art.** *n.* A human creative skill or its application'
Oxford Concise English Dictionary

'Life imitates Art far more than Art imitates Life'
OSCAR WILDE (1854–1900)

It can seem daunting to any student to try to grapple with the high-falutin idea of Art with a capital 'A'. Quite aside from the fact that many of the works themselves seem impenetrable or strange, artists and the world that surrounds them can appear like a closed book to those of us outside it. It's hard to have an opinion on artistic creations without any background knowledge, and the more modern art moves in an outré direction, the more we are encouraged to believe that our own interpretation is paramount. The greatest art has the power to move and improve, to teach and to torture, to bless and berate; it is the expression of the very best of human endeavour across the world. To dismiss the entire subject as too esoteric and unknowable is just plain idleness.

This chapter aims to equip you with the basics, so that you need never again feel small and obtuse when someone asks you what you think of the latest showing at the National and you tell them to back Kauto Star as a 9–4 odds-on favourite. Do you want to know your Vorticism from your da Vinci, your Cartier-Bresson from your Braque, your intaglio from your lithography and your Doric from your Ionic? Perhaps you've always wondered what on earth Egyptian frit is or which insects make the best paint or how our greatest scientist shaped the way artists see the world? The fascinating stories behind these questions are well worth investigating. In this chapter we'll also introduce you to some of the big brushes of the Renaissance – who knows, having acquainted yourself with the masters of the past, you might just feel the need to unleash the artist within . . .

A KALEIDOSCOPE OF COLOURS: THE COLOUR WHEEL

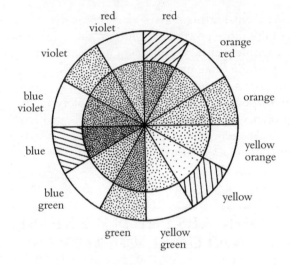

Before you set up your easel and whip out your beret and smock, you need first to familiarise yourself with the basics. Understanding the complexities of colour is key to understanding the visual arts.

Not content with grappling with gravity and the laws of motion, Sir Isaac Newton (1642–1727) also played a role in the realm of artistic endeavour. The colour wheel is based on Newton's colour circle, which he established when he split white light into a spectrum of different colours through a prism. In light, the three primary colours are red, blue and green, because mixing rays of these colours together can produce almost all other colours, and adding together **red**, **blue** and **green** in equal quantities creates white light. For this reason these are known as the **additive primary colours**. In painting, we use the **subtractive primary colours** of **cyan**, **magenta** and **yellow** (in school you tend to be taught the three colours you can use to mix all other colours are blue, red and yellow, but these are just for easy reference). Colour printing today is usually called CMYK printing, which stands for cyan, magenta, yellow and key (black). Mixing together pairs of primary colours creates, you guessed it, **secondary colours**: cyan and magenta mixed together make violet; cyan and yellow make green and magenta and yellow make orange.

Clever experimental artists noticed that certain colours placed next to each other look more powerful because of the contrast between them. These are **complementary colours**. Complementary pairs of colours are made up of the three primary colours and their secondary colours, i.e: magenta–green, cyan–orange, yellow–violet. Impressionist paintings often show shadows in the complementary colour of the light creating them – so orange light casts a cyan shadow. The colours used to cast a shadow on a face rendered in paint are a far cry from what we might expect: artists use blues, yellows and oranges to give a convincing effect.

OUR AESTHETIC EARTH: NATURAL PIGMENTS

Before the days of clever-whizz technologies and Dulux colour charts, our ancestors made use of what they found around them for artistic expression. The earliest cave paintings were created from paints made by grinding up stones, clays, charcoals and chalk. Amazingly, Stone Age painters were sophisticated enough to make oil-based paint – they mixed up vegetable oil with ground-up rock – and things got even better with those gifted ancient Egyptians, who used an incredibly advanced level of chemistry to create pigments. The oldest synthetic pigment is the famous blue Egyptian paint called **Egyptian frit** which was made of a careful blend of different minerals that was fired in kiln. In ancient Greece and Rome, in contrast to the mistaken Victorian belief that sculptures were all the pure white of the original marble, artworks were highly decorated using a palette of black, white, red and yellow. For some reason, the Romans didn't experiment with the chemistry of the pig-ments as much as the Egyptians, perhaps they were too preoccupied with trying to decide what to do with their increasingly insane emperors.

Crimson (also called kermes and vermilion): Crimson was used by the early Egyptians as a red dye. It was made of an insect known as *Kermes vermilio* from which we get the terms crimson and vermilion.

It was later used throughout ancient Greece, Rome and medieval and Renaissance Europe.

Ultramarine: A brilliant-blue pigment made from the semi-precious stone lapis lazuli. It was extremely important in medieval painting: as the most expensive paint available, it was used only for the most extravagant or holy commissions. It was a particular favourite for artists depicting the robes of the Virgin Mary.

Indigo: Indigo seems to have been in use for over 2,000 years in Europe, the Middle East and India. It's obtained from an extract of the *Indigofera* plant or the *Isatis tinctoria*. The *Isatis tinctoria* grows in Northern Europe and was used in a dye called woad, which the Celts used to paint on their faces before going into battle to make them an even more formidable foe.

Tyrian purple: A highly valued pigment, mentioned in the *Iliad*, which was obtained from the secretions of the sea snail *Murex brandaris* (called *purpura* by the Romans), and also of the *Thais haemastroma*. The most expensive Tyrian purple was made by mixing the secretions of both species, and in its time it was worth three times the price of gold – each shellfish produced only one solitary drop of dye. Despite its name, Tyrian purple varied in colour from purple right through to red. In republican Rome only those of high rank were permitted to wear any form of this colour in their garments, and in Imperial Rome, only the emperor was allowed to wear it.

Cochineal: A red pigment made from the dried and ground bodies of the female of the insect *Dactylopious coccus* which was introduced to Europe from Mexico. This insect could only be harvested during a two-week period annually and, because of its rarity, in early fifteenth-century Florence cochineal was twice as expensive as kermes.

Gold: Used throughout the ages for its association with royalty and the fact that it doesn't deteriorate with age. It was particularly important to medieval artists, who would hammer down coins to make gold leaf. It was also popular in the Renaissance for adding lustre to haloes and decorating the robes of saints – Botticelli's Venus even has gold in her hair.

Burnt sienna: One of the ochre pigments, made from iron oxide, which has been in use since people began to paint. Raw sienna is yellow, but when the pigment is cooked it becomes the warm brown we know as burnt sienna. The siennas are named for the Italian city of Siena which particularly excelled at producing them during the Renaissance. The colours were even more popular during the high Renaissance, when the tone of paintings became darker.

Verdigris: The ancient Greeks wrote about verdigris, a green pigment, which was made by combining copper with vinegar. It was used in painting until the late nineteenth century but, because it was chemically unstable and could damage paintings over time, it was abandoned as more stable green pigments began to appear.

THE FAMOUS FIVE: CLASSICAL
AND NEOCLASSICAL ARCHITECTURE

Those clever Greeks and Romans! Even today, their beautiful and elegant architecture is much imitated, so it's worth learning the five different types of column design that contribute to defining the five major orders of architecture, along with the **entablature**. Just in case that last term threw you, the entablature is the top part of the building that is supported by the columns and is made up of the **architrave**, the main beam resting along the top of the columns; the **frieze**, which is the middle band; and the **cornice**, which is the top band that projects from the frieze.

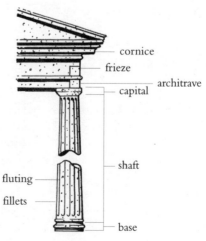

The five major orders of classical architecture are: **Doric**, **Ionic**, **Corinthian**, **Tuscan** and **Composite** and each has different characteristics of column and entablature.

* The Doric has fluted shafts and a distinctive frieze involving sets of three vertical bands that alternate with square panels.
* The Ionic has a more densely fluted shaft than the Doric and is distinguished by the scrolls (called **volutes**) that are carved on the capital.
* The Corinthian has a fluted column and a capital which is carved with two rows of acanthus leaves and scrolls.
* The Tuscan is a Roman adaptation of the Doric style and has a plain shaft with no fluting.
* The Composite style was developed by the Romans and included a capital that has both Ionic scrolls and Corinthian acanthus leaves.

An easy way to remember the five types is by repeating the words **Don't I Create Tall Columns?** Got it? Good. Then let's move on.

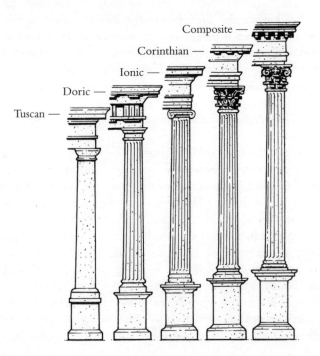

FROM CHIAROSCURO TO VELLUM:
A GLOSSARY OF PAINTING

You might think the world of painting is beyond your ken, but a basic familiarity with key terminology will make you sound like an art insider.

Bitumen: A tarry, dark substance which is naturally derived from petroleum. It was used in painting in the late eighteenth and early nineteenth centuries as a way of augmenting dark colours. Over time it damages paintings, causing the paint to crack.

Canvas: Cloth usually made of linen or cotton stretched over a frame as a base for painting.

Chiaroscuro: An Italian word meaning 'light–dark' which is used to refer to contrasts of light and shadow in paintings.

Composition: The arrangement of elements in an artistic work.

Fresco: A wall painting, particularly favoured in the Renaissance period, where the design is traced onto fresh plaster and painted on while wet.

Frottage: Derived from the French word '*frotter*' to rub, frottage is a technique of rubbing a pencil or other medium over an uneven surface to create an image of the surface.

Gouache: A type of paint invented in the eighteenth century using pigments suspended in water-soluble gum. Gouache is slightly more opaque than watercolour.

Iconography: The term used to refer to the symbolic elements of a painting.

Impasto: An area of thick or textured paint in a work of art, particularly common in works from the Renaissance and Baroque periods.

Oil painting: Oil paint is a mixture of pigment and oil which creates an extremely versatile painting medium. It appears as early as the eleventh century and reached its height in the Renaissance.

Pastels: A crayon comprised of powdered pigments bound with gum.

Pencil: Derives its name from the Latin word '*pencillum*' meaning a 'little tail' or brush. The first pencils, made of graphite sticks protected by wood, appeared around 1565 CE. People used to think graphite was a form of lead, which is why pencils were referred to as lead pencils, even though it has never been used in them. Graphite can be mixed with clay to give different levels of softness. There is a system of grading hardness in pencils that runs from 9H (the hardest) to 9B (the softest). H stands for hard, B stands for black and the F in the middle stands for fine point.

Plein air: A technique of creating an entire painting outside, in the fresh air.

Pointillism: Developed by Georges Seurat and Paul Signac in the late nineteenth century, pointillism is a technique of applying dots of paint next to each other to create an image that can be seen from a distance.

Still life: The still life is a genre common in Western art. The subjects of still lifes are inanimate objects such as flowers or fruit.

Tempera: Paints that can be oil- or water-based emulsions where the pigments are often bound together with egg. Tempera dries to a hard finish.

Triptych: A painting comprised of three panels linked in subject matter.

Vellum: Made from animal skin, as is parchment, though the animals used to make vellum are younger than those used to make parchment.

Watercolour: Paint comprised of pigment which is designed to be diluted with water and not oil, and which creates a semi-transparent colour.

ROCOCO 'N' ROLL: KEY ARTISTIC MOVEMENTS

The -isms have always been a minefield to navigate, with plenty to trip you up and expose the embarrassing gaps in your knowledge. But this chronological guide should help you distinguish your Impressionism from your Expressionism, your baroque from your rococo and identify just what movement Man Ray is associated with.

Mannerism, *c.*1520–90. A European movement of painting characterised by complicated and artificial compositions involving figures with elongated limbs. Key artist: Parmigianino.

Baroque, *c.*1590–early 1700s. A varied European movement characterised by dramatic, vigorous paintings full of energy and emotion.
Key artists: Caravaggio, Bernini.

Rococo, *c.* early 1700s. Originating in France, this was a reaction to
French baroque, and was characterised by delicate, pastel-coloured,
curving decoration. Key artist: François Boucher.

Neoclassicism *c.*1750s–*c.*1850. A European and North American
movement that was heavily influenced by ancient Greek and
Roman art and architecture. Key artists: Jacques-Louis David, Jean
Ingres.

Romanticism *c.*1790s–*c.*1850s. A European movement characterised by
emotionally intense and imaginative paintings. Key artists: William
Blake, John Constable and J. M. W. Turner

Pre-Raphaelites, 1848–54. A movement of British artists headed up by
Dante Gabriel Rossetti, William Holman Hunt and John Everett
Millais. They were particularly inspired by the Italian painters who
came before Raphael and their pictures were generally of religious
and medieval subjects.

Arts and crafts, *c.*1850–1900. A movement in reaction to the Industrial
Revolution, which celebrated craftsmanship. Key artist: William
Morris.

Art nouveau, *c.*1890–1910. A movement in Europe and America rejecting traditional artistic forms, characterised by organic, elegant lines
often involving flowers and natural objects. Key artist: Charles
Rennie Mackintosh.

Impressionism, *c.*1867–86. A major movement developed in France
that set out to reproduce the impression given by light on objects,
landscapes and figures, using textured and innovative painting
techniques. Key artists: Claude Monet, August Renoir.

Expressionism, *c.* late 1800s–early 1900s. A European movement that
aimed to express emotional states through distorted and exaggerat-
ed images, rather than reflect objective reality. Key artists: Edvard
Munch, Egon Schiele, Vincent Van Gogh.

Fauvism, *c.*1905–07. A French movement named after the French word
for 'wild beast' that celebrated the explosive and aggressive use of
colour. Key artist: Henri Matisse.

Cubism, *c.*1907–19. A movement that rejected traditional rules of
perspective and realism; for example, figures were sometimes

represented as broken geometrical shapes. Key Artists: Pablo Picasso, Georges Braque.

Futurism, *c.*1909–30. An Italian movement heavily influenced by cubism that celebrated representations of movement, technology and force. Key artist: Umberto Boccioni.

Vorticism, *c.*1912–16. The first British modern art movement, Vorticism developed from Futurism but rejected its celebration of technology, emphasising instead the negative implications of power and force. Key artist: Wyndham Lewis.

Constructivism, *c.*1913–30s. A Russian modern artistic movement that brought together engineering and art and celebrated modern industrial materials and technology. Key artists: Alexander Rodchenko, László Moholy-Nagy.

Dada, *c.*1916–20. A European and American nihilist intellectual movement that did not have a distinctive artistic style but changed the way that artists worked. It embraced group projects and collectives and rebellion against the artistic establishment. Key artists: Marcel Duchamp, Man Ray.

Art deco, *c.*1920s–1930s. A movement in Europe and America that embraced modernity though the use of elegant, geometric forms often using machine-made materials. Key artist: René Lalique.

Surrealism, *c.*1920s–1930s. A European artistic movement that grew out of Dada and sought to find a new means of expression that would depict both the conscious and the unconscious in a new type of reality: a surreality. Key artists: Salvador Dalí, Joan Miró.

Bauhaus (House of Building), 1919–33. An influential German school of design, architecture and applied arts set up by the architect Walter Gropius. It emphasised the union of art and craftsmanship. Bauhaus changed the face of modern design by aiming to marry function and form to create useful and beautiful objects that could be mass-produced so that design would be for the common man, rather than just for the rich. Key artists: Paul Klee, Wassily Kandinsky.

Abstract expressionism, *c.*1940s–1960s. A wide-ranging American movement characterised by spontaneity, rejection of conventional painting techniques and composition and depiction of abstract forms. Key artists: Mark Rothko, Jackson Pollock.

Pop art, *c.*1950s–1960s. A mainly British and American movement characterised by the portrayal of objects from popular culture not previously treated as suitable subject matter for art – television, comic strips, film images, soup cans, etc. Key artists: Andy Warhol, Roy Lichtenstein.

Minimalism, *c.*1960s–1970s. A mostly American movement that embraced simplicity and aimed to evoke a solely visual response. Key artists: Barnett Newman, Dan Flavin.

Stuckism, 1999–. A British movement that celebrates painting and rejects conceptual art. Key artists: Billy Childish, Charles Thompson.

THE GREAT REAWAKENING: THE RENAISSANCE

'*Renaissance*' is a French word meaning 'rebirth' but it is most commonly used to describe the extraordinary European cultural movement that occurred between the 1300s and 1600s. A vast number of glorious developments in science, literature and art came out of the Renaissance, which focused on a return to the principles of learning and art established by the ancient Greeks and Romans. The powerful Florentine Medici family, and in particular Lorenzo de' Medici (1449–92), supported the arts, and secured many patrons and in turn commissions for artists. Key artists of the time include those hallowed names Michelangelo, Leonardo da Vinci, Raphael, Brunelleschi, Giotto, Donatello, Piero della Francesca and Botticelli. 'Renaissance man' is a term used to describe a model worth emulating: a person with a multitude of different skills spanning different disciplines. The original Renaissance men are Leonardo da Vinci and Michaelangelo; both men achieved great success in areas as diverse as painting, technology and literature.

LEONARDO DA VINCI (1452–1519)

Leonardo da Vinci was a true polymath: a painter, architect, engineer, sculptor, draughtsman, theorist and scientist. From humble beginnings he grew to greatness: he was the illegitimate son of a Florentine lawyer and a peasant girl and was brought up by his grandfather on his father's estate. At the age of fifteen he was apprenticed to the sculptor Andrea del Verrocchio, from whom he learned painting, sculpture, technical drawing and metalwork. In 1482 he moved to Milan to work for Duke Ludovico Sforza. He lived in Milan for seventeen years and worked on a range of extraordinary projects, including *The Virgin on the Rocks* altarpiece for the church of San Francesco and *The Last Supper* painting for the refectory of the monastery of Santa Maria delle Grazie. Leonardo's paintings are famous for his use of *sfumato*, a technique he developed to show depth in his images using soft 'smoky' shadows.

In 1503 Leonardo returned to Florence where, as well as working on artistic projects such as the *Mona Lisa*, he also produced maps and plans to show how Florence could be connected to the sea by a huge canal. The canal was never built but, incredibly, centuries later the autostrada from Florence to the coast was built over the exact route that Leonardo had mapped. During this period he also carried out dissections to explore the structure of the human body and investigated the physics of flight by observing birds (a study which led to him drawing up plans for a helicopter).

Between 1508 and 1516 Leonardo worked in Florence, Rome and Milan. In 1516 he moved to Cloux in France under the patronage of King François I where he lived in a house next to the king's palace. He died there in 1519 and was buried in the palace church which was damaged in the French Revolution and later demolished. His grave can no longer be found.

MICHELANGELO BUONARROTI (1475–1564)

Michelangelo was apprenticed as a young boy to the painter Domenico Ghirlandaio, but it soon became clear his interests lay in the masters of the past – especially the Greek and Roman sculptors. He wanted to bring the human body to life in sculpture, and dedicated himself almost to the point of obsession to uncovering the secrets of sinew and the mysteries of muscle. He studied anatomy and dissected corpses until he was able to draw the human form in any pose. One glance at his marvellous *David* will convince you of his mastery.

When the Pope commissioned Michelangelo to create a tomb for him, the artist travelled to the marble quarries of Carrara where he found inspiration. However, on his return to Rome he found to his disappointment that the Pope's plans for the mausoleum had fallen by the wayside. Michelangelo left Rome for Florence in a huge huff, and was only persuaded to return after many letters of diplomacy had been exchanged. Finally, the Pope forced him to accept another commission, to paint the ceiling of the chapel which Pope Sixtus IV had built: the Sistine Chapel. Michelangelo protested, saying he was a sculptor not a painter, but then at some point he relented, shut the doors to the chapel and for the next four years worked alone on the vaulted ceiling. What he produced astonished the Renaissance world and continues to astonish today, even if the experience of visiting the famous chapel is nowadays marred slightly by Italian security guards who shout at you should the slightest gasp of admiration escape your lips.

CAPTURING REALITY: THE RULES OF PERSPECTIVE

Since time immemorial, perfectionist painters have struggled with the challenge of representing our three dimensional world on the mere two dimensions provided by canvas or paper. Efforts to depict three-dimensions in art led to the ancient Egyptian system of showing people with their chests face on but their legs and heads in profile. The Greeks and later the Romans moved this on with the first uses of foreshortening, but it was during the Renaissance that artists came up with a beautiful and elegant solution to the problem. At this time artists moved away from the idea of symbolic and stylised paintings towards representing what the human eye actually observes. A **linear perspective** system was developed to help painters give a sense of space and depth in their pictures. The system was based on the observation that objects that are far away seem smaller. Sounds simple, doesn't it?

Another observation that painters made was that parallel lines appear to converge on the horizon in one point; the '**vanishing point**'. If you're struggling with this concept, imagine a railway track stretching out in front of you; as your eyes move further along it into the distance, the two parallel tracks seem to converge into one single point. Painters began to work with pictures that were based on one **vanishing point** (as if the viewer were facing the scene head-on), **two-point perspective** (as if the viewer were looking at the scene from an angle) or **three-point perspective** (as if the viewer were looking down or up at the scene).

Although ancient Greek and Persian mathematicians had worked on the concept of perspective, the Florentine architect and sculptor Filippo Brunelleschi (1377–1446) is credited as being the first person to mathematically investigate and calculate its principles. *Della Pittura* (1436) by Leon Battista Alberti (1404–72) was the first work to lay out these laws in writing, and once the artists of the Renaissance got their hands on this fantastic formula there was no stopping them.

Foreshortening

Foreshortening is a technique used to depict an object or figure with a sense of depth. It involves distorting an image to accurately replicate the experience of the human eye. As we've already mentioned, we perceive that which is closer to us as being larger than that which is further away. Artists were aware of this as far back as 500 BCE, when Greek vase painters dared to break from Egyptian techniques and began representing images such as hands or feet face-on, and therefore foreshortened. The technique was perfected in the Renaissance, and *The Lamentation over the Dead Christ* by Andrea Mantegna (1431–1506) is a famous example of it.

THE BEST OF BRITISH:
TURNER AND CONSTABLE

Before Joseph Mallord William Turner (1775–1851) and John Constable (1776–1837) hit the scene, landscape painting had not been taken particularly seriously in Britain. In fact, the majority of landscape painters simply worked on commissions to paint landowners' houses in a similar way to those people who try to sell you aerial photographs of your home nowadays. However, these two artists are now considered among the greatest that Britain has ever produced and both of them had a profound influence on the later Impressionists, particularly in the vibrant and naturalistic depiction of light in their works.

The two were competing in the same field at the same time but their careers had markedly different trajectories. Turner was born in London, the son of a barber. He studied at the Royal Academy and first exhibited there when he was fifteen years old. He began by working in watercolours but moved to oil painting in the 1790s. His landscapes are characterised by a sense of action and fervent and dramatic depictions of light and weather. Turner travelled widely and attracted various aristocratic patrons; he was also championed by the art critic John Ruskin, although many other art commentators criticised his techniques. At his death he left all his work as a gift for the nation, with specific instructions on how it should be displayed.

In contrast to Turner's dramatic emotional scenes, Constable was fond of painting ordinary rural scenes that were very true to nature. His paintings are mostly depictions of locations in Suffolk near to his home. Constable would sketch outside from life and then complete his works in his studio. Constable's most famous painting, *The Hay Wain* (1821), is a restrained depiction of the millpond at Flatford in Suffolk featuring agricultural workers harvesting hay. It was first exhibited at the Royal Academy but was left unsold. However, this work brought him great critical acclaim, and a gold medal, in France when it was exhibited in Paris in 1824. Despite this, his genius was not recognised in Britain until after his death.

VINCENT VAN GOGH (1853–90)

Van Gogh was born in the Netherlands, the son of a Protestant pastor. Like his father, Vincent was deeply religious, and worked as a preacher in England and then among miners in Belgium. This stint caused him to lose his faith, but, happily for us, he found another: art. His early works were full of dark, brooding, poverty-stricken landscapes and characters but after he moved to Paris to live with his brother Théo, who had a job with an art dealer, his output changed dramatically as he was introduced to the Impressionists.

Théo was a model older brother, tirelessly supporting Vincent emotionally and, crucially, financially, even though he was not well off himself. He paid for him to travel to Arles in southern France, and it was there, among the vivid fields and rustic elements of the extraordinary landscape that Van Gogh's painting really came to life, marked by the characteristic swirls and intense colours associated with him today, and much in evidence in paintings such as *Landscape with Cypresses near Arles*. Tragically, however, Vincent was plagued with anxiety, self-doubt and depression, infamously cutting off part of his own ear after a fight during which he threatened Gauguin with a razor. He shot himself on 27 July 1890, and died, penniless and virtually unknown, two days later.

IS IT A RABBIT OR A BANANA?: HOW TO DRAW

- The first step to drawing the perfect picture is to choose your subject well – be it a still life of your fruit bowl, the view from your bedroom window or a sleeping partner or friend (ask permission first in this case or you may cause alarm). Then you must make sure that you are sitting or standing comfortably and you have a well-supported sketch pad and all the drawing materials you need, be it pencil and rubber, pen and ink, or charcoal.
- Take a few minutes to look carefully at your subject and break the image down into its component shapes. This is a very useful trick – if you can see the simple circles, ovals, triangles and squares in the composition in front of you, then you can sketch these out to form the basic structure of your drawing very easily.
- Begin by drawing these shapes lightly on your paper, being aware of the space you have to work with. Don't be afraid to make mistakes – the point of sketching is to get an approximation of what you want and then tidy it up with bolder lines later on. Don't start adding in any detail until you have the full architecture of the whole composition sketched out on your paper. What you are focusing on at this stage is getting everything in proportion. Remember the rules of perspective discussed earlier in the chapter.
- Once you have everything laid out correctly you can start fiddling around, making things look three-dimensional, smoothing out lines and then finally adding details of light and texture. Try to use gentle, swift strokes rather than slow, heavily pressed lines as this will make the picture look more natural and lively. In no time at all you will have a finished piece. And don't worry if your first attempt looks like a dog's dinner: practice makes perfect!

ART
TEST PAPER

1. **Which of the following is not a complementary colour combination?**

a) magenta–green
b) yellow–magenta
c) yellow–violet

2. **What does K stand for in CMYK printing?**

3. **What is Tyrian purple made from?**

a) the secretions of a sea snail
b) beetroot
c) the semi-precious stone lapis lazuli

4. **Why has verdigris fallen out of fashion as a pigment in art?**

5. **How many types of classical column design are there?**

6. **What is chiaroscuro?**

a) the morning song of a small, wren-like bird
b) the arrangement of elements in an artistic work
c) an Italian word meaning 'light-dark' which refers to light and shadow in paintings

7. **What is the hardest type of pencil?**

8. Georges Braque is most associated with which artistic movement?

a) pop art
b) surrealism
c) cubism

9. Vorticism is:

a) an art movement that emphasised the negative connotations of power and force
b) an art movement that celebrated modern industrial technology
c) the study of black holes

10. Name a technique that Leonardo da Vinci was famous for employing in his paintings?

11. How did the ancient Egyptians attempt to show perspective in their art?

a) using the method of foreshortening
b) showing figures with the chests face-on but faces in profile
c) they had no idea what perspective was

12. How many points of perspective does *The Last Supper* by Leonardo da Vinci have?

13. What does the term 'papier mâché' actually mean?

a) the dog ate my homework
b) chewed paper
c) cheese on toast

14. What is tempera?

a) a Japanese dish of fish or vegetables deep-fried in batter
b) a modernist technique of splashing paint at random on canvas

c) oil- or water-based emulsions where the pigments are often bound together with egg

d) a technique whereby paints are heated to a moderate temperature before use

15. What is the 'vanishing point'?

a) the point during an evening out when your eyesight becomes blurred

b) the point where two parallel lines appear to converge

c) the technique Michelangelo used when sculpting his *David*

16. What is woad?

17. What is ultramarine made of?

18. If you are looking at the façade of a building, where would you find the architrave?

a) at the bottom of the columns

b) on the roof

c) on the top of the columns

19. What kind of column is this?

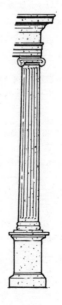

20. What is pointillism?

21. If someone was admiring your fresco, what would they be looking at?

22. Which artistic movement is John Everett Millais associated with?

23. Who painted the Sistine Chapel?

∽ HOMEWORK ∽
FOR
GROWN-UPS

ANSWERS

ENGLISH

1. There are no words that rhyme with these words.

2. The correct spellings are underlined:

misspelt/mispelled/<u>misspelled</u>   <u>millennium</u>/milennium
<u>parallel</u>/paralell   <u>accommodate</u>/acommodate
cemetry/<u>cemetery</u>   wierd/<u>weird</u>
<u>friend</u>/freind   calender/<u>calendar</u>
liesure/<u>leisure</u>   <u>daiquiri</u>/daquiri
<u>drunkenness</u>/drunkeness   liason/<u>liaison</u>
rythm/<u>rhythm</u>   embarassment/<u>embarrassment</u>
concience/<u>conscience</u>   <u>fiery</u>/firey
arguement/<u>argument</u>   <u>harass</u>/harrass
<u>eighth</u>/eigth   <u>inoculate</u>/innoculate

3.

a) Foxes sometimes fight in the Browns' garden, as if staging a wrestling match, but they always make up in the end.

b) 'We always have been, we are, and I hope that we always shall be, detested in France.'

c) 'I don't know what I said, but I know what I think, and, well, I assume it's what I said.'

d) 'To lose one parent, Mr Worthing, may be regarded as a misfortune; to lose both looks like carelessness.'

4. Uriah, who was <u>a bright spark</u> [metaphor], had his head <u>buried in a book</u> [metaphor] when we <u>bumped into</u> [metaphor – unless Agnes and David literally collided with Uriah] him in the park. 'Agnes!' he simpered, 'How <u>impossibly beautiful</u> [hyperbole] you look today. <u>It makes my life worth living</u> [hyperbole] to see you arrayed <u>like a princess</u> [simile] in all your <u>seductive silks</u> [pathetic fallacy] and satins.' 'Excuse Uriah,' I whispered to David, 'he's a bit of a <u>fruitcake</u> [metaphor and euphemism].'

5. As he walked [verb] slowly [adverb] away from Brookfield School [noun] Mr Chipping [noun] thought [verb] fondly [adverb] of his many years [noun] of service [noun].

6. b)

7.

a) Between you and <u>me</u>, that new hairdresser is terrible.
b) Our boss was sure that Mildred and <u>I</u> would both be successful in the promotion review.
c) It is <u>I</u> alone who must take responsibility for the downturn in sales this month.
d) All the team, save <u>me</u>, were good public speakers.

8.

a) The only ladies' gym in our town has had to close.
b) A men's working club has taken up the lease.
c) The three naughty girls' homework was closely monitored.
d) Father returned to work yesterday after a few days at a gentlemen's health resort.
e) The car's bumper was more damaged than the lorry's.

9.

a) 'Good heavens!' she cried. 'What do you think I meant to do, eat the whole pie myself?'
b) 'I'm so, so sorry!' she wailed. 'It wasn't my fault the jug's handle was broken.' Or 'It wasn't my fault. The jug's handle was broken.'
c) 'How queer it seems,' Alice said to herself, 'to be going messages for a rabbit.'
d) Ladies prefer well-cut silk-lined dresses.

10.

a) The boy <u>who</u> stole the apple had to confess.
b) <u>Whom</u> did you meet at the bus stop this morning?
c) To <u>whom</u> should I write for a new bus pass?
d) To <u>whom</u> does this bicycle belong?
e) The police kept an eye on the boys, <u>whom</u> they suspected of stealing the apples.

11.

a) My mother and father have gone to Skegness for a <u>well-earned</u> rest.
b) The dentist's surgery was reached by an <u>ill-lit</u> staircase.
c) The ball gown was <u>sky blue</u> in colour and reached her <u>nicely shaped</u> knees.
d) <u>Sleeping-cars</u> are available on the night train to Edinburgh.

12. They say that <u>practice</u> makes perfect, but still I don't have time to <u>practise</u> guitar every day.

13. When the bus was finally <u>stationary</u>, I jumped off and went to the <u>stationery</u> shop to stock up on pencils.

14. It was a very exciting cycle race. Tom quickly <u>passed</u> Stuart, and was first <u>past</u> the post.

15.

a) murder
b) clutch
c) parliament
d) wilderness
e) business
f) cete
g) drunkship

16.

a) daughter
b) a road
c) one
d) your breath

17. d)

18. <u>I was not overjoyed</u> to hear that the light of my life, my innocent, fresh-faced sixteen-year-old daughter, was with child.

19. It is a word that occurs only once in a language's recorded texts or in an author's body of work.

20. They are all onomatopoeic.

21. 'Gaudy' comes from the Latin verb 'gaudere' meaning 'to rejoice' and in Middle English the word 'gaud' came to mean a rosary bead as the rosary was considered a joyful prayer. It eventually came to refer to the bead itself as an ornament rather than a tool of prayer. And finally in modern English it has come to mean tasteless and showy.

22.

Jay Gatsby	Daisy Buchanan	*The Great Gatsby*
Rhett Butler	Scarlett O'Hara	*Gone with the Wind*
Humbert Humbert	Dolores Haze	*Lolita*
Vicomte de Valmont	Madame de Tourvel	*Les Liaisons Dangereuses*
Dante	Beatrice	*The Divine Comedy*
Count Vronsky	Anna Karenina	*Anna Karenina*
Romeo	Juliet	*Romeo and Juliet*
Aeneas	Dido	*Aeneid*
Mr Darcy	Elizabeth Bennet	*Pride and Prejudice*
Heathcliff	Catherine	*Wuthering Heights*

23. 'As Gregor Samsa awoke   *Metamorphosis*   Franz Kafka
one morning from uneasy
dreams he found himself
transformed in his bed
into a gigantic insect.'

'It is a truth universally   *Pride and Prejudice* Jane Austen
acknowledged, that a
single man in possession
of a good fortune, must
be in want of a wife.'

'Call me Ishmael.'   *Moby-Dick*   Herman Melville

'Happy families are all   *Anna Karenina*   Leo Tolstoy
alike; every unhappy
family is unhappy in its
own way.'

'It was the best of times,   *A Tale of*   Charles Dickens
it was the worst of   *Two Cities*
times ...'

'All children, except one,   *Peter Pan*   J. M. Barrie
grow up.'

'It was the afternoon of   *Earthly Powers*   Anthony Burgess
my eighty-first birthday,
and I was in bed with my
catamite when Ali announced
that the archbishop had come
to see me.'

24. c)

25. 14

26. d)

27. that they should never walk upright

28. iambic pentameter

29. four

30. The indicative is a realis mood. Realis moods indicate that something is, or is not, actually the case, as opposed to irrealis moods which
indicate uncertainty.

31. *Ulysses* by James Joyce

32. Adam and Eve – the weather on Earth was made inhospitable as
part of their punishments for disobeying God and eating the fruit of
the tree of knowledge.

33. c)

34. b)

35.

a)   George Eliot
b)   Magwitch
c)   Elizabeth Bennet, *Pride and Prejudice*
d)   Prince Andrei is engaged to her but Pierre Bezukhov marries her

36. a) Mina (Elizabeth gets killed by the monster in *Frankenstein*)

37.

a)   *The Turn of the Screw* by Henry James
b)   *Robinson Crusoe* by Daniel Defoe
c)   *The Hound of the Baskervilles* by Arthur Conan Doyle

c) *Brighton Rock* by Graham Greene

38. Eight – Polonius (stabbed), Ophelia (drowned), Rosencrantz and Guildenstern (killed in England), Gertrude (poisoned), Laertes (poisoned/stabbed), Claudius (poisoned/stabbed), Hamlet (poisoned/stabbed). (Hamlet's father is murdered before the action of the play begins)

39.

a) *Antony and Cleopatra* (V:2), Cleopatra
b) *Hamlet*, Hamlet (I:2)
c) *Henry V*, King Henry V (IV:3)
d) *King Lear*, Lear (I:5)

40. Joseph Conrad

ᏫᏬ MATHEMATICS ᏫᏬ

1.

a) sherbet lemons
b) 8
c) 12
d) 24

2. c)

3. 224

4.

a) To calculate area of a rectangle you multiply the length by the width. Roger and Hal's kitchen floor area is 96m².
b) The perimeter is the outside of a shape. The perimeter of a rectangle is the length x 2 + the width x 2. The perimeter of their kitchen measures 40 metres.
c) Each tile is 0.25m² and you have 96m² area to cover. 96 x 4 = 384. Roger needs 384 tiles.

5. 2.76cm

6. 14.42

7.

a) You owe ⅕ of the bill of £80. To express this as a percentage value you need to divide 100 by 5. This shows that you owe 20% of the bill.

b)   To calculate 20% of £80 you need to divide £80 by 100. This gives you £0.80, which is 1% of the bill. Multiply this by 20 and you get your share, which is £16.

8.   To work out your percentage you need to divide 7 by 12 and multiply the result by 100. This shows that you have achieved 58%.

9.   20

10. b)

11. 116, 168

12. 9

13. c)

14. 3.5

15. 162

16. 36

17. 66

18. heptagon

19. b)

20.

a)   right angle
b)   hypotenuse

c) acute angle

21. 80

22. 12 and -12

23. positive

24. the distance from the centre of a circle to its edge

25. These numbers are the first in the Fibonacci sequence. Each number is the sum of the two previous numbers. This sequence is special because the ratio of each successive pair of numbers is roughly φ. The further up the sequence you go, the closer you get to an accurate expression of φ.

26. ¾

27. red

28. 260 steps

29. 5 noughts, 15 ones, 6 fives

30. Tuesday

31. 3.58p.m.

32. 6 minutes

33. 90 degrees

34. 34 days, 11 hours

35.

a) £79.35
b) 16 laps

⟶ HOME ECONOMICS ⟵

1. 1½ hrs

2. b)

3. Make sure you and any casualties are free from further danger.

4. a)

5. c)

6. c)

7. get to your fallout room

8. b) tumble-dry – high heat

9. 364

10. See p.89 for food hygiene procedures you should follow.

11. Probably in the north of England or Scotland. Shepherd's Pie is made from lamb, as that's what shepherds look after. Cottage Pie is made from beef.

12. front

13. To calculate your body mass index, you need to know your height in metres and your weight in kilograms. Square your height in metres, then divide the result with your weight in kilos. The resulting figure is your BMI.

14. carbohydrates, protein, lipids, vitamins, minerals

15. amino acids

16. Lipids store energy and are essential for cellular health. They are used in the production of hormones and in the absorption of certain vitamins and they provide a cushioning protective layer for the organs.

17. a third

18. swelling of the body, pot belly, discoloration of the hair and digestive difficulty

19. oxygen, heat and fuel

20. See your doctor for advice on nutrition to aid gradual weight loss – you are seriously overweight and damaging your health.

21. A nuclear attack is imminent.

22. Dry the garment you are washing flat.

23.

a) 3 teaspoonsful – a teaspoon holds approximately 5ml
b) approximately 15ml

24.

a) beating the ingredients until they are a light and creamy consistency
b) gently but decisively mixing lighter and heavier ingredients without taking the air out of the lighter ingredients

∽ HISTORY ∾

1. aqueducts, underfloor heating, advertising, wine, coins, calendars, roads, law, baths, peas

2.

1. 1969 – Neil Armstrong and Buzz Aldrin land on the moon
2. 1969 – The first Woodstock festival
3. 1533 – Henry VIII marries Anne Boleyn
4. 1930 – First World Cup final played in Uruguay
5. 1963 – Death of John F. Kennedy
6. 1215 – Signing of the Magna Carta
7. 1787 – American Constitution signed
8. 1959 – Outbreak of the Vietnam War
9. 1981 – Marriage of Prince Charles and Lady Diana Spencer
10. 1976 – Concorde's first commercial flight
11. 1824 – Death of Lord Byron
12. 1919 – Treaty of Versailles signed
13. 1948 – Israel declares indpendence
14. 1925 – Publication of *Mein Kampf*
15. 1989 – Fall of the Berlin Wall
16. 1265 – Birth of Dante Alighieri
17. 1947 – Partition of India
18. 1943 – Birth of Mick Jagger
19. 1534 – Passing of the Act of Supremacy
20. 1997 – Death of Mother Teresa
21. 1865 – Abolition of slavery in the United States
22. 1587 – Mary, Queen of Scots executed
23. 1977 – Death of Elvis Presley
24. 1936 – Abdication of Edward VIII
25. 1945 – The atom bomb is dropped on Hiroshima
26. 1707 – Act of Union between Scotland and England passed
27. 1990 – Resignation of Margaret Thatcher

28. 1928 – Universal suffrage for all adults over 21 years of age

29. 1914 – Archduke Franz Ferdinand shot

30. 1170 – Thomas à Becket assassinated

3. Egbert

4. a primary source

5. c)

6. February/March

7. a 1955 agreement that allowed Soviet military units to be stationed in the Communist bloc countries

8. an aeon

9. werwulf

10. the white rose

11. the Romanovs

12. b)

13. 2005

14. Sir Robert Walpole

15. 1845

16. during the first Battle of the Somme

17. 1961

18. the period of history from which no written records exist

19. Ordovician, Devonian, Jurassic, Paleogene

20. The area in northern Britain where the Vikings were allowed to settle in the ninth century CE.

21. William the Conqueror

22. Bishop Odo, half-brother of William the Conqueror

23. Lackland

24. It documented the idea that the king's power could be constrained by a constitution or law rather than the monarch being solely answerable to himself.

25. Hundred Years War

26. Jane Seymour (although this depends on your opinion on the legitimacy of his marriages after his first to Catherine of Aragon)

27. In trying to convert England back to Catholicism, she was responsible for 300 Protestants being burnt at the stake.

28. 18 June 1815

29. It was considered a painless and egalitarian punishment, as previously only aristocrats had been privileged with being executed by decapitation.

30. Nicholas II

31. the industrial and agricultural workers

32. It was a programme instituted by Chairman Mao in Communist China whereby the intelligentsia were re-educated by being forced to move to the countryside and work alongside the peasants.

33. He assassinated the Austro-Hungarian Archduke Franz Ferdinand, setting in train the steps to World War I.

34. the judges who sit in the House of Lords

35. House of Commons, House of Lords, Monarch

36. 'ourselves alone' in Irish Gaelic

∾ SCIENCE ∾

1. c)

2. 19.3 g per cm^3

3. c)

4. d)

5. b)

6. b)

7. 81.25 newtons

8. c) and d)

9. f)

10. Count the number of protons in the nucleus.

11.

a) Mr Dadier eats a bowl of spaghetti and goes for a run – transfer of chemical into kinetic (and heat) energy.

b) A pendulum inside a grandfather clock swings back and forth – gravitational potential energy being changed into kinetic energy and back again.

c) A football is kicked towards goal, hits the crossbar and bounces back off – gravitational potential, kinetic, elastic potential and kinetic again.

12. the moment at which a falling body ceases to accelerate

13. b)

14. Cold can't seep into bones – it's the heat leaving your body that makes you cold. Absolute zero can never be attained.

15. Conduction and convection both move heat through the molecules of substances. Thermal radiation occurs using waves rather than molecules.

16. It is colourless

17. c)

18. c)

19. a)

20. See diagram:

21. mollusc

22. b) or c)

23. a)

24. a)

25. in a testicle

26. 78% nitrogen, 21% oxygen and 1% other gases

27. collagen and calcium phosphate

28. in your pancreas

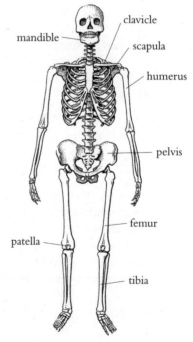

❧ RELIGIOUS EDUCATION ❧

1. Shiva

2. *kesh* (uncut hair), *kirpan* (the sword), *kangha* (a comb), *kara* (a steel bracelet), *kachera* (shorts worn as underwear)

3.

a) Samsara means wandering and refers to the Hindu belief in reincarnation.

b) Karma is the Hindu belief that every action a person takes causes a result that they are responsible for and will experience in their current or future life.

4. a Hindu rite of passage

5. Bartholemew, James the Less, Andrew, Judas or Matthias, Peter, John, Thomas, James the Great, Philip, Matthew, Thaddeus, Simon

6. St David

7. St Erasmus

8. 1. right views, 2. right intentions, 3. right speech, 4. right action, 5. right livelihood, 6. right effort, 7. right-mindedness, 8. right contemplation

9. a concept common to most religions which states that you should only do to others what you would like done to yourself

10. a bodhi tree

11. the spiritual state where a person is free from suffering

12. The focusing of the mind to achieve spiritual serenity

13. The Catholic faith does not accept the use of contraception.

14. Abraham

15. Reuben, Simeon, Levi, Judah, Issachar, Zebulun, Gad, Asher, Dan,
Naphtali, Joseph and Benjamin
or the Twelve Tribes who controlled separate territories in Canaan:
Reuben, Simeon, Judah, Issachar, Zebulun, Gad, Asher, Dan,
Naphtali, Massaneh, Ephraim and Benjamin.

16. 586 BCE by the Babylonians and 70 CE by the Romans

17. King Solomon

18. The menorah's candles represent the sacred flame that miraculously
burned in the Temple for eight days after it was reconsecrated by
Judas Maccabeus in 165 BCE.

19. They are not kosher foods and therefore forbidden in the Jewish
faith.

20. pride, avarice, lust, wrath, gluttony, envy, sloth

21. See p.259 for a full list of the Ten Commandments.

22. the first five books of the Jewish Bible, also known as the Law

23. a Roman Catholic doctrine which states that the Virgin Mary was
conceived without original sin (the essential sinfulness of mankind
passed on to each human being through procreation right back to
Adam and Eve)

24. submission

25. struggle

26. There are many but some of the most well known are listed below:

a) Roman Catholics believe in the authority of the established Church and its representatives, and at the head of this sits the Pope; but Protestants believe in the priesthood of all believers, which states that all people have equally direct contact with God and do not need the clergy to mediate for them.

b) Catholics depend on the traditions of the Church where Protestants believe in the primacy of the scriptures in deciding Christian belief and practice.

c) Catholics believe that partaking of the sacraments and doing penance and good works all help to invite God's grace where Protestants believe in justification by grace alone through faith (grace is God's favour, which He can grant to individuals and which 'justifies' them or redeems them from their sins).

d) Catholics and Protestants have slightly different books and orders of books in their Bibles.

e) Catholic priests must remain celibate but Protestant vicars may marry.

f) Catholic priests must be men whereas Protestant vicars can be women.

g) Rigorous Catholics believe that homosexual sex is a sin whereas some Protestants do not believe it sinful.

h) Catholics believe in transubstantiation: that the bread and wine change into the body and blood of Jesus during the sacrament of the Eucharist (Holy Communion – the moment in the Mass or church service where the priest re-enacts the Last Supper) and some Protestants do not.

i) Catholics are also opposed to contraception, abortion and divorce where many Protestants are not.

27. Joseph (son of Jacob)'s son and leader of one of the twelve territories of Israel

28. 3 – keeping the Sabbath holy, having no other god but God and making graven images

29. *shahadah* (declaration of faith), *salah* (prayer), *zakat* (giving alms), *sawm* (fasting), *hajj* (pilgrimage)

30. It is the ninth month of the Muslim calendar – which is lunar so changes in relation to the Gregorian calendar every year.

31. food, drink and sex

32. 90% are Sunni

33. Guru Nanak

34. Sikhs worship in buildings called gurdwaras.

35. Mecca

36. Bethlehem

37. in Christianity, the sin passed down to all people as punishment for the first human beings, Adam and Eve, eating the fruit of the tree of knowledge in the Garden of Eden

38. the pains of childbirth

✂ GEOGRAPHY ✂

1. b)

2. c)

3. d)

4. a)

5. Pangaea

6. Pacific, Atlantic, Arctic and Indian

7. Africa, America, Antarctica, Asia, Australia, Europe or Africa, Antarctica, Australia, Eurasia, North America and South America

8. Mount Everest – at 8,850 metres.

9. Officially spring runs from the night of 20 March to 21 June.

10. frozen droplets of water that are suspended in the sky because of changes in temperature that take place in the Earth's atmosphere

11. nephology is the study of clouds, nephrology is the branch of medicine dealing with kidneys

12. Timbuktu is a city in Mali in north-west Africa.

13. c)

14. Hide under a door frame or sturdy piece of furniture, away from windows.

15. the similarities he saw in fossils in different continents

16. rainy, overcast weather

17. Dar es Salaam

18. Burkina Faso

19. the outer layer of the Earth's atmosphere

20. ozone

21. rain, sleet, snow, hail

22. Nile

23. the ridges or hills that divide up the drainage basins of rivers

24. the hypocentre

⚛ CLASSICS ⚛

1.   Julius Caesar, Galba, Otho, Domitian

2.   *Amat canem*

3.   Creusa, Dido, Lavinia

4.   'I sing of arms and the man': it is the opening line of Virgil's *Aeneid*.

5.   the Belgae

6.   54 CE – he was killed with a poisoned mushroom.

7.   c)

8.   32

9.   Bucephalus
     Pegasus – a mythological winged horse; Incitatus – the Roman Emperor Caligula's horse, whom he appointed to the senate; the Trojan Horse.

10. Carthage

11. She stabbed herself in the heart on a funeral pyre she had built for herself as Aeneas sailed away from her.

12. Julius Caesar

13. He split the Roman Empire in half, into eastern and western areas of control.

14. Constantine's city or city state

15. Marc Antony and Julius Caesar

16. *Ferox canis bonae puellae*

17.
a) Zeus – Jupiter
b) Hera – Juno
c) Hermes – Mercury
d) Apollo – Apollo
e) Dionysus – Bacchus

18. Apollo or Asklepius

19. Athene

20. love of wisdom (philosophy)

21. that nothing can be truly known

22. that you should take the criticism with a pinch of salt

23. 10 years

24. Ithaca

25. First, that Agamemnon took Briseis away from him, and then that Hector killed his best friend Patroclus.

26. He is sitting under a tree.

27. She needs to change her clothes.

28. into the midst of things

29. purgation – referring to the experience of strong emotion while watching a play

30. a)

31. the satirical poet Juvenal

32. Hephaestus – as he is crippled and Ares is the god of war.

33. Socrates

34. a) Orestes and c) Sophocles

∽ PHYSICAL EDUCATION ∽

1. d)

2. 13

3. A player is in an offside position if he is nearer to his opponents' goal line than both the ball and the second last opponent when the ball is played to him. A player cannot be offside if he is in his own half and nor can he be if the referee deems him to be 'inactive' to the play.

4. b)

5. different number of players and length of match, also physical contact only permitted in the men's game

6. at a cricket match, when one of the fielders thinks that the batsman is out

7. b)

8. d)

9. Native Americans

10. 11

ᥴ ART ᥲ

1. b)

2. key (black)

3. a)

4. because it damages paintings over time

5. five

6. c)

7. 9H

8. c)

9. a)

10. *sfumato*, the use of smoky shadows

11. b)

12. one

13. b)

14. c)

15. b)

16. blue paint used by the Celts to paint their faces before going into battle

17. lapis lazuli

18. c)

19. Ionic

20. a technique of applying dots of paint next to each other to create an image that can be seen from a distance

21. your wall painting

22. Pre-Raphaelites

23. Michelangelo

ACKNOWLEDGEMENTS

We are very grateful to:

Rosemary Davidson, Gemma Avery, Tom Avery, Isabel Barter, Marcus Bates, Dr Lynsey Bennett, Anna Bowden, Emma Buttle, Hannah Carter, Yen Chong, Shah Chowdhury, Lyndsey Clegg, David Coates, Geraldine Coates, Jo Coates, Morgan Coates, Rachel Cugnoni, Suzanne Dean, Tom Drake-Lee, Benjamin Evans, Dr Eleanor Foley, Isabel Foley, Thomas Foley, Dan Franklin, Kathy Fry, Noel Gillett, Emily Greenfield, Jamie Goodman, Leo Humphries, Mary Instone, Ilana Jackman, Chloë Johnson-Hill, Spike Lacey, Dr Francis Lambert, Penny Liechti, Alastair Lockhart, Lucy Luck, Chris Lyon, Patrick Mackie, Zoë MacLachlan, Frances Macmillan, Ross Milne, Emily Morley, Clare Murphy, Helen Murphy, Marcus Parker, Owen Parry, Rosalind Porter, Liam Relph, Simon Rhodes, Asif Salam, Reshmin Salam, Jonathan Smith, Christopher Stephenson, Peter Ward, Kyra Watkins, Stuart Williams, Claire Wilshaw and particularly to Oliver Bebb and Jack Murphy.

∾ CREDITS ∾

Excerpt from *Modern Man in Search of a Soul* by C. Gustav Jung (Routledge Classics, 2001), by Permission of Taylor and Francis Books Ltd.

Excerpts from *The Two Cultures and a Second Look. An Expanded Version of the Two Cultures and the Scientific Revolution* by C.P. Snow (Cambridge University Press, 1964), by permission of Cambridge University Press.

Dictionary definitions from *Oxford Concise English Dictionary* by kind permission of Oxford University Press.

Whilst every effort has been made to obtain permission from holders of copyright material reproduced herein, the publishers would like to apologise for any omissions and will be pleased to incorporate any missing acknowledgments in any further editions.

The authors have endeavoured to ensure that all the information in this book is accurate and relevant. However, if you have any corrections or suggestions please send them to the authors care of Square Peg, Random House, 20 Vauxhall Bridge Road, London, SW1V 2SA.